THE BUSINESS TRAVELER'S SURVIVAL GUIDE ™

DALLAS FORT WORTH

Business Travelers, Inc.
New York 1982

Published in the United States of America by Business Travelers, Inc., and simultaneously in Canada through its distributor, Franklin Watts, Inc., New York, London, Toronto, Sydney.

Library of Congress Cataloging in Publication Data

Main entry under title:
The Business traveler's survival guide, Dallas/Ft. Worth.
Includes index.
1. Dallas (Tex.)–Description–Guide-books.
2. Fort Worth (Tex.)–Description–Guide-books.
3. Business travel–Texas–Dallas. 4. Business travel–Texas–Fort Worth. I. Business Travelers, inc.
F394.D213B87 917.64'28120463 81-21633
ISBN 0-531-09851-6 AACR2

FIRST PRINTING

Design and cover by Antler & Baldwin, Inc.

CONTENTS

This book was researched and written by
Polly Freney Rea who gratefully acknowledges
the assistance of Sandy Humphrey, Debbie Goldie
and Jeannie Clark.

PREFACE

THE BUSINESS TRAVELER'S SURVIVAL GUIDE: DALLAS/FORT WORTH has been researched, written, organized and edited for the business traveler. It will prove useful to the more than two million people who will attend the 1,600 conventions and meetings held annually in Dallas/Fort Worth and for the person whose business itinerary includes a day or a week in the area.

There are other guides to Dallas and Fort Worth but we are not aware of any written specifically for the business traveler whose needs are quite different from those of the vacation traveler. We know you do not have the time to search through unfamiliar Yellow Pages. The hotels, restaurants and services listed in this guide are divided into specifically detailed geographic areas. By using the maps in the earlier portion of the book you can determine those most convenient to where you will be doing business. We will guide you through arrival, help you choose the best hotel to suit your needs, suggest appropriate places to eat a gourmet meal or grab a quick sandwich. We have given you information on car rental, copy shops, shoe repair service, sightseeing and health care facilities. We think you will find it all useful.

This guide is not meant to be a comprehensive listing of all services available in the Dallas/Fort Worth vicinity. Rather it is meant to be a briefcase or pocketbook companion for the business traveler. We have listed well-established and reputable firms–there are others but these are our choices for the Metroplex area.

The fares, fees and other prices listed are current as of publication and should be used as approximate charges subject to change. Because so many business travelers use credit cards for expense records we have provided extensive credit card information throughout the book–a feature omitted in other guides. Each service listed will indicate the credit card policy of that establishment. Credit card abbreviations are: American Express (AE); Carte Blanche (CB); Diners Club (DC); MasterCard (MC); Visa (V). "All major credit cards" indicates all five of the above are accepted. "Most major credit cards" means at least four.

Business Travelers, Inc., accepts no fees or services in exchange for listings or reviews. Businesses were selected on the basis of their relevance to the business traveler's needs—location, services offered, hours and credit card acceptance policy. All meals and drinks were paid for by Business Travelers, Inc. There was no promise or guarantee of listing and no privilege of editorial review offered.

The services and firms listed were selected specifically for their suitability for business travelers. If any business or service fails to meet your expectations based on our recommendation, we would appreciate hearing about it. We would also love to know about new or unlisted services you especially like so we may include them in future guides. Write to us at 730 Fifth Avenue, New York, N.Y. 10019.

Since Dallas/Fort Worth is a major Sunbelt business center expanding at an unbelievable rate, it is impossible to print a guide which is absolutely current. Entire new business complexes, huge new hotels and completely new shopping malls are being built and opened weekly. By next year there will be areas of the Metroplex which will need to be added to the guide. As this book is going to press there are buildings springing out of the flat hard earth at an astonishing pace. There will be continual updating of information in our revised guides.

Business Travelers, Inc., publishes guides to major cities throughout the United States which are important to business travelers. Look for guides to many major cities and use them to make your business travels more organized and less harried.

WELCOME TO BIG D

WHEN actor Larry Hagman's face graced the cover of *Time* with the blaring headline, Who Shot J.R.? *Time* had finally caught up with what everyone had known for quite some time–Americans have Dallas fever. Since the days of the Alamo and Davy Crockett, no area of the U.S. has quite captured the imagination of Americans as Texas has. Is there anyone who doesn't know where longhorns come from? Is there anyone who hasn't seen Tony Dorsett score a touchdown for the Dallas Cowboys? No one made a movie about the Washington Redskins cheerleaders.

Founded in 1841 by John Neely Bryan, Dallas probably got its name from Bryan's friend, the then vice president of the United States, George Mifflin Dallas. The fledgling city must have seemed to some a strange choice for Mr. Neiman and Mr. Marcus to open their emporium, but apparently, they knew what they were doing, for today Neiman-Marcus epitomizes luxury with western charm. What other store can offer an $8,000 TV dish-antenna and a pair of snakeskin cowboy boots to wear while you sit back and watch *Dallas?*

Downtown Dallas looks like any other major U.S. city. (The 15,000-acre ranches are miles away.) You won't see many cowboy hats, but you may see some well-polished (and expensive) boots sticking out from under the three-piece suits that many Dallas business executives wear.

Dallas is not a country town. It has a resident symphony orchestra and an exciting night life which includes country and western music, dancing, theater and ballet–not to mention the already-mentioned Dallas Cowboys. Dallas boasts a wonderful parks system which operates and maintains bike paths, tennis courts, running tracks and swimming pools–all available to visitors.

Like any American city, Dallas has its share of crime and there are areas one should avoid after dark. We have attempted to identify problem areas, but generally, we have focused our attention on areas that we consider safe. We doubt that you will encounter any problem if you exercise normal caution. Dallasites are friendly and outgoing, whether they are natives or transplanted Yankees. Southern hospitality prevails and you will find shopkeepers, bus drivers, restaurant workers and anyone else you meet anxious to give you directions or help out.

The city is really a twentieth-century development. It has grown at such a remarkable pace, that natives are often as confused as the newcomers. The feeling of growth and progress is everywhere, even as you enter the terminal at Dallas/Fort Worth airport.

The terrain of this north Texas city is very flat and there are relatively few trees. At one time, the general feeling was of wide open spaces, but now, many of those spaces have been filled in with business complexes, industrial parks, shopping centers and housing developments. In fact, the area is spreading so rapidly, that the media has coined the word, Metroplex, to refer to this large area of Dallas, Ft. Worth, the so-called "Mid-Cities," and the suburbs to the south. Dallas is the seventh largest city in the U.S. Downtown Dallas boasts many shiny, mirrored buildings and skyscrapers, but few historical buildings. Many of these have fallen victim to the wrecker's ball. The skyline changes almost weekly.

The area's major businesses include insurance, banking, oil, electronics, data processing, and convention and trade shows. Dallas's large Market Center includes an apparel mart, a trade mart, and a furniture mart. A giant computer mart is planned to open sometime in 1983.

If you need more convincing to dispel the notion of Dallas as a small, southwest town, more national firms are headquartered in Dallas than in any other city in the country. These include the Boy Scouts of America, the American Heart Association, American Airlines and Braniff Airlines.

You won't see rich oil barons lighting imported cigars with $1,000 bills, but you will see miles and miles of luxury cars. There won't be any doubt in your mind that MONEY is the name of the game in Dallas. Big D epitomizes free enterprise, and young and old have caught that frontier spirit that allows each individual to set his own mark on the world. Enjoy the spirit.

CLIMATE

Even Texans joke about how rapidly the weather changes. "If you don't like the weather–just wait a few minutes!"–is the often heard refrain.

Most business travelers will find Dallas/Fort Worth's weather generally pleasant. The legendary 100°–110° summer days do certainly grow tedious, but they are offset by mild and generally dry winter weather. Seasons change less dramatically here and therefore medium weight or nine-month clothing is almost always a good choice.

TEMPERATURE RANGES

MONTH	FAHRENHEIT (HI-LO)	CELSIUS (HI-LO)
January	56–35	13–2
February	59–38	15–3
March	68–46	20–8
April	76–55	24–13
May	83-63	28–17
June	91–71	33–22
July	95–74	35–23
August	95–74	35–23
September	88–67	31–19
October	79–57	26–14
November	67–46	19–8
December	58–37	14-3

Average yearly temperature: 65.5° F

Weather phone number: 357-4643
Time and Temperature: 844-1111

We certainly do not want to alarm you but an important aspect of the local weather here is tornado season. Tornadoes (or "twisters" as they are often called) are most likely to occur in April, May and June and result from winds whirling in a counterclockwise direction at a tremendous speed.

For the person visiting this area during tornado season it is important to know the warning system and some very basic safety rules.

Tornado Watch: A National Weather Service bulletin indicating conditions are ripe for tornadic activity. You should continue your regular activities but keep the radio or TV tuned in for further information.

Tornado Warning: This is the most serious stage and indicates that a tornado has been sighted in the area. You should immediately follow these instructions:

1. if walking outside, immediately enter the nearest sturdy building and keep away from windows and glass doors.
2. if inside a building or home, move to the central part

of the house in a bathroom or closet away from glass and windows.

3. if driving, head at right angles to the storm cloud as fast as possible or if you feel you cannot outpace the twister, stop by the side of the road and head for the nearest ditch or culvert and lay down flat until the twister has passed.

ZONES

This guide focuses on those areas which the majority of business travelers will visit. There are many surrounding areas which have fine hotels, restaurants and business services available. We have chosen key clusters of hotels and have selected the services and restaurants most convenient to them. Future guides, of course, will include other areas but we feel those we have selected will give you, the business traveler, a broad range of hotels, locations, services and restaurants to choose from.

For your general information there are within the city of Dallas itself two small communities which are separately incorporated: University Park and Highland Park–known to natives as "The Park Cities." This is one of the most attractive and wealthiest areas in the city, with many beautiful homes. It is a residential area so we have not included it in our zones.

Other surrounding areas include: Arlington, Grand Prairie, Irving, Bedford, Hurst and Euless to the west; Lewisville, Carrollton, Farmer's Branch, Plano and Richardson in the north; and east of Dallas–Garland, Rowlett, Rockwall, Sunnyvale and Mesquite; on the south are Duncanville, DeSoto and Lancaster.

We have used for our zones areas which are clearly recognizable to local residents including: D/FW Airport, the Market Center, Downtown, North Central and LBJ-North.

Fort Worth will not be divided into separate zones as we have divided Dallas. A separate chapter at the rear of our guide will tell you all about Fort Worth. Most of the listings in Fort Worth are located in the central business section downtown or at least within easy access. Travel from center-city Fort Worth to center-city Dallas should take about 40–50 minutes and is very convenient along the Dallas–Fort Worth Turnpike (Route 30). Though it is called a turnpike, there are no tolls! Once the road was paid for the toll booths were removed and it is now just a well-maintained state highway.

Obviously, weather, currency and other general information contained in our guide is applicable to both cities.

DALLAS

For Fort Worth, *see map in introduction to Fort Worth, p. 230.*

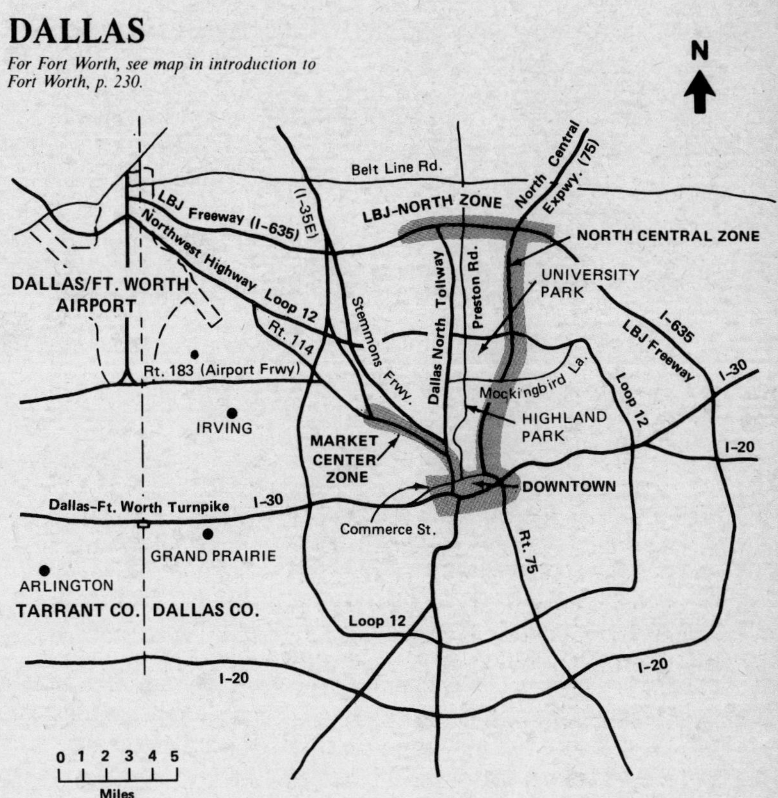

D/FW AIRPORT

For purposes of this guide this zone will include areas within and immediately surrounding the almost 18,000-acre area known as the Dallas/Fort Worth Regional Airport. As with the rest of the Metroplex, buildings are going up daily but there are already several fine hotels around the Airport area with wonderful facilities. One could easily arrive and depart from D/FW, stay in a fine hotel, play golf or tennis, shop and conduct business meetings without ever leaving the physical area of D/FW Airport.

The Airport is located almost exactly equidistant from both Dallas and Fort Worth and to the north of both. It should take approximately 20–25 minutes to get downtown to either city. There are no services available in the Airport zone except those listed under hotels. The only restaurants are located in the hotels but they offer a variety of eating fare. If you have a lot of business in other areas of the city, you might want to choose a hotel in another area because D/FW is an inconvenient location if you need to reach office buildings or restaurants in other zones.

MARKET CENTER

This area is named for the activities that take place here in the Dallas Market Center complex. As you approach Dallas on the west side of the city along Route 35E (Stemmons Freeway) you will encounter a series of large buildings known as the Market Center and including: the Apparel Mart, Decorative Center, Home Furnishings Center, Market Hall, Trade Mart and the World Trade Center. In a 2–3 mile stretch on either side of Route 35, there are numerous office buildings, medical facilities and hotels. The Market Center is only 5–10 minutes from Downtown Dallas. There are fewer services in this zone since it is an industrial area and there are some sections that are not safe. Downtown services are easily accessible from hotels in this zone and to the north LBJ-North zone listings are within 10–15 minutes of hotels in the Market Center. You will also find that the hotels we review in this zone are very complete so it is a good zone to choose.

DOWNTOWN

Dallas is unusual because the central Downtown area is quite small and for a major city it is relatively inactive after 6 P.M. For purposes of our guide we will include in this zone

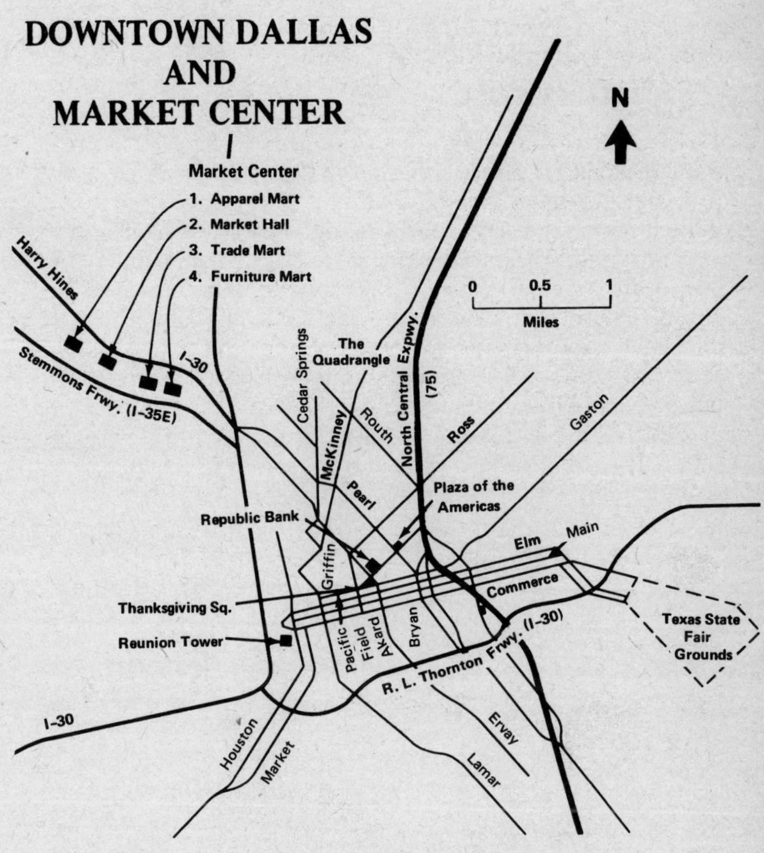
DOWNTOWN DALLAS
AND
MARKET CENTER
N
Market Center
1. Apparel Mart
2. Market Hall
3. Trade Mart
4. Furniture Mart
Harry Hines
Stemmons Frwy. (I-35E)
I-30
0
0.5
1
Miles
Cedar Springs
The
Quadrangle
North Central Expwy.
(75)
McKinney
Routh
Ross
Gaston
Pearl
Plaza of the
Americas
Republic Bank
Griffin
Elm
Main
Commerce
Thanksgiving Sq.
Reunion Tower
Pacific
Field
Akard
Bryan
R. L. Thornton Frwy. (I-30)
Texas State
Fair
Grounds
I-30
Houston
Market
Ervay
Lamar

hotels, services and restaurants in an area bounded roughly by Thornton Freeway (Route 30) on the south; Stemmons Freeway (Route 35E) on the west; along McKinney Avenue on the north, and North Central Expressway on the east. Except during rush hour it should not take longer than 15 minutes to get from one point to another in the Downtown area.

NORTH CENTRAL

This area runs along the most heavily traveled north–south route in Dallas (North Central Expressway–Route 75), from north of Ross Avenue out to LBJ Freeway (I-635). In some instances we have extended the area a few blocks east or west of North Central Expressway. This zone includes the Greenville Avenue "Strip," the road running parallel to North Central Expressway and a block to the east which is the busiest restaurant and nightlife area in the city. An area known as Old Town is a huge shopping and restaurant complex on Greenville Avenue at Lovers Lane.

Everything in this zone is easily accessible to Downtown within 15–20 minutes, except during rush hour when North Central Expressway is one huge parking lot.

LBJ-NORTH

This is our northernmost section including services, hotels and restaurants along the Lyndon B. Johnson (LBJ) Freeway–Interstate 635. LBJ Freeway is a circumferential highway around Dallas and it is the easiest route to travel from east to west especially on the northern edge of the city. Our zone is the area from Stemmons Freeway (Route 35E) at LBJ on the west to just east of North Central Expressway at LBJ on the east.

The next edition of our guide will extend its coverage to the north beyond I-635 but we feel that currently you will find this area fully developed with many fine hotels and restaurants. There are numerous office complexes and malls being developed along LBJ now and in the next few years this LBJ-North area should become almost a second Dallas.

PRACTICAL INFORMATION

The cost of living in Dallas is as high as in most major American cities, but hotels and restaurants here will be less

NORTH CENTRAL AND LBJ–NORTH

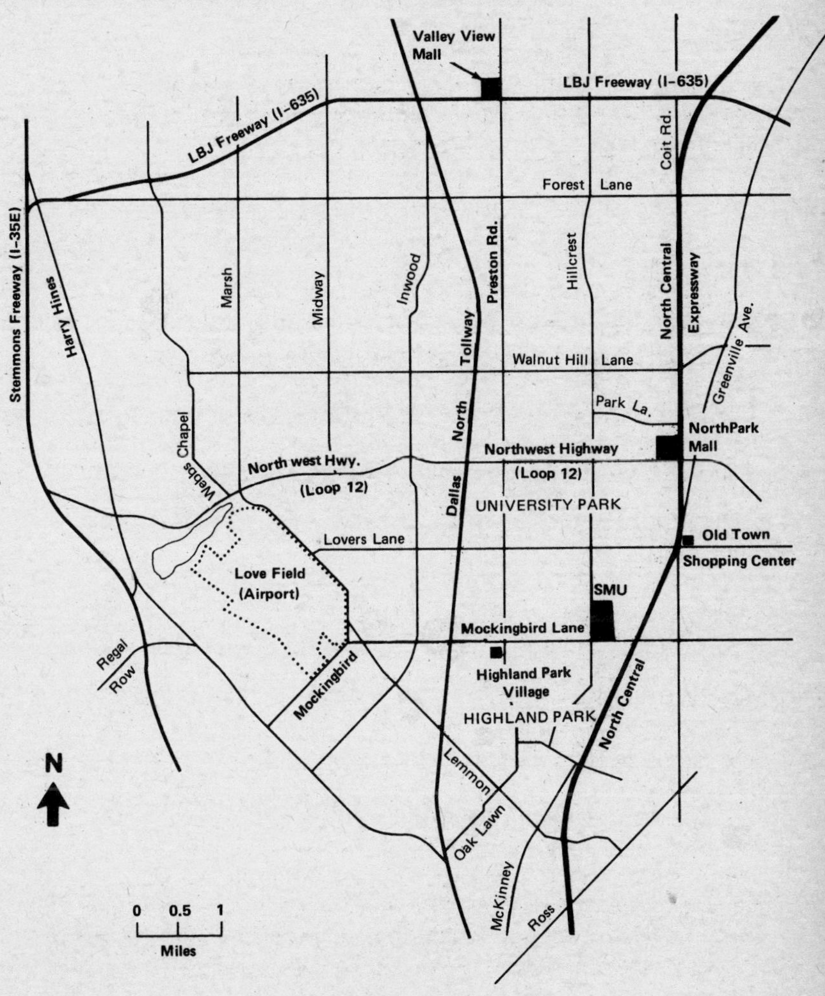

expensive than in many. Tipping and other customs are much the same here as anywhere else in the U.S. A 15% tip in restaurants is standard (but always check the menu to be sure that this has not automatically been added to your bill), with up to 20% for exceptional service. Nevertheless, remember that tips are a reward for good service; we believe that they should not be given if in fact poor service made the meal an unpleasant or exasperating experience.

All service people in hotels are tipped, e.g. the doorman, bellman, room maid, and room service waiter, and, for special favors received or extra attention given, so are the people on guest service and concierge staffs.

Cab drivers expect to be tipped 10% to 15% of the fare. Again, however, if the driver has been surly or unresponsive to your requests or directions, we don't believe the tipping courtesy applies.

In Dallas/Fort Worth the basic coin-operated telephone costs 25¢. Instructions for dialing are usually printed above the telephone or inside the phone booth. If you have any difficulty you can dial "O" and the operator will assist you with your call. The area code for Dallas is (214); the code for Fort Worth is (817).

You will find practical information about prices, hours of business and services in the appropriate chapter. The Dallas Convention and Visitor's Bureau is at 1507 Pacific Street (651-1020).

FOR FOREIGN TRAVELERS

Unlike Europe, the major cities of the United States provide very few visual aids for non–English-speaking travelers. Gradually international signs are appearing but generally foreign business travelers in Dallas and Fort Worth must rely on friendly natives to point in the right direction. There are, of course, many Spanish-speaking people in this region because of the proximity to Mexico. Some hotels, banks and stores (but not many) have multilingual staff members.

Standard American currency is the dollar, available in $1, $5, $10, $20, $50, and $100 denominations. Coins in use are the penny (1¢), nickel (5¢), dime (10¢), quarter (25¢), and half dollar (50¢).

Foreign currency is not easily usable in Dallas/Fort Worth. It is wise to carry travelers checks in U.S. dollars for dining, shopping and other purchases. Look for the chapter on banking services later in this guide for further information. Hotels which provide foreign currency exchange service will be identified in that section. Generally speaking, downtown banks are the most likely spots to exchange foreign currency.

Public telephones are available both indoors and outdoors and are generally located near or inside restaurants, shopping areas, gasoline stations and other public areas.

American cities do not have public toilets as most European cities do and those which are available may not be clean or safe. For clean, safe restrooms one should ask in a department store, hotel, restaurant or in an office building. Many office buildings in this area require a passkey for the door to the restroom. Ask a receptionist for the key.

The best source of help to foreign visitors is a "language bank" sponsored by the Dallas Council on World Affairs and located in the World Trade Center (744-3109). You can telephone and a volunteer will provide you with the name of someone who speaks the language you need. There are over a hundred different languages spoken by "language bank" volunteers on file.

ARRIVAL

YOU may be surprised when you arrive in Dallas not to see any horses tied to hitching posts or cowboys herding cattle along Main Street. We hope you will use this guide to avoid other less humorous surprises. We have tried to give you an advance view of how best to travel to and around Dallas so your visit here will be enjoyable and well-planned.

For special needs the following information should be helpful:

FOREIGN VISITORS	Emergency Travelers Assistance, Dallas/Fort Worth Airport, 574-4420
	Language Bank, World Trade Center, 2100 Stemmons Frwy., 744-3109
	Dallas Council on World Affairs, 3409 Oak Lawn Ave. (near Downtown), 521-2171
HANDICAPPED VISITORS	Dallas Action Center, 670-4014

Most travelers to Dallas arrive by air and most air travelers arrive at Dallas/Fort Worth Regional Airport, 18 miles west of downtown Dallas. Some flights to and from other cities in the state arrive and depart from Love Field which is located within the city limits of Dallas. Major access roads to Dallas are Route 20 along the south; Route 30 across the middle; and Interstate 635 (Lyndon B. Johnson Freeway), a circumferential highway around Dallas. All are multilane, limited-access highways.

DALLAS/FORT WORTH REGIONAL AIRPORT

This airport covers 17,800 acres almost exactly midway between Dallas on the east and Fort Worth on the west (17–

18 miles from each city). It is one of the largest and busiest air traffic centers in the world and is rapidly becoming an international "port" city despite the fact that it is totally landlocked. D/FW handles in excess of 25 million passengers a year making it one of the busiest airports in the world.

Access to and from the airport is very convenient from both Dallas and Fort Worth—Route 114 is the north exit and Route 183 is the south exit. Both are clearly marked as you leave the airport.

You will find this airport one of the best in terms of finding your way as a visiting stranger. The roads are all clearly marked with overhead signs indicating airlines and parking areas. The design is exceptionally functional with all terminals lining International Parkway, the six-lane road which divides the complex running north-south (all access to and from terminals is from this one road and all exits are from your left).

Airlines which service D/FW currently include: Air Canada, Air Jamaica, American, Braniff, Thai International, U.S. Air (formerly Allegheny) Frontier, General Aviation, Ozark, Texas International, British Caledonia, Chaparral, Eastern, Jamaire, Metro, Mexicana, Lufthansa, Delta, Piedmont, Rio, Skyways and Trans-Central.

All terminals are identical in design with arrivals on the upper levels and departures on the lower levels. There are both escalators and elevators. Airtrans service (a computer-operated rail system between air terminals and long-term parking facilities) is located on the lower level and is color-coded with complete operating instructions posted prominently. There is a 25¢ charge for Airtrans (quarters only). Airtrans also takes you to the Amfac Hotel complex located within the airport and to rental car areas.

All baggage claim areas have direct phone lines to each of four rental companies serving D/FW. Pickup and return of rental cars is handled in the remote parking area which is clearly marked in Airtrans cars and along the Parkway. Cars must be returned there so allow yourself plenty of time to drop off and ride Airtrans to your departure terminal.

Ample short-time parking is available for pickup and delivery of travelers immediately outside each terminal. Curbside luggage check-in is another helpful feature. Baggage claim areas are a few short yards away from exit ramps and should you have the misfortune to arrive without your baggage, airline personnel are on duty right there to track it down by computer. If they are not able to get it for you immediately, be sure to have them deliver it to you at your hotel; they are responsible for seeing that your luggage is delivered at no charge to you.

Security check points are now located at the top of each escalator and all persons—traveling or not—must go through the security check point prior to entering the arrival or departure area.

All terminals have gift shops, newsstands, coffee and snack shops and bars. Though hours vary there is usually a spot to buy a snack or cup of coffee within easy walking distance of your departure gate. Waiting areas are clean and comfortable and there is amazingly little hassle involved in arriving or departing from the airport.

Ground transportation between D/FW and Dallas and Fort Worth is provided by Surtran, a bus system run by the two cities and serving hotels and three terminals: Downtown, Union Terminal Bldg.; LBJ & Coit Rd.; and Love Field (closest to Market Center), Mockingbird and Cedar Springs. Schedules and route information is available 24 hours, seven days, 574-2142. General operating hours for Surtran are 6 A.M.–12:30 A.M. Sun.–Fri. Saturday service is more limited. Cash or travelers checks are accepted as payment of fares which currently are $5–$6 one way depending on destination. Tickets may be purchased near baggage claim areas and signs are posted at the exits from the upper level platforms. Throughout the hotel section of this guide we will indicate which hotels provide Surtran service.

One special note of caution regarding Surtran. Since it serves all airline terminals and hotels the routes are circuitous. If you get on at the first terminal and your hotel happens to be the last drop-off spot, you could be an hour and a half on the road. You can ask at the ticket counter for an approximate arrival time.

Should you be tired and not want to wait for the bus there are taxi stands immediately outside each terminal with cabs available at all times. A cab ride into Downtown costs approximately $18 and takes about 45 minutes. This is probably the best method to use if you want to conserve your energy and don't care to ride around to six or eight hotels before you reach your own resting spot. Taxis are air conditioned, relatively reliable and regulated by the city so you can depend on the meter's accuracy. Drivers are friendly and generally honest. Cabs and drivers must display registration numbers so if you have a complaint be sure to note the identifying numbers.

Airport telephone numbers you may need:

Police/Fire Emergency 9911
Police/Fire Non-Emergency 574-4454
Doctor (on call 24 hrs.) 574-6666
Emergency Car Service 251-1741
Emergency Traveler & Handicapped Assistance ... 574-4420
Lost & Found 574-3112

LOVE FIELD

Located in west central Dallas, this inner-city airport is bounded by Mockingbird Lane, Denton Drive, Northwest Highway and Lemmon Avenue. The airport is limited to air travel within the state, and to neighboring states. Its hours of operation are much more limited than D/FW, and because the airport has no general telephone number, you must call individual airlines for flight information. It is in the middle of a residential area and is always the source of local controversy because of noise level and general nuisance complaints.

Texas International, Southwest and Muse Air are the three major airlines using this airport and there are terminals located off the main tower building which are well-marked and easy to get to. This airport will be important for the business traveler who has come to Dallas and might have to travel to Houston, Austin, San Antonio or another major Texas city. It provides relatively inexpensive flights to other cities in Texas and it is closer to many of the hotels. There is plenty of parking, both long- and short-term, and Surtran service is also available. Cab stands are located in front of the main entrance.

ARRIVAL BY CAR

As is true of most urban centers, Dallas has peak traffic times from 7–9 A.M. and 4–6 P.M. weekdays so it is best to avoid travel on major arteries at those times whenever possible. Arrival around midday is probably best.

Route 30 to the northeast is the major highway coming in from Arkansas. Route 20 runs east-west from Shreveport, La., all the way across the northern half of Texas. Access from Texas cities to the south is best using Route 45 from Houston and Route 35 from San Antonio and Austin.

One great asset is the beautiful condition of Texas roads and the fact that highways are very well-marked so you should have little trouble navigating your car into Dallas. Generally speaking, all roads lead to downtown or to I-635 (LBJ Freeway). Check the maps for the most direct routes to our various zones.

ARRIVAL BY BUS

If you travel by bus to Dallas you will arrive in downtown Dallas and due to the rather unsafe nature of center-city bus terminals, you should plan to arrive in daylight. The two major bus stations are within a very short distance of the central business district and major center-city hotels.

GREYHOUND BUS TERMINAL, Commerce at Lamar, 741-1481
TRAILWAYS, 1500 Jackson Street, 655-7000

ARRIVAL BY TRAIN

So few people arrive in Dallas by train that we could almost eliminate this reference. However, Reunion Station is located at the lower end of Downtown in a newly restored area which includes the Hyatt Regency hotel and the Reunion Tower complex. Train service is by Amtrak and information can be obtained by calling 653-1101. The main train route is north to St. Louis and Chicago. Service has now been reduced to one train a day, three days a week.

HOTELS

CONVENTIONS, meetings, seminars–all roads seem to lead to Dallas, which hosts 1,600 conventions per year with over two million attendees. It doesn't take a veteran business traveler to realize what a strain so many visitors place on hotel accommodations, not to mention car-rental agencies, restaurants and taxis. As a business traveler, you can't afford to drag yourself from one hotel to another in search of a bed for the night. If you intend to come to Dallas you should book your hotel as soon as possible. Chances of finding a room on a day or two's notice are slim to none.

In general, Dallas hotels are very busy during the earlier part of the week, and less fully booked over the weekends. If you want to enjoy sightseeing or shopping along with your business trip you might wish to take advantage of one of the many package deals offered by Dallas hotels for weekend guests.

For purposes of our guide we have included the best that Dallas has to offer the out-of-town business traveler from luxury suites to basic double rooms in zones which are carefully aligned with major business activity centers. Every hotel listed is recommended so that you can be assured of clean, safe, comfortable accommodations. We have excluded any facility which was unsafe or which offered unpleasant facilities or services.

Every major national motel chain is represented in each of our zones. Days Inns, Quality Inns, Howard Johnsons and Holiday Inns are as familiar a sight on major highways as are the chains of fast-food franchises. You can rely on the nationally known motel chains for clean, safe and generally economical accommodations. We have included some special ones in our reviews but generally we have not reviewed basic motels.

RATINGS

General eye appeal and comfort are important, but we have also given consideration to location, security, and business and personal services available. Some hotels have absolutely everything and others are lacking in some services; our criteria are objective but our analyses must be somewhat subjective, so hotel ratings are based on overall impressions of a hotel as much as on how many of our listed criteria it meets. You will find that in Dallas, hotels often do not have the large lobby areas familiar in older hotels in other parts of the country, and as a result there are fewer lobby shops, barber and beauty shops (so we have had to alter our criteria slightly to fit the city). You will find that most Dallas hotels have convenient parking (usually free), swimming pool or other health facilities, small but well-stocked newsstands, and some restaurant facility. Most have laundry and dry cleaning weekdays only.

We have rated Dallas hotels according to what we feel most business travelers want. We have visited most hotels several times, both by appointment and anonymously. Still, there is no way to rate the quality of certain services. As in any business, there are good days and bad; you may be disappointed when a desk clerk is inattentive or room service is slow. Should you find that a listed service is no longer available or of inferior quality, please let us know.

All hotels listed have individually controlled air conditioning and heat, color TV and bath in all rooms. In Dallas, most suites have only one bathroom, usually with access only through the bedroom.

★★★★ **Superb.** These hotels are the finest in Dallas. All conveniences for business travelers are provided and decor and rooms are outstanding. All include the following (except when noted):

1. Good room service hours.
2. Same-day laundry and dry cleaning service.
3. Food and beverage facilities on the premises.
4. Newsstand or lobby shops that sell basic items.
5. Meeting rooms with equipment rental and catering service.
6. Accept all major credit cards.

★★★ **Excellent.** Hotels in this category are of high quality but are lacking in business services or some other area which places it below our "Superb" listing.

★★ **Very Good.** Adequate services and generally comfortable, convenient accommodations identify these hotels though they may be lacking in a specific service. Usually mid-priced and a good choice.

★ **Good.** Clean, reliable but perhaps without business services. Usually less expensive but safe and comfortable.

OK. Hotels in this group are very basic—clean, safe and convenient but offering no services. A good choice if your other selections are all booked.

PRICES

Dallas hotels are reasonable compared to those of other major cities. Prices, of course, change rapidly so we have given you a range which should prove a useful guide. Categories will remain accurate even though inflation may alter the dollar figures. Prices are for single-person occupancy in a regular double, with no meals, tax, or tips included.

$$$$	Luxury	$80 or more
$$$	Very Expensive	$60–$80
$$	Expensive	$40–$60
$	Moderate	$40 or less

Your quoted price from the reservation clerk can represent the best room in the range—meaning a fine view or perhaps a few extra square feet. If price matters be sure to indicate your wish to have a room at the lower end of the range.

LOCATION

A word is in order about the choice of hotels in Dallas and their location. Obviously, you will want to stay in a hotel which is closest to the main scene of your business transactions. Here are some tips which may help you decide which zone to choose.

The airport hotels are useful if you need to fly in and out

of Dallas on a tight time schedule. There are no outside services or restaurants in this zone, but the hotels we have included here have very complete facilities. A trip Downtown for a meeting or dinner will cost about $36 round trip by taxi.

The Market Center zone is made up mainly of the buildings of the Market Center complex, surrounded by industrial and hospital buildings. There are few service or shopping areas here and you will find that most hotels in this zone have very complete in-house facilities, including many restaurants. You should choose this area if you have business at the Market or if you are content to use your hotel for most of your needs. This area is not far from Downtown or LBJ-North by car, but it would be inconvenient if you had to depend on taxis to get you around town.

For the first-time Dallas visitor, the zones with the most complete services, restaurants and generally more active nightlife are LBJ-North and North Central. As you will note from the maps these two zones are in the heart of Dallas geographically and are probably the most centrally located zones for business travelers who want to get a full view of all that Dallas has to offer. The trip downtown from either of these zones takes about 15–20 minutes depending on traffic. Many major office complexes are located in these zones also.

Downtown Dallas is very busy during office hours but is relatively quiet at night except in the major hotels. There is plenty of fine dining in town but it is not the kind of city which lends itself to nighttime strolls for window shopping. It is literally closed after dark.

The choice of location is one only you can make depending on your business needs and the location of offices you must visit. Try to pick the most central location for your needs and you will probably find hotels and restaurants to suit your taste and expense account.

As for room location, most hotels have their quiet side and if concentration and solitude are important to you, you should request such a room. You won't want a poolside room if you are feverishly ironing out details of a contract. And do try to avoid locations near ice and soda machines too.

SECURITY

Room security does not seem to be as big an issue in Dallas as in other major cities. Most hotels use ordinary keys, many with the room number right on it. Only one hotel, the Anatole, uses the computer card key system at this time (guests are issued cards programmed by computer to open only their door; there is no room number on the card and cards are reprogrammed at check-out so that each guest actually receives a brand new key). As of this writing, only the Mansion on Turtle Creek uses the Winfield rotating cylinder lock system, where locks can be changed immediately in an emergency and are periodically rotated to change keys. Most rooms have chains and deadbolt locks.

Fire security, with all its recent publicity, is a bigger issue. Since many hotels have been built within the last few years fire and safety feaures including sprinklers, smoke detectors and advanced communications to all guest rooms are provided. We found an increased awareness on the part of hotel managers and staff regarding guest safety and most are currently reviewing their policies and procedures to provide the best preventive measures possible. For your own sake, be sure to locate the nearest exit, carry a flashlight in your luggage and be aware of the layout of your room. It could save your life.

BUSINESS CLASS SERVICES

This is relatively new to Dallas hotels, and where it exists it generally consists of a top-quality room, complimentary continental breakfast and morning newspaper, and extra amenities such as bathrobe, special soaps and nightly turndown service. It does not usually include separate check-in. Some hotels are now providing separate floors for this area, with separate lounge areas and concierge on duty. Only a few now provide complete concierge service and we have indicated those that do.

RESERVATIONS

Whenever possible, we have listed toll-free telephone numbers (800) for your convenience. Toll-free numbers may be dialed only from the continental U.S. Try to remember that hotel reservation clerks are not highly paid and often are not able to cope with your questions or needs. We have found this to be true especially when using centralized toll-free calls to large chains.

Whenever possible, get the name of the person who takes your reservation and note the date and time of your call. Always insist on being mailed a confirmation slip. If there is not enough time, insist on a telegram or cable confirming your reservation. Always let the hotel know if you expect to be arriving quite late, so that your room can be held for you. Some credit cards now guarantee rooms for you, but you should know that if you do not arrive until the next day, you will be charged for the missed night's stay. In any case, if a hotel knows that you are coming from quite far away and will be depending on airline connections, they will make an effort to keep your room for you. If you require a suite, we suggest you call the hotel directly and speak personally to the director of sales. This way, you will get quality service and knowledgeable information about available facilities. When you do this, always identify yourself as a corporate traveler. Virtually every director of sales in Dallas knows us and we suggest strongly that you mention our book as your source. We feel that this may get you better service.

D/FW AIRPORT

★★★ **AMFAC HOTEL AND RESORT**
$$$$ **Dallas/Fort Worth Airport**
(214) 453-8400; (800) 227-4700; Telex 9108605932
All major credit cards

Texas's largest hotel has some of the best business services and facilities we have encountered. The hotel is really two separate hotel buildings, an East and a West Tower connected by a quarter-mile footpath across the Airport's main road. There are golf carts which run back and forth from one side to the other and guests may hop a ride if there is space available. Each side of the hotel has a huge lobby area where registration desks and cashiers are available at all times. At least two bellmen are on duty 24 hours and luggage is never seen piled up in the lobbies. Registration desks can be converted to cashiers for fast check-out service during a rush, and in spite of the masses of arriving and departing conventioneers, we've always seen this area handled quickly and efficiently. An information desk is staffed by two people at all times and there is also a concierge desk.

Although they function so well, we do find the lobbies here unattractive, highlighted by gaudy purple carpeting and a cold and transient feeling. Large wall hangings post the hours of all available services and eating establishments in the complex and there are many car-rental and airline desks.

Accommodations

There are 1,450 rooms in the two towers and 75 suites. The rooms are attractively decorated and amazingly quiet considering the location of the hotel—right next to the runway! Each room has a wall unit with fold-down desk, a leather recliner, color TV with remote control for closed-circuit films, UPI wire news service, stock market reports and flight schedules, and AM/FM radio and alarm clock. Standard rooms are quite spacious with a full-length mirror and conversation area including a couch, chair and table. Bathrooms and closets are also spacious. All regular suites have a parlor, bedroom, and one and a half baths.

The penthouse level on the 13th floor of the East Tower (which the hotel calls the 33rd floor) has both regular doubles and suites. All rooms on this level are exceptional and each is decorated differently. All rooms have full component stereos and marble bathrooms in addition to the ordinary amenities. This floor also has four Club Suites, larger than other suites in the hotel, with two bedrooms, two and a half baths, and each with wet bar, refrigerator and Jacuzzi bath. The two-story Townhouse Suite has even more: elevated platform bed, stereo in every room and crystal chandelier. The best things about this penthouse floor, though, are the guard to check passes, the 24-hour concierge, 24-hour room service and free valet service.

Personal Services

Room service with no minimum charge is available 6:30 A.M.–1 A.M. Same-day laundry and dry cleaning service is available Mon.–Sat. Both a doctor and dentist are on the premises during business hours to answer calls; at other times the hotel is serviced by the D/FW Airport paramedic team. Babysitters, cribs and rollaways can be arranged. There are safe-deposit boxes and a cashier is on duty at all times. Deak-Perera in the West Tower can exchange foreign currency. A beauty and barber shop is open 9 A.M.–5 P.M. Mon.–Sat. The newsstand which sells incidentals is open seven days, 6:30 A.M.–10 P.M. Transportation to the various airline terminals is available free 24 hours.

Bear Creek Country Club, owned and operated by the hotel, is a few minutes away and includes facilities for golf, tennis, racquetball and jogging. The facility is large enough to accommodate 500 people for a tournament. This is truly a completely self-contained resort facility.

Business Services

The Amfac has the largest ballroom and exhibit hall in the state of Texas and it is perfect for large conventions. There are 70 corporate meeting rooms which can handle from 10 to 2,500 persons. The Convention Services Department can handle even the smallest meeting to the last detail.

The Enterprise Ballroom in the East Tower can accommodate 2,100 for banquets and 3,000 for meetings and can be divided into eight separate meeting rooms. The entire room is ringed by projection booths near the ceiling and there is a drive-in door for autos. An elaborate lighting system, including spotlights, can be controlled by a wall switch. A large prefunction area surrounds the ballroom with faceted mirrors and red carpeting. There are four separate wet bars and a coatroom.

Across from the ballroom are 13 breakout rooms and two exhibit areas. The West Tower has 30 meeting rooms. Slide projectors, tape recorders, and other equipment can be rented from the audiovisual department 24 hours a day. Secretarial services can be provided as well as business machines and translation service. A photocopier is available for guest use but the Telex machine is not.

Eating and Drinking

There are eight restaurants and five bars in the hotel and their hours of operation are posted in the lobby of each tower. One note: the hours are subject to rather frequent change and there are times when there will not be an open restaurant in one Tower so you will have to travel to the other. Check carefully in the lobby to determine exact operating hours.

The Branding Iron is open for dinner Mon.–Sat., brunch

only on Sunday. Also open for dinner every evening are Il Nonno's, Mister G's (see review in restaurant chapter), and Le Cassoulet. Papaya's serves breakfast and lunch seven days and Brighton Express serves lunch only. Harvey House is open seven days, 24 hours. Sullivan's Pub serves lunch and drinks and Whispers is open for cocktails and dancing.

★★ HOLIDAY INN-D/FW AIRPORT NORTH
$$ 4441 West Highway 114, Irving
(214) 255-7147; (800) 238-8000
All major credit cards

This hotel is in the process of remodeling all of its rooms. While it is certainly not a luxury hotel we feel the range of services provided makes it a desirable place for meetings. The lobby is large and attractive with a fountain and an atrium/garden. The front desk is well staffed and keys and mail are not visible. A bellman is on duty at all times to direct the flow of arriving and departing guests.

Accommodations

Hallways are long and lighted by industrial fluorescent lighting. There are 300 rooms and four suites. Decor here is depressing, caused by an uncontrolled use of orange in carpets, on walls and furniture. All rooms have color TV, AM/FM radio, an alarm clock, two comfortable chairs and a small table. There is no writing desk. There are several rooms with king-sized beds.

Some suites have refrigerators. The Presidential Suite, on two levels with four bedrooms and two baths adjoining a parlor, would be ideal for a company's president and several officers to share. Doors have chains and double lock against passkey.

Personal Services

Room service is provided from 6:30 A.M.–10:30 P.M. Laundry and dry cleaning, available weekdays, features same-day service if in by 9 A.M. Pets may stay in rooms with guests, and cribs and rollaways are available. There are safe-deposit boxes and a cashier is on duty 24 hours a day. The gift shop in the lobby is open seven days 8 A.M.–11 P.M. Free transportation is provided to D/FW Airport.

Business Services

There are seven large and five small meeting rooms, all of which are being remodeled. There is a catering department and meetings can be arranged for 50 to 1,000 persons. The largest meeting area, Convention Hall, has a loading entrance large enough for a car to enter. The International Ballroom has a nice pre-function area that leads to the Executive meeting rooms which all have glass sliding doors with a nice view of the lobby fountain. There is an audiovisual company on the premises and a typewriter and telecopier are available in the sales office weekdays from 9 A.M. to 6 P.M.

Eating and Drinking

GiGi restaurant is open seven days, 6:30 A.M.–11 P.M. Club GiGi, a bar with entertainment, is open 10 A.M.–2 A.M. and there is a membership fee.

★★ HOLIDAY INN-D/FW AIRPORT SOUTH

$$ 4440 West Airport Freeway, Irving
(214) 256-4541; (800) 238-8000
All major credit cards

Within the next year this recently remodeled hotel will be undergoing construction for an additional 175 guest rooms, 17 meeting rooms and a Holidome recreation center. The decor throughout is based on flying, with old photographs of flights on the walls and room numbers displayed on wooden airplanes. The rooms are among the nicest we have seen for the price but the meeting facilities are beginning to show signs of wear and tear with sagging ceilings and chipped moldings. We feel that the hotel's rating will probably change when renovation is complete.

Accommodations

There are 249 rooms and only two suites. Unlike the usual Holiday Inn decor, rooms are dominated by pale greens and brown, and have a feeling of comfort and ease. All rooms have color TV with free HBO movies but no radio or clock. One wall is mirrored, there is a wire rack for hanging clothes and some rooms have a writing desk with chair. Some rooms have doors leading to the parking lot or pool areas. Bathrooms are adequate with woodgrained formica counter tops.

Personal Services

Room service with a minimum charge of $1.50 is available 6 A.M.–10 P.M. Same-day laundry and dry cleaning service is provided Monday through Saturday if in by 8 A.M. Babysitters, cribs and rollaways can be arranged. A cashier is on duty 24 hours and there is a lobby car-rental agency. Safe-deposit boxes are available and free transportation to D/FW Airport is provided seven days every half hour around the clock.

Business Services

There are three large and two small meeting rooms holding 15 to 225 people. Screens, easels and blackboards are free and other audiovisual equipment and business machines can be arranged. Guests may make copies in the office Mon.–Fri. 9 A.M.–6 P.M. and Sat.–Sun. 9 A.M.–3 P.M.

Eating and Drinking

L'Escale is the only restaurant in the hotel and serves American food from 6 A.M.–10 P.M., seven days. Spirit de Corps is the bar which is open Mon.–Sat. until 1:30 A.M., Sun. from noon–midnight.

OK LA QUINTA MOTOR INN

$ 4105 West Airport Freeway, Irving
(214) 252-6546; (800) 292-5200
All major credit cards

Other than prime location (only five minutes from the airport) this hotel offers very little to the business traveler. The rooms are adequate for a good night's sleep but not conducive to working in your room since they have only a small desk and an uncomfortable chair. Parking is available right outside your room. The lobby is not a place you will spend much time.

Accommodations

There are 169 rooms and no suites in this hotel. Rooms are rather small and have one or two beds. There is color TV with VUE programs (cable) and an AM/FM radio in each room. Bathrooms are hidden behind accordion-pleated partitions and are not very appealing. Access to all rooms is from the outside like a motel. Doors have chains and double locks.

Personal Services

There is no room service but laundry and dry cleaning in by 8 A.M. is returned that day. Cribs, rollaways and sitters can be provided. There are safe-deposit boxes and a cashier is on duty 24 hours. Newspaper dispensers are in the lobby. There is free transportation to the airport 24 hours.

Business Services

The three meeting rooms can accommodate 15 to 60 persons. Beverage service is available for meetings but no food service, and there are no other business services.

Eating and Drinking

There is no restaurant in the hotel but there is a 24-hour one next door. A private club with free membership for hotel guests serves drinks 5 P.M.–2 A.M., seven days.

MARKET CENTER

★★★★ **LOEW'S ANATOLE DALLAS**
$$$$ **2201 Stemmons Freeway**
(214)748-1200; (800) 223-0880; Telex 730475
All major credit cards and personal check

The Loew's Anatole is a unique landmark along sprawling Stemmons Freeway. Like almost everything else in Dallas, the hotel is new, built only four years ago. It is part of the Dallas Market Center.

A red brick building supports a trio of glass pyramids. Under the pyramids are two spectacular atria filled with trees, woven tapestries and Texas sunshine. The spacious lobby has marble floors and green velvet couches on a rich wool rug shaped like the octagonal stained-glass dome overhead. Arriving guests are greeted here by several doormen and a bell captain. The registration desk, covered in a bright gold metal, is always staffed by knowledgeable people. The hotel uses the new computer card lock system, changing the "key" with each new guest (the management would not discuss other security measures). There is a Braniff and American ticket agency as well as a rental car desk in the lobby. Pay phones are hidden in a room off the entrance and the elevator bank is hard to find and poorly lit.

Accommodations

The hallways all overlook the atria and are flooded with light. The hotel has 900 rooms including 52 suites. Rooms are very large and have a light, airy feel to them. Chrome headboards, butcher-block tables, Breuer chairs and museum posters team up with natural-colored cotton drapes and spreads.

A standard guest room has either two double beds or a king-sized bed, a conversation area with sofa, chairs and table, a parsons-style desk, color TV and AM/FM digital clock radio. A full-length mirror covers the closet, and the bath has a separate dressing area with a lighted makeup mirror.

All regular suites are different from each other in size and decor, and all are located at the corner of each floor (affording extra windows). Each suite has a bedroom and parlor and one and a half baths. All bathrooms are large and have extra toiletries. The seven Presidential Suites have breathtaking views of Downtown. The feeling here is more New York than Dallas: parquet floors, plush Oriental carpets, Chinese furniture and original art work. There are extra large towels in the bathrooms and silver ice buckets.

The Anatole has separate business class floors with a separate concierge on duty most of the time. Extra amenities include complimentary continental breakfast, fruit, cheese and wine in the afternoon, and brandy and cigar in the evening. There is nightly turndown service as well as separate laundry, valet and shoeshine service, VIP toilet kit and bathrobe.

Personal Services

Room service is 24 hours a day and there is no minimum charge. The concierge in the lobby promises to provide everything from translation to getting tickets to Cowboys' football games, and running buses to the Stadium. There is one-day dry cleaning, laundry and tailoring offered weekdays. A doctor, dentist or babysitter can be recommended in the area. A cashier is open 24 hours and can exchange most foreign currencies. There is an indoor swimming pool, a health spa with saunas, Jacuzzis and a well-known masseuse. A few blocks away, there are tennis courts for a small fee. The barber and beauty shop are open Mon.–Sat. from 7 A.M. until 5:30 P.M. In the lobby, you'll find many elegant shops including a Western-wear shop, an art gallery, a florist and the Atrium Boutique. A drugstore is open from 7 A.M. until 10:45 P.M.

Business Services

The hotel has 32 meeting rooms on three levels and a catering department that can handle any group. The Grand Ballroom is the largest and can accommodate up to 2,800 for a reception. The room can be divided into five sections and is ornately decorated with dark green carpet and walls and gold seats. An impressive lobby area surrounds this room where people may relax on downy couches or catch a glimpse of themselves in the gilded mirror, before a meeting. The Stemmons Amphitheatre Auditorium holds 1,000 and is sleekly designed: narrow wood slats and bright red carpeting create a dramatic effect. Just off the Atrium II, on the main floor, the Jade Room is the hotel's premier reception room and holds 50 people for VIP use only. Exquisite jade objects from around the world, Danish tapestries and rugs and an eight-foot antique table provide most of the atmosphere. And if all these rooms are not enough for you, the hotel can arrange for space in the 3,000-square-foot Dallas Market, just a two minute walk away. There is an audiovisual company on the hotel premises, and a photocopier is available 24 hours a day. The

Telex is available on request, but the hotel has no secretarial or messenger service.

Eating and Drinking

There are three bars in the hotel generally open until 2 A.M.; two have excellent pianists. There are five restaurants. The Mirage Kiosk, occupying the center of Atrium II, serves light meals 24 hours. The Mirage Bar is directly across the marble lane and opens at 11 A.M. For disco dancing, there's Crocodile and for classical music try the Lobby Bar. Both are open until 2 A.M. L'Entrecote serves continental cuisine at lunch (buffet weekdays) and dinner. La Esquina is open for lunch weekdays, dinner nightly, and Saturday brunch. The Plum Blossom, an elegant Chinese restaurant, serves dinner only and is closed Sundays. The Chanticleer stays open until midnight daily for snacks and complete meals.

★ **DU PONT PLAZA**
$ **899 Stemmons Freeway**
(214)748-8161
All major credit cards

More like a large motel than a hotel, the DuPont Plaza remains almost as it was decorated in the 1960s and very little has been done to keep up with modern furnishings in the lobby or guest rooms. The lobby has 25-foot windows which light up the first level and there is a round of sunken couches in burnt orange prints. The registration area is well staffed and although we've seen lines it seems to run smoothly. Baggage is kept out of sight in a separate room off the lobby, and keys and mail are secure.

Accommodations

There are 800 rooms and only eight suites in the DuPont Plaza and hallways are wide and well-lighted. Rooms have a mirrored wall, large windows, a table with two chairs but no desk. Bathrooms are quite spacious and nicely tiled. There is a telephone next to the shower and a convenient electric outlet. A separate vanity area outside the bath is nice and has a separate chair so you could use it as a desk surface. Doors have chains, peepholes and pushbutton locks on the knobs.

Personal Services

Room service operates 6:30 A.M.–10 P.M. Same-day laundry and dry cleaning service is available as well as rollaways and cribs. There is a small exercise room and a barber shop in the basement open Mon.–Fri. 9 A.M.–5 P.M. A large gift shop which also sells clothing is open seven days 7:30 A.M.–9 P.M. Safe-deposit boxes are available and a cashier is on duty 24 hours.

Business Services

There are ten meeting rooms which can serve 12 to 700 in any type seating arrangement. The Crystal Ballroom is the largest room and can be divided into three separate rooms. There is a small pre-function area and a coatroom. Catering services are available and audiovisual equipment can be arranged. A photocopier is available for guest use during normal business hours.

Eating and Drinking

The restaurant, The Greenery, is open 6:30 A.M.–10 P.M. and has an excellent lunch buffet. Reflections, the lounge, is open seven days, noon–2 A.M.

OK **HOLIDAY INN-MARKET CENTER**
$ **1955 North Industrial Boulevard**
(214) 747-9551; (800) 238-8000
All major credit cards

The Holiday Inn is right down the street from the Apparel Mart and suitable for the business traveler on a budget who wishes to have a comfortable room and does not demand much in the way of services. Registration and cashier areas are small but well-staffed and there is a small lobby area with sofas and a few chairs. There is also a lounge area with electronic games.

Accommodations

There are 247 rooms and no suites in this hotel. All rooms have modern furnishings and are decorated in shades of brown and orange. Each room has a color TV and some rooms have an AM/FM radio. Bathrooms have ample counter space and electrical outlets near the sink. Doors have chains, double locks and peepholes.

Personal Services

Room service is available 7 A.M.–2 P.M. and 5–10 P.M. Same-day laundry and dry cleaning and emergency tailoring are available. A doctor and dentist are on call; babysitters and cribs are available as well as rollaways. Safe-deposit boxes are located at the front desk and a cashier is on duty 24 hours. There is free transportation to Love Field and hourly Surtran service around the clock to D/FW.

Business Services

There are four large and three small meeting rooms which are carpeted and can accommodate 25 to 300 persons. The largest room is divisible into three rooms so you can use it for a meeting, lunch and classroom simultaneouly. There are also some very small rooms off the main room suitable for exhibits. Catering is available on the premises and secretarial and translation services can be arranged. The hotel will arrange for audiovisual equipment rental.

Eating and Drinking

South Forty Restaurant is open seven days, 6 A.M.–2 P.M. and 5–10 P.M. The cocktail lounge is open 11 A.M.–midnight.

★★ LE BARON HOTEL

$$ 1055 Regal Row
(214) 634-8550 (800) 527-5208
All major credit cards

Located near Texas Stadium in Irving, the Le Baron is about a fifteen-minute drive from Downtown and ten minutes from the Market Center. The hotel has been open seven years and has a friendly atmosphere, in spite of a lobby that lacks comfort and space. The life-size portraits of presidents, kings and entertainers by Dmitri Vail, which hang everywhere there seems to have been an empty space, do not help to make the area—which includes a sunken bar lounge—distinctive, and unless you are waiting for someone, the small seating area near the registration desk is not an inviting spot for a repose. The front desk serves as both registration area and cashier and is well-staffed. A doorman and assistant manager are very visible.

Accommodations

All rooms we saw were clean, comfortable and spacious. The 11-floor high-rise building has 354 rooms and 15 suites. There are brown carpets, beige drapes and rust spreads. Each room has a writing desk, chair and brass-plated lamp. The bathrooms are adequate and have a separate vanity area and electrical outlet. All rooms have color TV, and a comfortable recliner but no alarm clock or radio, which makes it easy to go to sleep but hard to wake up. A guest has a choice of shower or bathtub, but not both, so be sure to state your preference when you make your reservation. There are electric kettles in each room with coffee fixings, and complimentary coffee is served in the lobby from midnight until 7 A.M. You should know that the hotel has a very popular discotheque on its 12th floor, so the top floors here are not necessarily the quietest.

Personal Services

The hotel offers room service between 6 A.M. and midnight. There is same-day service for laundry and dry cleaning in by 9 A.M. Babysitters can be arranged by the operator but there are no provisions for either medical or dental care. Pets are allowed in the rooms. There is an exercise room, a hot tub, a running track, two well-lighted tennis courts and an outdoor heated swimming pool. A cashier is on duty from 8 A.M. to 5:30 P.M. and foreign currency can be exchanged if arranged in advance. Limousine and bus service runs every half hour around the clock to Love Field and every hour to D/FW. Safe-deposit boxes are at the front desk. The newsstand in the gift shop is open from 7 A.M. until 8 P.M.

Business Services

From 10 to 1,000 persons can be accommodated in the 22 meeting rooms. Audiovisual equipment can be rented. The staff chef will arrange to cater any meeting. There is a photocopier for guest use available seven days around the clock and requests for secretarial and translation services are referred to a local agency.

Eating and Drinking

If you are a guest at the hotel, a membership fee for drinks will not be tacked onto your bill. A $10 fee per year covers the membership for all clubs in the hotel for nonguests. The V.I.P. Lounge in the lobby is open from 4 until 8 P.M. and features piano music in the evenings. The Jabberwocky Club, a favorite spot with locals on weekends, for disco and Country & Western dancing, is open Mon.–Sat. from 5 P.M. until 2 A.M. For a light meal, the Bakery is open from 6 A.M. to midnight serving American and creole food. High Cotten serves prime rib luncheon specials and dinners Mon.–Sat. from 11:30 A.M. until 8 P.M. On the 12th floor, the Italian Pavilion looks out over the Dallas skyline. The Italian food is very good and service is excellent. Open for dinner, drinks and dancing Mon.–Sat. 6 to 11 P.M.

★★ MARRIOTT MARKET CENTER
$$ 2101 Stemmons Freeway
(214) 748-8551; (800) 228-9290;
Telex 910 861 9313
All major credit cards

The Dallas Marriott is located directly across from the World Trade Center and the Apparel Mart and is only five minutes from Downtown. Rooms are comfortable if a bit on the small side and the hotel offers excellent meeting facilities.

The lobby is large and inviting, decorated in Spanish-style with high-beamed ceilings, an iron chandelier with yellow lights, tiled floors and a huge stone fireplace. Chairs are leather, and potted palms in terra-cotta containers seem to be everywhere. Just off the lobby, a door leads to the sprawling pool area with lush landscaping—one of the best in town. The electronic game room attracts business people as well as youngsters.

In spite of all the space in the lobby, bellmen often seem to be overrun with luggage that is stacked high and deep. This is a real problem during markets, since buyers tend to carry more than one suitcase. Check-in can be slow due to lack of help.

Accommodations

The hotel has 476 rooms and nine suites—all perfectly adequate for the price. Generally on the small side, rooms have one or two double beds, a writing desk attached to a bureau, a chair and lamp, nightstand, color TV and clock radio. Bathrooms are small with no vanity space. All rooms have a balcony. Suites are decorated as undistinctively as regular rooms, but have a small parlor and one or two standard bathrooms, each with bath. Some suites have wet bar and refrigerator.

Personal Services

Room service operates from 6:30 A.M. to 10:30 P.M. Laundry and dry cleaning in by 8:45 A.M. is back by 5 P.M. A doctor is on call and the hotel will recommend a dentist. Babysitters and cribs are available; pets can stay in the rooms. The cashier is open 24 hours and will exchange foreign money. There is a very nice gift shop open seven days from 7 A.M. until 11 P.M. that carries luggage and designer clothing. A Hertz car-rental agency in the lobby is open weekdays 8 A.M.–6 P.M. The barber shop is open Mon.–Fri. from 9 A.M. until 5 P.M. Guests may use the hotel's safe or safe-deposit boxes, and women traveling alone are given rooms closest to the lobby.

Business Services

There are 11 meeting rooms at the Marriott and the bullfighter theme is carried through in each one. Some are located on the balcony over the lobby and others are in a separate building. Full catering is available. There are blackboards, podiums, microphones and platforms available and audiovisual equipment is rented from Federal Progress. Secretarial services and use of a photocopier can be arranged with a little notice.

Eating and Drinking

The hotel has three restaurants and one bar. A coffee shop in the lobby is open from 6:30 A.M. until midnight. Allie's Pantry serves light meals from 6:30 A.M. until 11:30 P.M. Las Columnas has a dark, romantic setting and serves lunch from 11 A.M. to 2 P.M. and dinner from 6 to 11 P.M. Clancy's Saloon, open 4:30 P.M. to 2 A.M., is attractive, decorated in brass, antiques and memorabilia.

★★★ THE REGENT

$$ Mockingbird and Stemmons
(214) 630-7000; (800) 527-9510
All major credit cards

The Regent, a lovely 350-room hotel located a few minutes from Love Field, offers convenient and comfortable business headquarters. The decor here is modern with plenty of woodsy touches–brown and orange with much use of brick, oak and greenery. A stroll through the sunny atrium is a refreshing break on a busy day. The hotel has a staff of meeting assistants at your disposal and there is a homey feeling about the way things are done.

The registration area is small and luggage is often piled up in the lobby because of the limited space between the front door and the desk. There is a large room off the lobby with comfortable seating, to get away from the bustling lobby.

Accommodations

All rooms and suites at the Regent are spacious and attractive. They are decorated in earth tones with geometric patterns on spreads and drapes. Each room has a separate writing desk and comfortable chair and color TV. Bathrooms all have electrical outlets and extra towels, but are smaller than in other hotels.

The suites are appointed with the same fabrics and furniture as the regular rooms. Bedrooms (one or two) are the same size but the parlor is spacious with sectional couches, fabric-covered walls and tall plants. We like the suites overlooking the swimming pool with sliding glass doors and long balconies. The penthouse suites offer the best views, and also have stereo, wet bar and refrigerator, separate vanities in the bathroom and more expensive furnishings.

Personal Services

Room service operates from 6:30 A.M. to 11:30 P.M. and there is a $2.50 minimum charge. One-day laundry and dry cleaning is available. The hotel knows where to find a babysitter in a few minutes, but they cannot refer you to a doctor or dentist. Cribs and rollaway beds can be requested but pets are not permitted in rooms. There are safe-deposit boxes for guests. The kidney-shaped pool has a cabana bar open on weekends from noon until 5:30 P.M. Guests of the Regent may also use the Irving Athletic Club (just a few minutes away) free of charge. Free rides to Love Field are provided and there is hourly Surtran service to D/FW.

Business Services

Local businesses find the facilities at the Regent unsurpassed in providing the best space for the money. Off the atrium, heavy wooden doors open up to modern, tastefully decorated rooms. There is full catering service and the entire staff will outdo itself for a small group of 10 or a whole company of 700. Typewriters, copiers and secretarial services are available but there is no outgoing Telex. Receptions and conference registrations can be set up in the atrium.

Eating and Drinking

The hotel has two restaurants and two bars. A room key or membership is required to order drinks in the bar. The Brass Bull serves lunch weekdays from 11:30 A.M. until 2 P.M. and dinner nightly from 5:30 until 11 P.M., Pepper's is open from 6:30 A.M. until 11 P.M. for coffee shop fare. The Lobby Bar opens at noon and closes down around 9 P.M. The Cowboy Disco is known for the attractive waitresses and serves cocktails from 4 P.M. until 2 A.M. but changes hours so frequently that we recommend you check with the management ahead of time.

DOWNTOWN

★★★★ THE ADOLPHUS HOTEL (Amfac)
$$$$ 1321 Commerce Street
(214) 742-8200; (800) 227-4700
All major credit cards and personal check

Built in 1912 by the famous beer brewer, Adolphus Busch, this hotel has just undergone a $45-million restoration. This part of Commerce Street is in the center of Downtown and is being upgraded with new streetlamps, storefronts and sidewalks. There is not much activity Downtown after dark, but it is certainly safe. Neiman-Marcus and other top stores are just a few blocks away.

The motor entrance is well-serviced, with both doorman and bellman on duty 24 hours. Your baggage is taken immediately and the registration desk is right by the door. (There is also a special elevator here for handicapped guests.) The lobby is located on the second floor, an escalator ride up from the registration desk. It is large and opulently decorated with English antiques, and you can feel the excitement of international commerce amid the high ceilings, marble columns, dark-wood paneling and 12-foot tapestries. There is an elegant bar with a grouping of antique chairs, couches and cigarette tables. Tea is served daily at 4:30, accompanied by French pastries and finger sandwiches.

Accommodations

The Adolphus's 439 rooms, including 18 suites, are the most spacious in Dallas. Decor throughout the hotel is lovely and thick moldings add a touch of antiquity. Hallways are well-lighted and each floor has an elegant parlor area with tapestry rugs and Queen Anne furniture.

The large rooms are all beautifully decorated in pastel colors, and all rooms have four-poster beds with thick, fluffy down comforters, dust ruffles and matching drapes. Double rooms have a Chippendale-style writing desk, a separate seating area and often a dining table as well as a walk-in closet. All rooms are soundproof and have color TV, AM/FM radio, an alarm clock and a refrigerator. All bathrooms have marble floors and marble showers and two pedestal sinks with brass fixtures. The hotel provides a bathrobe and a Chinese porcelain soap dish and cup. The bathrooms all have a scale, heatlamp, clothesline and electrical outlet.

In general, suites have one or two bedrooms (usually a king and a double), and a large parlor area suitable for meetings and entertainment. There is a conference table, a desk and a nice conversation area. Most suites have one bathroom per bedroom and most have wet bars. There are several special suites, including one with a dining room on a different level and one with a 20-foot floor-to-ceiling skylight.

Personal Services

Facilitating the business traveler's needs is top priority according to Adolphus's general manager, and we believe him. Room service is available 24 hours a day and there is no minimum charge. A fresh flower comes with each order. Same-day laundry, dry cleaning and tailoring is available Mon.–Sat. 9 A.M. to 5 P.M. Babysitters and cribs are available, but pets may not stay in the rooms. A doctor and a dentist are on call 24 hours a day. There is a barber on premises and a hairdresser from Neiman-Marcus will come to the hotel on request. All guests may use Amfac's Bear Creek Resort, 30 minutes away at D/FW Airport, for tennis and golf, or the health club one block away for an added fee. The concierge will arrange for guided tours as well as theater tickets, airline tickets and car rental. A cashier is on duty 24 hours a day to exchange foreign currency. The newsstand is open from 6:30 A.M. until 10 P.M., seven days a week. Safe-deposit boxes are large enough for coats.

Business Services

Although the Adolphus is not a hotel for a large convention, it is perfect for smaller conferences and meetings. The famous Grand Ballroom has tapestry carpeting, high ceilings and a wall of white-paned windows. A large pre-function area provides an elegant entranceway for this truly grand ballroom. In addition, there are 11 conference rooms that can be set up in theater, classroom or banquet fashion. On the mezzanine level, there are three permanent boardrooms with high-backed leather chairs. The hotel supplies the PA system, lecterns, blackboards and 6′ x 8′ portable stages. Audiovisual equipment rental is arranged by the hotel. A photocopier is available around the clock, and a Telex machine is available during business hours and by arrangement. Secretarial services are available through the business office. The catering department is excellent.

Eating and Drinking

There are three bars in the hotel, generally open until around 1 A.M. There are three restaurants. The French Room is elegant with high muraled ceilings and serves classic and nouvelle cuisine dishes Mon.–Sat. from 6–11 P.M. The French Room Bar has about 40 overstuffed chairs open from 11 A.M. until midnight seven days. It is wise to order soufflés from the bar before dinner since they take extra time to prepare. The Grille serves breakfast, lunch and dinner from 6 A.M. until midnight, seven days a week. The Palm Bar serves salads and sandwiches for lunch from 11 A.M. until 2:30 P.M., seven days, and is open for drinks until midnight. The lobby bar stays open until 2 A.M. and high tea is a tradition each day at 4:30.

★★ THE BRADFORD
$$ 302 South at Houston Street (at Jackson)
(214) 761-9090; (800) 442-7292
All major credit cards

When Austin designer Jack Shaw created the decor of the Bradford, he definitely had the business traveler in mind (the telephone is on the desk, not next to the bed). This small hotel has an elegant lobby marked by hand-painted canvas walls at the registration desk and soft beige leather couches. The hotel is located across the street from the courthouse so there are always lawyers with clients in the lobby and restaurant. A doorman is on duty and keys and mail are concealed from view. A giant brandy snifter offers shiny red apples to guests and visitors. We like this hotel very much, and if it had more meeting rooms and met more of our criteria, we would be inclined to give it a three-star rating.

Accommodations

There are 140 rooms and seven suites in the Bradford. Hallways are well-lighted and no room is more than a few steps from the elevator. Everything smacks of newness since the hotel was totally refurbished last year. Rooms are all decorated alike with tan spreads and drapes and chairs and sofas in cranberry red. All rooms have color TV,' AM/FM radio and a comfortable writing desk and chair. There is a wooden valet in every room in addition to the closet. Bathrooms all have new fixtures as well as conveniently located electrical outlets.

Suites here are actually only large, L-shaped rooms with sofas that convert to sleepers, track lighting and live plants. Doors have chains and double locks against passkey.

Personal Services

Room service is from 7 A.M.–10 P.M. Same-day laundry, dry cleaning and tailoring service is available. There are cribs and rollaways and babysitters can be arranged with advance notice. There is a safe and safe-deposit boxes and a cashier is on duty 24 hours. Ice machines are located on even floors and soda machines on odd floors.

Business Services

The hotel provides few business services and has only one meeting room which handles up to 20 people. Catering for small banquets can be arranged. Audiovisual equipment can be rented from an outside company and secretarial services should be requested in advance.

Eating and Drinking

The restaurant is open seven days, 7 A.M.–10 P.M. The Hippopotamus Lounge, open noon–2 A.M., features a pianist and has a brass hippo and several interesting bird sculptures.

★★★ THE FAIRMONT
$$$$ Ross at Akard Street
(214) 748-5454; (800) 492-6622;
Telex 910-861-9051
All major credit cards

Centrally located to business and pleasure, the Fairmont has held the first position among Dallas hotels since it was built in 1969. But within the past two years, at least three other top-notch hotels have caused local "star wars" when it comes to the best rating in terms of food, rooms and services. By any scale, the Fairmont has excellent personal and business services.

The lobby is magnificent, dominated by three ten-foot Belgium glass chandeliers and a 24-foot woven tapestry entitled *In Celebration of Cabeza de Vaca* hung against a black marble wall. The registration desk is large, but not always adequately staffed. For a hotel this size, we think there is not enough staff. We have seen piles of keys on the counter, easy to grab—a sign that security here may not be as good as it should be.

ACCOMMODATIONS

There are 600 rooms in the two white towers, 50 of which are suites. That does not include the Fairmont Suite which is completely separated from the 25th floor by a private staircase. Decor is contemporary and tasteful. All rooms have floor-to-ceiling windows, color TV, AM/FM radio and alarm clocks and electric shoe buffers. On the beds, there are two types of pillows, soft and firm. Closets are spacious with good, strong wooden hangers. The bathrooms all have glassed-in showers, oversize towels and custom soaps in addition to scales, telephones and clotheslines. Counters are marble-topped and old-fashioned. There is nightly turndown service and room-straightening.

Suites in the South Tower have small parlors and large bedrooms, a design that makes them popular with family groups. Business travelers should ask for suites in the North Tower, which have smaller bedrooms and larger parlors (although no extra bathrooms), making them better for entertaining and holding meetings. Most of the suites in the South Tower have a minibar and refrigerator stocked with drinks as well as a liquor cabinet—charged by use. Extras in all suites include two televisions, linen hand towels and special toiletries. Some suites have dining tables.

Personal Services

Twenty-four hour room service is top priority and there is something special about the way a cart arrives laden with linens, crystal, china and silver when you only ordered a bagel. Same-day laundry, dry cleaning and tailoring is available Mon.–Sat. 8 A.M.–6 P.M. within a few hours. There is a house doctor on duty during the day and on call 24 hours. Babysitters are available as are cribs and rollaways. Dogs and cats are not permitted in the rooms but boarding services are provided for an additional charge. There are safe-deposit boxes and a cashier is on duty 24 hours and will exchange foreign currency. The drugstore is open seven days from 7 A.M. to 11 P.M.

For diversion or relaxation, the Hartmann Art Gallery with rare art from the Orient and the Neiman-Marcus Boutique display their treasures Mon.–Sat. 9:30 A.M.–5:30 P.M. in the lobby. There is a barber shop and a beauty salon downstairs open Mon.–Sat. from 9 A.M. until 5 P.M. For exercise, there is a beautifully landscaped outdoor Olympic-size swimming pool. Or guests may use the brand-new YMCA across the street for swimming, squash, jogging, or weightlifting, for a small fee. The hotel will arrange for golfers and tennis players to use the local country clubs during their stay.

Business Services

The Fairmont has 24 different meeting rooms accommodating from 10 to 3,000. There are eight meeting rooms on the terrace level overlooking the outdoor garden and a large swimming pool. On the second level, there are 14 other rooms located close to the kitchen for quick service of banquets. Each room is slightly different from the others. The Regency Ballroom on the banquet level is magnificent with 16,540 square feet of space. Red dominates the room from the vaulted ceilings to the velvet-covered walls and draperies.

Add to it chandeliers, gold arches and gilded columns for a feeling of elegance and importance. A service elevator nearby can accommodate 15,000 lbs. On the lobby level, the International Ballroom has room for 105 exhibitors' booths. Both rooms are fully equipped with the latest lighting and sound machines. The Fairmont is famous for its catering department. A 29-page booklet offers some of the menu suggestions from fresh seafood to French pastries and an extensive wine list. Every banquet or reception should have at least one candy creation from the chocolateer–we recommend the Cowboy boot.

The catering department can provide almost anything you might need, from sending a Telex to renting a typewriter.

Eating and Drinking

The Pyramid Room, one of the most elegant rooms in Dallas, serves lunch and dinner. The Venetian Room features top entertainers at the dinner shows with dinner starting at 7 P.M. On Sunday, there is a very good brunch in this room. Both rooms require reservations. The Brasserie is open 24 hours and serves delicious sandwiches as well as the best Eggs Benedict in town. The lobby bar opens around 11:30 A.M. and closes 1 A.M.

★ THE GRENELEFE
$ 1011 South Akard Street
(214) 421-1083; (800) 527-7606;
(800) 492-9510 (Texas only)
All major credit cards

The Grenelefe is a very small hotel, situated just south of Downtown and, according to the director, just 383 steps away from the Convention Center. The hotel is exceptionally clean and all the rooms have just been refurbished. For its size, there are many business services offered. The friendly staff believes in personal service and runs free van rides to anywhere Downtown. There is no lobby seating area, but there is a very nice indoor pool. From the Rooftop Restaurant, there is a remarkable view of Downtown.

Accommodations

There are 242 comfortable rooms of which eight are suites. The hallways are roomy and well-lighted. Rooms are large and furnished with good-quality (not basic motel) pieces. Colors are earth-toned which seems to be a favorite these days. There are no closets, just metal bars in the corner. Bathrooms are ordinary. The suites are located on the 10th floor and require a special elevator key. The hallway on this floor has parquet floors, fresh flowers and original art. All suites are nicely decorated with soft red-velvet couches and chrome and glass tables. A full bar makes entertaining easy. (One suite has a refrigerator too.) The bathrooms have separate dressing areas and two electrical outlets. All doors have chains and can be double locked against passkey.

Personal Services

This hotel offers many services to the business traveler. Room service is from 6:30 A.M. until 10:30 P.M. and there is a $2 minimum charge. Same-day laundry, dry cleaning and tailoring services are available. They will provide the names and telephone numbers of a doctor, dentist or babysitter. Pets are allowed in the rooms but there are no cribs. A large indoor swimming pool is open from 7 A.M. until 10 P.M. There is free van service to Love Field and hourly transportation to D/FW. A cashier is on duty 24 hours but will exchange Canadian currency only. A newsstand is open seven days from 7 A.M. until 10 P.M. Safe-deposit boxes are available.

Business Services

The Grenelefe has eight meeting rooms to accommodate from 15 to 500 persons. The Seasons Ballroom is the largest and is decorated in brown and orange colors with track lighting. Small conference rooms are bare and functional, each with its own bathroom and telephone. There is a catering service on premises. Audiovisual equipment can be rented from local vendors for a fee. There is a photocopier, available Mon.–Fri. 9 A.M.–5 P.M., weekends by special request, but no Telex machine. Secretarial services can be arranged as well as Spanish translation.

Eating and Drinking

The hotel has one bar open from 11 A.M. until 2 A.M. and offers piano accompaniment to a vocalist and hors d'oeuvres during happy hour. The Rooftop Restaurant, open from 6:30 A.M. to 10:30 P.M., serves an all-you-can-eat lunch buffet and is a good vantage point for seeing Dallas.

★★ DALLAS HILTON
$$ 1914 Commerce Street
(214) 747-2011; Telex 147180; Cable Teleserv Dal
All major credit cards

Located a few blocks from the Convention Center, the Dallas Hilton is clean, comfortable and cheaper than many other Downtown hotels. There is a convenient driveway entrance with plenty of bellmen on duty. The lobby is cheerful, decorated in a bright pink and purple motif that is carried up the two staircases to the meeting rooms. There are several seating areas with fresh flowers, pink couches, red chairs and marble and brass tables. The front desk is well-staffed and there is Hilton Quick Check-In service.

Accommodations

The building is Y-shaped, and although the hallways are dimly lighted, there is an unobstructed view to your room from the elevators. The hotel has 782 rooms–ranging in size from singles to double doubles–and 54 suites. Corner rooms (there are about 170) are preferred by many guests since they are somewhat larger and don't cost much more than other rooms. All rooms are attractive with off-white walls, beige carpeting, and bedspreads and curtains in soft shades of mauve, peach and pink; some have modern furnishings and others are traditional. All rooms have color TV and good-sized closets with full-length mirrors (but no skirt hangers). Bathrooms here are very small with no counter space, but they do have electrical outlets, bottle openers and used razor blade disposal. There are soda and ice machines on every floor (including club soda and tonic) and a mail chute.

Double doubles have two double beds as well as two

baths, and suites have parlor, dining area, and a choice of one or two bedrooms. Each bedroom has its own TV and AM/FM radio. All suites are decorated in modern style, with many attractive color schemes.

Personal Services

Room service is available from 6 A.M.–11 P.M. No doctor is on call. There is same-day cleaning service if in by 8 A.M. Monday–Friday. Cribs and rollaways are available. On the roof, there is a sundeck with two hot tubs. The newsstand is open Mon.–Fri. 9 A.M.–6 P.M. There is a drugstore on the basement level that sells newspapers and magazines seven days from 9 A.M.–7 P.M. American and Delta airlines have offices in the lobby (Mon.–Fri. 8:30 A.M.–5 P.M.) and Surtran service to and from D/FW airport is available every half hour around the clock.

Business Services

The hotel offers many business services and has 18 meeting rooms on the mezzanine level with a banquet capacity of up to 1,600. In addition, the fourth floor has about 20 converted rooms serving as small meeting rooms and hospitality suites. They are very comfortable and have the same services as elsewhere in the hotel. The Grand Ballroom has a large stage and a recent remodeling includes a sophisticated sound system. The pre-function area is attractive and there is a separate registration booth available. Audiovisual equipment can be rented for you and there is a copier operated by desk personnel available 24 hours (can be charged to your room). The hotel provides blackboards, podiums and movie screens at no charge. Kosher catering is available.

Eating and Drinking

The Library bar, serving from 11 A.M.–2 A.M., offers lunch and Happy Hour hors d'oeuvres. Gatsby Bicycle Bar is open from 11:30 A.M.–2 A.M., and also serves sandwiches at lunchtime. The Beef Baron restaurant is open for lunch and dinner. The hotel's coffee shop, El Cafetel, is open from 6 A.M.–11 P.M.

★★★★ HYATT REGENCY
$$$ 300 Reunion Boulevard
(214) 651-1234; (800) 228-9000; Telex 732748
All major credit cards and personal check

Located next to the spectacular Reunion Tower on the city's southwest side, the Hyatt Regency is a distinguished part of the Downtown skyline and the hub of activity at the Reunion complex. The hotel offers many personal and business services and is located minutes away from the Convention Center, Market Center and the Reunion Arena sports complex. The registration area is usually filled with conventioneers of some sort and at times there seems to be a shortage of personnel. Keys and mail are visible from the front desk but the hotel uses coded keys as part of the security.

On the next level, an atrium rises to the 19th floor and visitors always delight in riding up through it in the three glass elevators.

Accommodations

The hotel has 1,000 rooms including 49 suites. All of the rooms have color TV, AM/FM radio and alarm clock. Most suites have a refrigerator. Hallways have red carpet and paper and are generally not well-lighted except around the atrium. The rooms we saw were clean with modern furnishings, a full-length mirror, and a writing desk with a rattan chair as well as a conversation area. Bathrooms are unremarkable except to say that they have plenty of counter surface around the sink. All doors have chains and can be double locked against a passkey.

A typical suite can have one or two bedrooms–some with king-sized beds and some with twins. The parlor is very nicely decorated in deep shades of red and burnt orange, with hooked rugs and weavings on the walls. Each parlor has a sofa, two chairs, coffee table and a large writing desk.

The Regency Club on the eighth floor has a comfortable lounge where guests are served hors d'oeuvres from 5–7 P.M., cordials after 8 P.M., and there is an honor bar. A concierge is on duty here to assist with everything from full breakfast service to airline tickets, but there is no separate check-in. Extra amenities include complimentary fruit and cheese on arrival, Godiva chocolates, Perrier in a copper ice bucket, and special toiletries and bathrobe.

Personal Services

Room service operates 24 hours a day with no minimum charge. Same-day laundry and dry cleaning is available weekdays if in by 9 A.M. There is a health club with sauna, outdoor jogging path and tennis courts. The outdoor swimming pool is a little too close to a major highway interchange for comfort. A doctor is on call and there is dental referral. Babysitting can be arranged, and cribs are available. Dogs and cats may not stay in the room with you. There is a cashier on duty to exchange foreign currency 24 hours a day although the hotel does not encourage it. An Avis car-rental agency (Mon–Fri 9 A.M.–5 P.M.) is next door in Reunion Tower. There is no barber or beauty shop in the hotel. The newsstand is open from 7 A.M. until 11 P.M. seven days a week.

Business Services

This hotel offers some of the best facilities for meetings and conventions. There are 25 meeting rooms. The largest is Reunion Ballroom, located on the main floor, which can accommodate up to 2,800 persons. Brown and yellow velvets cover the walls and floor under sparkling chandeliers. The foyer is carpeted in red with wall sculptures picking up the colors of the walls, ceiling and doors. Just off the atrium, along a long corridor covered with heavy gray woven fabric, there are a number of rooms including a boardroom with high-backed velvet chairs, an icicle chandelier and dark-paneled walls. The hotel supplies blackboards, flipcharts and podiums and there is an audiovisual company on the premises to provide equipment. The hotel does not have a Telex machine for guest use and typewriters and other business machines can be rented from outside. Secretarial, but not translation, services are available.

Eating and Drinking

There are three bars and three restaurants in the hotel. Antares, the revolving restaurant atop Reunion Tower, serves good food but there is often a long waiting line. Hours are 11 A.M. to 2 P.M., seven days, for lunch; Sun. to Thur. 6 to 11 P.M. and Fri. and Sat. 5 P.M. to midnight for dinner. The Top of the Dome, revolving atop Antares, is open Mon. to Fri. 2 P.M. to 2 A.M., and Sat. and Sun. noon to 2 A.M. This bar features live entertainment and a magnificent view but crowds up on weekends. Park Place, forming the central core of the atrium, serves drinks from 11:30 A.M. daily. The Cafe Esplanade stays open 24 hours, seven days, and is popular for late-night snacks. Fausto's Sea Catch serves fine seafood in a nautical setting Mon.–Fri. for lunch, and seven days for dinner; Fausto's bar is open daily and the restaurant serves an excellent Sunday brunch.

The hotel also manages the bars and restaurants located in Union Station, connected by an underground tunnel. Station Master serves family-style meals for lunch Mon.–Fri. and dinner Mon.–Sat. The Dispatcher deli and Lone Star Ltd. Grill serve sandwiches Mon.–Fri. 11 A.M. to 2 P.M. Casey's bar is open at 11 A.M.

★ **HOLIDAY INN**
$$ **1015 Elm Street**
(214) 748-9951; (800) 238-8000
All major credit cards

Considering the amount of business this Holiday Inn does, we wonder why this hotel doesn't offer more to the business traveler. Linked to many of the major financial institutions and office buildings by clean and safe underground tunnels, this is a prime location for business travelers. (We should warn you, however, that outside, the area is bustling by day, deserted evenings and weekends.)

The 316 rooms and 10 suites here are like every other motel we've ever seen and the meeting rooms are simply all right. Unfortunately, the lobby staff is not always all right.

Accommodations

All rooms are small and the decor is unimpressive. Suites are all the same size–small. A couch, chair and card table, relics from the early sixties, are not conducive to meetings.

All rooms have color TV and all bathrooms have electrical outlets. Doors all have chains and double bolts.

Personal Services

Room service is available from 6:30 A.M.–10:30 P.M. with a $2 minimum. Same-day laundry and dry cleaning is available weekdays. Cribs and rollaways are provided but there are no doctors, dentists or babysitters on call. The cashier is on duty from 6:30 A.M. to 10:30 P.M. and there are safe-deposit boxes available. There is free parking for hotel guests in the garage.

Business Services

There are 11 meeting rooms on the lower level available to groups of 20 to 450. Most audiovisual equipment can be rented through the manager's office. There are no secretarial or translation services available.

Eating and Drinking

The Gazebo Room serves from 6:30 A.M. until 10:30 P.M. The Sundance Lounge on the 9th floor is open from 11 A.M. until midnight.

★★★★ **PLAZA OF THE AMERICAS**
$$$$ **650 North Pearl Boulevard**
(214) 747-7222; (800) 223-5672; Telex 791620
All major credit cards

Europe in the middle of downtown Dallas, Texas? Smack in the middle of some of the newest buildings and shopping atria, Plaza of the Americas, although itself brand new, has all the feel of a fine Continental hotel, from its expensive decor to the flurry of foreign accents among the concierge staff. The lobby's pale-pink walls and pink and green carpet are accented by a large vase of vibrant flowers, and the lobby bar, with its granite walls, white leather couches and soft fleur-de-lis carpet is just as understated as the rest of the decor. Every afternoon in the two salons, with their Louis XVI furniture, crystal chandeliers and oil paintings, guests raise Wedgwood china teacups and chat about the day's events.

Service here, from check-in and baggage handling to room service and sightseeing arrangements, is just as smooth as the decor. Outside, the area which is dominated by office buildings is safe and clean, but the covered walkway connecting the hotel with Bryan Tower, the Southland Life Building and other hotels and offices makes it possible to stay here without ever going outside. The adjoining 15-story atrium has many places to shop and dine, as well as an ice skating rink.

Accommodations

Even hallways here are exquisite; at the elevators you'll find large vases of flowers and the doorway to each room is recessed and individually lighted. There are 407 rooms and 37 suites in the hotel, and the walls of even the standard doubles are covered with a lovely beige fabric that resembles silk. The plush wool carpets and down pillows and comforters are quietly unobtrusive in pale shades of pink and green. Color TV is concealed in sleek cabinets. Each room has a separate writing desk and lamp as well as a sitting area. Bathrooms are very nice with a vanity area and plenty of light. There are two electrical outlets. The sink and counter are quite large and the hotel provides a special soap set for each guest. All baths have telephones.

The suites are the finest we've seen, some combining the sleek look of Art Deco designs with touches of the Orient, and others attractively decorated with coordinated prints. Regular suites have one or two bedrooms, one and a half baths, and walk-in closets as well as parlors. Bathrooms are large with marble floors and the bath off the parlor also has a shower and telephone.

Personal Services

Room service is offered 24 hours a day. Same-day laundry, dry cleaning and tailoring are available weekdays. The hotel will refer you to a doctor or dentist. Babysitters are always available and the hotel will provide cribs but no rollaways. Pets are restricted from the rooms. Although the hotel does not have a pool, a health club does provide saunas and a weight room in addition to outdoor tennis courts. A concierge and Manager of "Guest Relations" are on duty to arrange anything from securing airline tickets to renting a private jet.

A cashier is on duty 24 hours in a separate office and will gladly exchange your foreign currency. There are safe-deposit boxes. The newsstand is open from 6 A.M. until 10 P.M.

Business Services

The hotel wishes to attract business travelers from all parts of the world. Although this is not the place for a large convention, there are 12 meeting rooms that can accommodate from 15 to 650 persons. The Plaza Ballroom can seat 800 for banquets and as many as 1,200 arranged theater style for a general session. It has an attractive foyer and terrace adjoining it. All meeting rooms have telephones and the hotel will supply quite a bit of equipment at no charge including a microphone, podium, blackboards and direction signs. The hotel will arrange other audiovisual equipment rental. Telex machines and photocopiers are available during business hours and a secretary will generally be provided for small typing jobs. The hotel caters meetings of all sizes.

Eating and Drinking

The Plaza of the Americas has three bars and two restaurants. Cafe Royal is an excellent French restaurant serving nouvelle cuisine at lunch from 11:30 A.M. until 3 P.M. and dinner from 6:30 until 10:30 P.M. Reservations are required. Le Relais, a sort of formal coffee shop, is open 24 hours. Passerelle, forming a foot bridge that spans the atrium, is a comfortable place to enjoy cold oysters and shrimp from 11 A.M. until 2 A.M. For dancing to live music in a tropical setting, Windows is the place atop the hotel serving drinks only from 5:30 P.M. until 2 A.M.

NORTH CENTRAL

★★★★ DOUBLETREE INN
$$$ 8250 North Central Expressway (at Caruth Haven)
(214) 691-8700; (800) 528-0444
All major credit cards

One of three tall gleaming gold-toned buildings at Campbell Centre on the east side of North Central Expressway, the

Doubletree Inn has one of the most convenient locations in Dallas, and whatever shops and services the hotel lacks can be found in the adjoining building. The hotel is a very short distance from Greenville Avenue's "strip" of restaurants and night clubs, as well as from Old Town and NorthPark malls, which are among Dallas's best. Business travelers with business near this hotel need not rent a car for extracurricular activities, since cab fares and distances to good selections are minimal.

The decor of the Doubletree is classy–rich gray velour and marble registration desk–and the service is too. The registration desk is well-staffed and the bell-captain desk is right at the front door. A quiet and comfortable lobby bar is a popular spot after working hours for office workers in the adjoining buildings.

Accommodations

The building is oval-shaped, and the 302 rooms and 19 suites are arranged along one wide and well-lighted hallway, and each floor has only 16 rooms and one suite. Double rooms are larger than usual and include extra chairs and coffee table. Floor to ceiling windows give guests a marvelous view of the city night and day, and the color schemes are attractive, with matching geometric print drapes and spreads. All rooms have color TV, AM/FM radio, alarm clock and in-room movies for a small fee. There are folding luggage racks and skirt hangers in the open closet areas and a spotlighted dressing table with large mirror located outside the bathroom. All bathrooms are carpeted, have an electrical outlet next to the sink and tub/showers.

Suites include minibar, refrigerator and full-length mirrors but have only one bathroom. The sitting room has a comfortable sofa, occasional chairs and coffee table as well as double windows. Each floor has ice and soda machines.

Personal Services

Room service is open daily 6 A.M.–11 P.M. and same-day laundry and dry cleaning service is available Mon.–Fri. 9 A.M.–5 P.M. Pets are permitted in rooms but a large deposit is required. Babysitters and rollaway beds are available. Safe-deposit boxes are available and a cashier is on duty around the clock. A notary public is available weekdays during business hours. The lobby shop is open seven days 7 A.M. to 10 P.M. The hotel does not have a separate business class floor, but there is VIP service which includes complimentary newspaper, turn-down service and an extra portable TV in the bathroom. There is an outdoor club with shuffleboard, putting green, four Jacuzzis and a tennis court.

Business Services

The Doubletree is a wonderful place for a meeting whether you use the three Board Rooms on the 21st floor which hold from 8 to 100 people or the Doubletree Ballroom which can handle 900. The Ballroom can be divided into smaller meeting rooms each with full audiovisual capacity and completely soundproof. There is a catering department which can handle requests for kosher service and a convention service staff. A photocopy machine is available for guest use during normal business hours.

Eating and Drinking

Peter B's restaurant is located to the right of the main lobby and is decorated with wicker and plants. It is open for breakfast, lunch and dinner seven days 6 A.M.–11 P.M. Seafood specialties are outstanding. The lobby bar is open seven days 11 A.M.–11 P.M., and for a spectacular view of the city you can ascend to the Cirrus Lounge, open 3:30 P.M.–2 A.M. seven days, with live entertainment nightly.

★★★ DALLAS HILTON INN

$$$ 5600 North Central Expressway (at Mockingbird)
(214) 827-4100
All major credit cards

From the perky fresh flowers at the entrance to the huge arrangement of gladiolas gracing a table in the lobby seating area you will find this Hilton warm and hospitable. It has 400 rooms and 10 suites and is centrally located halfway between Downtown and LBJ Freeway on North Central Expressway. There is a doorman and bellman who will park your car and carry your bags into the large well-staffed registration area, where check-in is usually efficient. This is one of the few hotels in Dallas where it is pleasant and fun to sit in the lobby and watch the hustle of people from a comfortable over-stuffed chair surrounded by plants and flowers.

Accommodations

Rooms are oversized and each has color TV, AM/FM radio and separate alarm clock. In-room movies are available for a fee. Coordinated drapes and bedspreads in prints of beige and earth tones are accented by attractive wallpapers in bedrooms and baths. All rooms have a nice closet and a retractable clothesline in the bathroom. There is a desk with chair and a small table with two comfortable chairs. Rooms have chains and can be double locked against a passkey.

Suites include a very large sitting room with dining table and four matching chairs, a wet bar with refrigerator and ice-maker and a built-in stereo system. Each suite has two large bedrooms and two full baths. All are decorated in muted soft colors with attractive geometric wallpapers and have double doors onto a balcony overlooking the city. Some of the more recently refurbished rooms have designer fabric headboards and matching drapes in the bedrooms.

Personal Services

All rooms have automatic coffeemakers in the bathrooms and complimentary morning papers are delivered to your door. A cashier on duty 24 hours will also exchange foreign currency. Safe-deposit boxes are available. Room service operates 6:30 A.M.–11 P.M. and same-day laundry and dry cleaning service is available Mon.–Fri. 9 A.M.–5 P.M. Babysitters are on call and cribs and rollaways are available. Pets are permitted in rooms. Parking is free and there is a very attractive outdoor swimming pool with deck. The barber shop in the rear of the lobby area is open Tues.–Sat. 8 A.M.–6 P.M. and the gift shop is open seven days 7 A.M.–10 P.M.

Business Services

There are five large and seven small meeting rooms which can handle 40 to 1,000 people and all types of audiovisual equipment is available for rental. Translation services can be arranged through the meeting staff and there is provision for kosher catering service. Meeting support services are arranged in the offices to the right of the registration desk.

Eating and Drinking

The attractive French Market to the left of the main entrance of the hotel serves breakfast, lunch and dinner 6:30 A.M.–11 P.M. Trader Vic's, like its namesakes throughout the country, serves Polynesian specialties in an island setting complete with waterfall 5–11:30 P.M. seven days. The Penthouse Supper Club now under construction will serve intimate suppers with dinner dancing at the top of the hotel. The Tavern of the Fierce Sparrow serves drinks 11 A.M.–2 A.M. right off the lobby.

OK LA QUINTA MOTOR INN

$ 10001 North Central Expressway (at Meadow Rd.)
(214) 361-8200; (800) 531-5900
All major credit cards

Conveniently located and exceptionally clean, this is a terrific bet if you are looking for a comfortable room and don't care about services. The lobby, decorated with Mexican tiles, is small but efficient. There are no lobby shops and no bellhops. The three-story section of the hotel has an elevator. Courtesy van is provided to the Surtran station. Toll-free reservation for other hotels in the chain is available by lobby telephone.

Accommodations

There are 129 rooms and only one suite. A standard room has generous floor space, AM/FM radio, color TV and desk with extra chair. There is a separate dressing/vanity area and closet outside the bathroom. Skirt hangers are standard. All rooms have chains and double locks.

Personal Services

There is no room service, but there are ice and soda machines on all floors. There are safe-deposit boxes and a cashier is on duty 24 hours. Same-day laundry and dry cleaning service is available Mon.–Fri. 9 A.M.–5 P.M. Babysitters, cribs and rollaways are provided and small pets are permitted in rooms. There is an outdoor swimming pool.

Business Services

There is one small meeting room which could handle 40–45 people and no other business services.

Eating and Drinking

There is no restaurant within the hotel.

★★ NORTHPARK INN AND CONVENTION CENTER
$$ 9300 North Central Expressway
(214) 363-2431; (800) 528-1234
All major credit cards

This huge complex, which includes a complete convention facility, was built 17 years ago when Dallas was still a small town. It was purchased recently by a local developer who is doing a total refurbishing which should return the Center to its former status as a high point of Dallas activity. Right now the facility seems more a motel than a hotel, with its six garden-type buildings and separate convention facility. Some buildings are connected to the lobby, but from others you must walk outside. It is centrally located within easy access of several of Dallas's finest shopping and dining areas and convenient to many new office complexes.

The lobby area is small and rather bland. There are few seating areas and it does not seem a place you will want to linger for very long. A bellman and several desk clerks are on duty 6 A.M.–11 P.M. and are pleasant and efficient. Security guards are on duty from 11 P.M.–7 A.M. On request, women business travelers will be given rooms close to the lobby when available.

Accommodations

Northpark Inn has 350 rooms (many with parking right outside your door) and 10 suites. The rooms have a definite motel feel but many offer a nice view of the pool and all are easy to get to from the public areas of the hotel. All rooms have color TV, radio, clock and offer HBO movies for an extra fee. There are a desk and two side chairs in each room but there is no separate dressing area. Bathrooms have tub/showers and single sink. Outlets in all bathrooms are attached at the doorway light switch—rather inconvenient if your razor or hair dryer has a short cord.

Suites or junior suites are a trifle larger than double rooms and have small refrigerators and a well-lighted dressing mirror. Parlors have sofas and armchairs, a small desk and extra small tables. All regular suites have two bathrooms. You may also reserve parlors alone on a daily basis when available. They are suitable for small cocktail parties, group discussions or even for an interview spot during daytime hours when you have no office available.

Personal Services

Room service is available 7 A.M.–10 P.M. with no minimum charge and each room has a courtesy coffee maker. Same-day laundry and dry cleaning service is available Mon.–Fri. if in by 9 A.M. Rollaways and cribs are available and pets are permitted in guest rooms. There is cashier service 24 hours and safe-deposit boxes are available. All rooms have double locks and chains. Mr. Peabody's Newsstand is open Mon.–Fri. 6 A.M.–10 P.M. and Sat.–Sun. 9 A.M.–9 P.M. It sells liquor, snacks, toiletries, magazines and local newspapers. There is hourly Surtran service and the bellman will arrange transportation to local restaurants and shops. There are two tennis courts and two outdoor swimming pools.

Business Services

The separate Convention Center building houses 13 large meeting rooms on the upper level and an 8,500 sq. ft. exhibition hall and 7,100 sq. ft. ballroom on the lower level. The hotel itself has smaller meeting rooms handling 25 to 1,200 people. All meeting rooms have chalk board, flip chart and retractable screen. Other equipment rental is arranged for you by the hotel with Hoover's. There is a catering department and photocopy equipment is available for guest use during business hours.

Eating and Drinking

The small coffee shop is open 6:30–11 A.M. The Garden Terrace, the attractive main dining area, serves meals seven days 6:30 A.M.–10 P.M. The Old New York Tavern is open 4 P.M.–2 A.M. and has dancing and live entertainment.

OK TROPICANA INN
$ 3939 North Central Expressway
(214) 526-8881
All major credit cards

The Tropicana has a terrific location, very close to Downtown and right on North Central Expressway, but it has absolutely no eye-appeal and is surrounded by old buildings in a generally seedy neighborhood. The lobby has several comfortable sofas and a small in-ground goldfish pond. There are no lobby shops or other services available.

Accommodations

The 98 rooms have color TV, AM/FM radio, and free breakfast and happy hour are complimentary for all guests. The room decor is orange and rust and rather drab. There is a an open closet area and no skirt hangers or full-length mirrors. Bathrooms are equipped wtih stall-enclosed bath and shower and the separate vanity area is right in the bedroom. All rooms have chains and double locks.

Personal Services

Room service is available 7 A.M.–9 P.M. with $1.50 minimum. The free breakfast is served in the restaurant with a full menu. Cribs are available. There is a single cashier on duty 24 hours and safe-deposit boxes are available. There is an outdoor swimming pool.

Business Services

There is one meeting room which can hold 75 people but no other business services.

Eating and Drinking

The small, bare-tabled restaurant overlooks the swimming pool and is open 6:30 A.M.–10 P.M. It is here that you have your complimentary breakfast. A cocktail lounge the size of a closet is located directly off the restaurant and is open 4 P.M.–midnight.

★★ TWIN SIXTIES INN

$$ 6060 North Central Expressway (at Yale)
(214) 691-3600; (800) 527-6800
All major credit cards.

Located next to the Dallas Cowboys Building and very close to Downtown, this 300-room hotel looks like just another office building. The registration desk is large but not well-staffed and the bellman is located right inside the front door. The lobby area with tables and chairs as well as sofa seating separates the hotel rooms from the meeting areas and public space.

Accommodations

Rooms are equipped with color TV, AM/FM radio and in-room movies are available for a fee. Decor is muted beige and blue and all rooms have two side chairs with a small table, desk and luggage rack. There are open closet areas and no skirt hangers or full-length mirrors. Bathrooms have counter sinks, tub shower and electric outlet next to the sink. All rooms have sprinklers, door chains and can be double-locked against a passkey, and each floor has ice and vending machines. There are eight suites and all include a parlor, two connecting bedrooms (one double double and one king-sized) and two and a half baths. Each suite has a wet bar, living room with sofas and a full dining area with table and chairs. They are attractively decorated in beige with nice greenery. VIP service on the ninth floor offers separate concierge service, complimentary breakfast and newspaper, extra amenities such as velour towels, alarm clock and live plants in rooms, but no separate check-in.

Personal Services

Room service is available 6:30 A.M.–10:30 P.M. and same-day laundry and dry cleaning service is available Mon.–Fri.

8:30 A.M.–5 P.M. Complimentary coffee and newspapers are offered in the lobby each morning. Babysitters, cribs and roll-aways are available and there is a sauna, health club, and outdoor swimming pool. A cashier is on duty 24 hours and safe-deposit boxes are available. Surtran service to airports is operated from the lobby. The gift shop is open seven days 6:30 A.M.–10:30 P.M.

Business Services

There are six small and one large meeting rooms which can accommodate 14 to 750 people. A very attractive Board Room with director's table and comfortable seating for 14 has a vaulted ceiling and is done in wood and beige tones. It has a built-in screen, blackboard and incoming telephone line. The other meeting rooms are created by dividing the ballroom, and partitions are quite thin so noise carries from one to the other. There is a catering department and all types of audio-visual equipment is available for rent. A notary is available weekdays during business hours.

Eating and Drinking

Half Time is a small dining room that serves breakfast, lunch and dinner 6:30 A.M.–10:30 P.M. Cassidy's Steak and Spirits, named for the famous Butch Cassidy, is open for dinner only 5:30–10:30 P.M. It looks like an old Western saloon. The Time Out Bar, located on the lower level, serves drinks 11:30 A.M.–1:30 A.M. Guests of Twin Sixties are also welcome for a fee to the Playboy Club located in the Cowboys Building next door.

LBJ-NORTH

OK **BEST WESTERN INN-LBJ**
$$ **8051 LBJ Freeway (at Coit Rd.)**
(214) 234-2431; (800) 442-4545
All major credit cards and personal check

The convenient location is probably the most attractive feature of this motel. The lobby is the size of a coat closet and there is only one desk clerk on duty. There are safe-deposit boxes and a cashier is on duty 24 hours (you may have to look!). Rooms here are pretty dismal, but the hotel is redecorating.

Accommodations

There are 206 rooms and only one suite in the Inn and all have color TV with free in-room movies and AM/FM radio. Double rooms have a desk and a small round table with side chairs. The room sizes are claustrophobic and a majority of the rooms have a parking lot view. Bathrooms are medieval with a single sink with no counter, a tub shower and cold, ugly tile floors. The closet is a hanging rack which the manager explained "saves a lot of money"! All rooms have double locks and chains.

Personal Services

Room service is available Mon.–Fri. 10 A.M.–10 P.M. with a $2.50 minimum. Same-day laundry and dry cleaning is available Mon.–Fri. 9 A.M.–5 P.M. Babysitters are on call and cribs and rollaways are provided. Pets are allowed in rooms. Safe-deposit boxes are available and a cashier is on duty 24 hours. There is an outdoor pool and a courtesy car will take you to the Surtran Terminal.

Business Services

One large and three small meeting rooms can handle 10 to 135 people. Audiovisual equipment rental is arranged and a notary public and photocopy equipment are available to guests during weekday business hours.

Eating and Drinking

JoJo's Restaurant is located directly next door and is open seven days, 24 hours. The Wayfarer Lounge in the motel is open for drinks Mon.–Fri. 4:30 P.M.–2 A.M. and Sat.–Sun. 6 P.M.–midnight with free membership to motel guests.

★★★★ CENTRE PLAZA-HOLIDAY INN
$$$ 4099 Valley View Lane (LBJ at Midway)
(214) 385-9000; (800) 238-8000
All major credit cards

Opened in January 1981, this luxury Holiday Inn is outstanding architecturally and breathtakingly beautiful. Entering the huge open-air, multi-level lobby you immediately feel a special sense of service, quiet good taste and comfort. During lunch piano music quietly entertains those in the lobby and those dining below in the Court which is dominated by huge metal bird sculptures suspended from the multistory atrium.

The bell captain's desk is located directly inside the front door and is very well staffed. The registration desk is fully manned and a special express check-out service allows you to drop off your room key without having to wait for check-out procedures.

A special feature in the lobby is a total information station completely computerized and operated by placing your finger directly on the screen to select information needed. Movies, shopping areas, business centers, hotel services and maps of Dallas for house-hunters or sightseers are all indicated at the touch of a finger. It is so much fun to use you may want to just play with it as you wait in the lobby for your dinner guest or business associate. If you can drag yourself away from the lobby you have more treats in store for you.

ACCOMMODATIONS

There are 298 rooms and 10 suites all equipped with color TV, AM/FM radio and alarm clock. HBO (Home Box Office) movies are provided free. All rooms have double locks and chains. Standard double rooms have king-sized or two double beds and a seating area with separate desk and chair. Bathrooms have convenient electrical outlets and sinks located in an outer room off the bathroom which has a tub/shower. Skirt hangers are provided. Three rooms are specially equipped for handicapped travelers.

Parlor suites have one bedroom, one sitting room with a sofa bed and one bathroom, and have exceptionally attractive furnishings. Drapes and spreads are coordinated. All suites are equipped with minibars with sinks, and parlor rooms may be reserved separately for use as interview or meeting rooms. There are a few special suites which have huge bedrooms, with dressing room with full-length mirror, full living room complete with large bar, refrigerator and conference table, and special bathrooms with Jacuzzi bathtubs. The Presidential Suite is a duplex with a picture window overlooking the pool and atrium.

The Concierge Floor, accessible only by key-operated elevator, provides extra services such as separate concierge service from 7 A.M.–11 P.M., a message center, and amenities such as complimentary breakfast, honor bar for evening cocktails with free hors d'oeuvres, terry cloth robes, playing cards, backgammon sets, foreign newspapers and complimentary late-night cocktail and turn-down service.

Personal Services

Room service is available 6:30 A.M.–11 P.M. seven days and same-day laundry and dry cleaning service is offered Mon.–Fri. Cribs and rollaways are available and pets are allowed in guest rooms. Ice machines and soft drink machines are located on each floor. There is an exercise room, game room and indoor and outdoor pools. An outdoor jogging track is available to guests by arrangement with nearby Brookhaven College. The gift shop is open seven days 7 A.M.–10 P.M. and a car-rental agency is located in the parking lot. A notary public is available Mon.–Fri. 9 A.M.–5 P.M.

Business Services

There are three large and 11 small meeting rooms which hold from 10 to 1,000 people. The catering and sales department is located on the second floor and audiovisual equipment for rental is right on the premises. A photocopy machine is available to guests Mon.–Fri. 8:30 A.M.–5:30 P.M.

Eating and Drinking

Cafe in the Court in the delightful Atrium with its pool and fountains, serves breakfast, lunch and light meals seven days 6:30 A.M.–11 P.M. Dr. Feelgood's, a steakhouse with salad bar, serves lunch and dinner. Judge's Chambers serves dinner Mon.–Thurs. 5:30–10 P.M. and Fri. & Sat. 5:30–11 P.M.

Cocktail lounges with free membership to guests of the hotel include the Cascade Lounge open seven days 11:30 A.M.–1 A.M. and Isadora's, which is rapidly becoming the "in" spot, open Mon.–Sat. 11 A.M.–2 A.M.

★★ THE HILTON-LBJ
$$ 4801 LBJ Freeway (at Inwood Rd.)
(214) 661-3600
All major credit cards

This Hilton is conveniently located on the north side of LBJ Freeway, amidst hundreds of office complexes and several large shopping malls including the soon to be completed Galleria. The sunken lobby seating area in Mexican decor is right outside the Silver Saddle Saloon and can be noisy after dark. There are plenty of front desk personnel and bellmen who are not always in evidence. Entry from the street level parking area is easy. Three elevators off the lobby are ample for guests since meeting rooms are at the rear of the first floor. Fire precautions are outstanding with sprinklers and smoke detectors in every room and all stairwells have heavy-duty exhaust fans to keep the air safe in case of fire. There is also a hotel-wide intercom system which would be used to alert guests by voice command should there be an emergency.

ACCOMMODATIONS

There are 323 rooms and 11 suites all with color TV, AM/FM radio and alarm clocks. Hallways are wide and well-lighted. All rooms have chains and double locks. Double rooms have two double beds, desk, chair and small round table with two additional chairs. All closets are open but have plenty of hangers including skirt hangers. For the best night-time view of downtown Dallas ask for a room with a south-east view.

Alcove suites include a king-sized bedroom and separate seating area with sofa and extra chairs. Executive suites come with one or two bedrooms. All suites have colored towels, hair dryers, shampoo and colored sheets. They also have a clothesline in the bathroom, electrical outlets by the sink, and some have an extra sink in the outer area. There is a room equipped for handicapped travelers.

Personal Services

Room service with no minimum is available seven days 6 A.M.–11 P.M. and there is same-day laundry and dry cleaning service Mon.–Fri. if in by 8:30 A.M. Cribs and rollaways are available and babysitters can be arranged. There is a sauna and attractive glass-enclosed swimming pool. The bellman can arrange tennis and racquetball reservations at a local club and also provide free transportation. Outdoor tennis at the club is free but there is a fee for indoor court time. Rental cars from a local dealer are kept on the premises and can be arranged for in the lobby. American Airlines has a lobby desk. The gift shop is open seven days 7 A.M.–10 P.M. and sells *The New York Times* and local papers. Free transportation is provided to the nearby Surtran Terminal (allow an hour from the airport). There is a notary available.

Business Services

Meeting rooms located at the rear of the building hold from 35 to 370 people. There are nine small rooms and one large room. Audiovisual equipment rental is arranged through an outside firm. There is a large pre-function area and a photocopy machine is available for guest use during business hours. The catering and sales departments are located to the right of the registration desk.

Eating and Drinking

Sadie's Silver Saddle Restaurant has the same Mexican decor as the lobby and comfortable large tables where it serves breakfast, lunch and dinner from 6 A.M.–11 P.M. Sadie's Silver Saddle Saloon, right next door off the main lobby, serves lunch, dinner and drinks. Guests of the hotel receive complimentary memberships since this is a dry area. You may bring outside guests without paying a fee ($3/3 days or $12/year). The Saloon is hopping after hours!

★★★ MARRIOTT INN-PARK CENTRAL
$$$ 7750 LBJ Freeway (at Coit Rd.)
(214) 233-4421; (800)228-9290
All major credit cards

The lobby of the Marriott is beautifully decorated in rose and green and looks like a private living room. There is a bell captain's desk and a rather small check-in desk which is well staffed. A total renovation of the hotel is proceeding gradually and all facilities are scheduled to be completely refurbished by 1983. A new complex of buildings is going up next door, but not much else is within walking distance; it is not far by car from here to several malls and the North Central area.

Accommodations

The hotel has 447 rooms and 19 suites located in a long narrow building which makes hallways endless; but they are bright and clean. All rooms have sprinklers. Standard rooms have print spreads and drapes to match, a full-length mirror outside the bathroom and comfortable side chairs and game table. Each room has color TV with free HBO movies, AM/FM radio and alarm clock. Bathrooms have marble vanities and tub/showers with tile floors. Shower caps, high quality soaps and skirt/pant hangers are standard in all rooms.

Suites are attractively done in beige with grasscloth wall coverings. Fresh plants add a warm touch. Each parlor has a living/dining room combination with a complete dining room set, two sofas and console TV and large closet. The bedroom is separated by louvered doors and has a king-sized bed, comfortable chair, TV and electric shoeshine machine. The one bathroom has separate dressing area with vanity and glass enclosed tub/shower.

Personal Services

Room service is available Sun.–Thurs. 6:30 A.M.–10 P.M. and Fri. & Sat. until 11 P.M. Same-day laundry and dry cleaning is available Mon.–Sat. Doctors and dentists are on call. Cribs are provided at no charge and pets are permitted in guest rooms. There is a beautiful large outdoor pool area with a separate Jacuzzi.

Business Services

Many meetings are held here in the 14 meeting rooms which can handle 10 to 400 people. There is a catering department located on the second floor and a kosher kitchen. All types of audiovisual equipment are available for rental, and photocopy and Telex are available for guest use weekdays during business hours. Secretarial services can be arranged. Through arrangement with American Express foreign visitors can receive help 24 hours a day; the hotel also makes an effort to hire staff members who speak Spanish, French and several other languages.

Eating and Drinking

The Currency Club Restaurant is open 6:30 A.M.–11 P.M. seven days and has a wonderful buffet lunch which provides a good place for a business luncheon meeting with good food. Friday and Saturday nights the Royal Feast Buffet with all you can eat is offered at $8.95 from 6–11 P.M. Sunday brunch is another treat served 10 A.M.–2 P.M.

The Currency Club Lounge is open 4 P.M.–2 A.M. seven days with live entertainment Mon.–Sat. Registered guests receive free memberships. The Quiet Bar off the main lobby is open seven days 11:30 A.M.–11 P.M.

★★★★ THE SUMMIT HOTEL

$$$ 2645 LBJ Freeway (at I-35)
(214)243-3363; (800)228-3555
All major credit cards

This hotel is lovely to look at, exceptionally convenient to both D/FW and Love Field airports and the service and amenities are great. The lobby has piped-in music, an atrium foyer called the Parke with lobby bar and comfortable seating areas in and around the indoor-outdoor pool which is the focal point of the first floor entrance area. There is plenty of counter help for registration, bellhops are available and there is actually a concierge on duty every day 7 A.M.–10:30 P.M. just to the left of the front desk. All personnel must wear name tags and are eager to serve you and to make your stay pleasant. The Summit is geared to business travelers and is able to provide whatever service is required.

Accommodations

Three separate buildings of six stories each are connected by covered walkways. There are 378 rooms and 11 suites and many rooms have thermo-control units which automatically adjust heat and air-conditioning according to body heat in the room. Many rooms face the indoor-outdoor pool and Parke area; some first floor rooms have sliding glass doors and some upper level rooms have balconies overlooking the pool.

Double rooms are attractive and sizable with a desk and chair and an extra table and chairs. Bathrooms have convenient electrical outlets and countertop sinks as well as tub/showers. Suites have color-coordinated towels and sheets, Neutrogena soap and shampoo, and king-sized suites even have a recliner. The International Suite consists of a very large room with a boardroom table and chairs as well as a separate coffee table and sofa seating area in a most attractive oriental motif. This room connects to a king-sized bedroom. All suites have a sink, refrigerator, glasses and serving dishes for cocktail hour. Some suites have Jacuzzi bath. All rooms have chains and double locks.

The handicapped traveler will receive the best care here that we have seen in Dallas. A huge room is provided with all switches and sinks lowered, a sliding door to the bathroom and a directly connecting double room for traveling companion. There are rails in the tub and hooks in the ceilings for assistance in moving in and out of bed and bath. All elevators in the hotel have Braille markings.

Personal Services

Room service is available 7 A.M.–10 P.M. daily. There is same-day laundry and dry cleaning service Mon.–Sat. Small pets are permitted in guest rooms. Cribs and rollaways are available and babysitters are on call. The first floor gift shop is open seven days 7 A.M.–9 P.M. and has a “Dallas Cowboys” corner. There are safe-deposit boxes and a cashier is on duty 24 hours. American Airlines has a staffed lobby desk (Mon.–Fri. 8 A.M.–6 P.M.) and Hertz has a direct phone line. There is free hourly van service to Love Field and D/FW Airport seven days.

Business Services

There are eight large and three small meeting rooms all attractively paneled and very well-lighted. There is an audiovisual service on the premises and a new auditorium has theater-type seating. Secretarial services can be arranged and there is a photocopy machine for guest use during business hours. There is plenty of open area near meeting rooms for pre-function registration and receptions.

Eating and Drinking

A full menu buffet breakfast is served around the pool area from 6–11 A.M. daily and the Sunday brunch is a special treat. Lunch is served in the flower-laden restaurant to the left of the lobby bar (the pool area is reserved for banquet luncheons only). Gabriel's Restaurant and Club is one of the finest restaurants in Dallas serving lunch and dinner daily. See our review in the restaurant section of this guide. The Club has a membership fee.

LOVE FIELD

★ **DUNFEY DALLAS**
$$ **3800 West Northwest Highway**
(214)357-9561; (800)228-2121
All major credit cards

This sprawling hotel is adjacent to Love Field, about 20 minutes north of Downtown and the Convention Center and a little out of the way of most Dallas activity. The motif of thc entire complex is English Tudor, and the lobby has beamed ceilings, a high brick tower and a seating area that is warm and inviting with wood paneling and overstuffed couches.

The registration desk is well-staffed and keys and mail are not visible. The hotel is huge but only two stories high, so corridors throughout the hotel are very long and give you the feeling you will never get to your room. Many of the hallways are steeply inclined and very tiring to traverse.

Accommodations

There are 604 rooms and 56 suites. All rooms offer comfortable, spacious quarters and many have nice wood paneling. Standard rooms have color TV, AM/FM radio and a hanging rack for clothing. There is a small vanity outside the bathroom but no counter around the sink.

There must be about 40 different kinds of suites here. All suites have wet bar, couch, table and two extra chairs. Suites have large bedrooms and an extra half-bath connecting the rooms. Six bi-level suites each have a small balcony with a bedroom area overlooking the parlor. All doors have chains and peepholes. Some rooms have deadbolt locks but most have simple pushbutton knobs which we found rather flimsy.

Personal Services

Room service hours are 6 A.M.–10 P.M. Same-day laundry, dry cleaning and tailoring are available Mon.–Sat. Pets are permitted in guest rooms. There are safe-deposit boxes and a cashier is on duty 24 hours. There is a liquor store (Mon.–Sat. 10 A.M.–9 P.M.) and gift shop and an electronic game room. Delta Airlines has a lobby desk open Mon.–Fri. 9 A.M.–5 P.M. The newsstand is open seven days 7 A.M.–10 P.M. Parking is free and there is Surtran service to Love Field and D/FW.

Business Services

The 38 meeting rooms can handle 10 to 2,000 people. The ballroom with its 17-foot ceiling and wood paneling is Tudor style. There are several breakout rooms with a spacious reception area and coatroom. The Top of the Castle is located at the top of a long hallway and is fine for banquets with its own bar and dance floor. The catering department offers an extensive menu and an audiovisual company is on the premises. Guests may use the photocopier during working hours and the hotel provides many meeting supplies including PA system, lectern, podium, projection screen, blackboard and easels.

Eating and Drinking

Poppies restaurant serves meals seven days 6 A.M.–11 P.M. The Cafe serves New York delicatessen-type foods. Tingles Disco, located in the lobby, is open 11 A.M.–2 A.M. and is a great gathering spot at Happy Hour.

OK EXECUTIVE INN

$$ 3232 West Mockingbird Lane
(214) 357-5601; (800) 528-1234
All major credit cards

The area around the entrance to Love Field Airport is not attractive, but this hotel is especially suitable for business travelers who are coming to Dallas for a brief meeting—and the catering department is capable and used to tough schedules. The hotel itself is a multistoried nondescript building, but has a well-staffed check-in desk.

Accommodations

There are 300 rooms and six suites in this hotel. Rooms located in the Tower portion are more spacious, but in all rooms furnishings and decor are definitely "motley motel," as are the bathrooms. Several rooms we visited had a musty odor. Rooms all have color TV with cable movies and Tower rooms also have coffeemakers. Suites have a wet bar and refrigerator. Hallways are long and poorly lighted. Doors have chains and double locks against passkey.

Personal Services

Room service is available 6 A.M.–10 P.M. and same-day laundry and dry cleaning is available weekdays. Pets may stay in guest rooms, and cribs, rollaways and babysitters can be arranged. A cashier is on duty 24 hours and there is a barber shop open 9 A.M.–4:30 P.M. except Sunday. There are safe-deposit boxes but no lobby shops. Newspaper dispensers are in the lobby.

Business Services

There are 30 meeting rooms available which can accommodate from 10 for a conference to 400 for a banquet. Some of the rooms have a definitely well-used appearance and could use some redecorating. There is an audiovisual firm on the premises and a photocopy machine is available for guest use during business hours.

Eating and Drinking

The Harvester, a coffee shop, is open seven days 6 A.M.–10 P.M. The Black Garter Lounge is open 11:30 A.M.–2 A.M.

PARK CITIES

★★★★ **THE MANSION ON TURTLE CREEK**
$$$$ **2821 Turtle Creek Boulevard**
(214) 559-2100; (800) 527-5432; Telex/Cable 794946; TWX 9108614352
Most major credit cards

From the moment you drive into the circular drive with its lovely fountain you will be treated royally at the Mansion. The name refers to the restored mansion which houses The Mansion on Turtle Creek restaurant managed by "21" Management Company of New York. The restaurant entrance is opposite the canopied entrance into the recently constructed nine-story hotel. The lobby is a huge rotunda decorated in muted beige and blue with a huge urn of fresh-cut flowers and spectacular individual arrangements on side tables in the waiting area. An enormous Oriental rug and breakfront with Meissen china dominate the seating area which is filled with comfortable sofas and chairs. Outstanding artwork and a framed tapestry decorate the walls.

Service here is excellent, from the concierge desk right inside the front door to the marble registration desk where check-in is accomplished with grace by people who act as if it really matters that you chose the Mansion. There are 24-hour security guards and the hotel uses Winfield cylinder locks that are rotated frequently.

This elegant hotel caters to the business traveler who does not need shops or enormous meeting rooms. It does not meet all our criteria for a top listing, but the sheer opulence of the rooms and the personal attention lavished on guests by a large staff make it impossible to give the hotel less than a four-star rating.

Accommodations

Everything from the flower arrangements to the Verona marbles and top-quality furnishings makes this a special place to stay. The hotel includes 144 rooms and 14 suites each beautifully decorated and furnished.

Standard double rooms decorated in beige and rose include a private little terrace area through French doors. Each room has a love seat, chair with ottoman, armoire with concealed color TV and a king-sized bed. Bathrooms have separate vanity with light-surrounded mirror, free-standing marble sink with brass fixtures and tub/shower. All rooms come with bathrobe, special soaps, shampoo and shower cap and each room has a small foyer with large closet.

There are three types of suites. Executive suites come with one or two bedrooms and an adjoining sitting room; master suites have the same configuration but are much larger; terrace suites are like small apartments, with dining area, living room with bar counter and sink, complete kitchen with microwave oven, bedroom and one and a half baths. All suites, decorated in peach and beige, have canopy beds, and all suites have extra-large bathrooms with marble fixtures and brass fittings, as well as separate powder room in the entry.

Personal Services

Full restaurant menu service is available through room service 24 hours, seven days. Guests receive complimentary morning newspapers daily. Same-day laundry and dry cleaning is available Mon.–Fri. 9 A.M.–5 P.M. but special arrangements can be made for weekend service. Babysitters, cribs and rollaways are available. Safe-deposit boxes are available and foreign currency is exchanged by the cashier on duty 24 hours. There are no lobby shops but newspapers and toiletries are available at the front desk. There is a concierge to arrange for car rental, limousine service, barber shop and beauty salon appointments, and in general, the staff to guest ratio here is the best we've seen in Dallas.

Business Services

There are five large and three small meeting rooms which can handle 10 to 200 people for meetings or meals. Guest services personnel can arrange for audiovisual, secretarial or translation services. A photocopy and Telex machine are available for guest use during normal business hours. There is a catering department on the premises.

Eating and Drinking

The adjoining Mansion on Turtle Creek restaurant is one of the most elegant dining spots in Dallas. Lunch and dinner are served seven days with high tea served in the Promenade Lounge afternoons 3–5:30 P.M. and supper available from 10:30 P.M.–midnight. See our review of this fine restaurant in that section of our Guide. Breakfast is available daily in the garden room connecting the hotel with the restaurant.

ARLINGTON

If you have business in both Dallas and Fort Worth, you might find it easiest to stay in one of the following hotels in Arlington on the Dallas-Fort Worth Turnpike, almost equidistant from the central business districts of each city.

★★★ FLAGSHIP INN
$$ 601 Avenue H East, Arlington
(817) 640-1666
All major credit cards

Formerly the Inn of Six Flags and named for the amusement park nearby, this hotel has recently been transformed into a major meeting and resort facility. In order to attract business travelers and convention clients, the new hotel has incorporated excellent meeting facilities and flexible room arrangements. The registration area is well-staffed and a cashier is on duty 24 hours. There should be no delay in registering despite large groups arriving regularly. This is a great spot to bring your family along since the Six Flags amusement park is so close and there is free transport to and from the park.

Accommodations

The Inn has 301 rooms and six suites and two villas. Standard rooms have coordinated drapes and spreads and include color TV, desk space and extra table and chairs. Good closets have full-length mirrors on doors but no skirt hangers. Ceramic tile bathrooms have convenient electrical outlets and tub/showers. All rooms have double lock against passkey. Suites feature king-sized bedroom and an adjoining sitting room large enough for meetings of 30 people, but no extra bath or powder room. Rattan dividers and wicker furnishings are very attractive.

A special feature at the Inn is the addition of two villas with two and three bedrooms respectively, large parlors with refrigerators, ice makers and wet bars, and their own private outdoor swimming pool. These are perfect for the company executive who needs to entertain during meetings at the Inn.

Personal Services

Room service is available seven days 6:30 A.M.–11 P.M. and same-day laundry and dry cleaning is available Mon.–Fri. 8 A.M–5 P.M. Babysitters, cribs and rollaways are available. Pets are permitted in guest rooms. Budget and American Airlines each have a lobby desk (Mon.–Fri. 7:30 A.M.–4 P.M.) and the gift shop is open seven days 7:30 A.M.–8 P.M. There is a notary public and a photocopy machine is available for guest use during normal business hours. Guests of the Inn have access to nearby Great Southwest Golf Club's 18-hole course and transportation is arranged. There are three outdoor swimming pools and two lighted tennis courts on the premises.

Business Services

With five large and seven small meeting rooms the Inn can handle 25–800 people in any meeting arrangement. A full range of audiovisual equipment is available and there is a catering department on the premises. The Crystal Palace, the largest meeting room, has a professional stage with theater lighting, dressing room, projection and sound equipment and can handle up to 800 people.

Eating and Drinking

The Signature Room serves dinner Mon.–Sat. 6–11 P.M. Indigo is the more casual restaurant which serves meals seven days 6:30 A.M.–11 P.M. For cocktails and live entertainment try the Cactus Moon Mon.–Sat. 11 A.M.–2 A.M. and Sunday noon–2 A.M.

★★ RODEWAY INN AND CONFERENCE CENTER

$$ 833 North Highway 360, Arlington
(817) 265-8241; (800)228-2000
All major credit cards

This motor hotel is one of the more fully equipped in the area. The lobby/registration area is very small but the desk is well staffed and service is friendly. While it is definitely not an elite atmosphere it is very functional for large group meetings or for the business traveler who must travel to both Fort Worth and Dallas. There are often large groups of students and young people because of its closeness to Six Flags Amusement Park, a popular stopoff for touring youth groups.

Accommodations

All 350 rooms and 42 suites have deadbolts. Standard rooms have small side table and chairs and a desk area, color TV with AM/FM clock radios attached. Some rooms overlook the outdoor pool. Decor is subdued beige, earth tones and tweeds. Bathrooms have convenient electrical outlet but no separate dressing area. Suites have sinks, refrigerators and minibars. Some have stoves and all overlook the pool and have patios.

Personal Services

Room service is available 7 A.M.–10 P.M. Same-day dry cleaning and laundry service is available Mon.–Fri. 7 A.M.–6

P.M. Pets are allowed in guest rooms, and cribs and rollaways are available. Car-rental phone lines are available in the lobby. Taxi to D/FW airport is available from the front door but there is no Surtran service. The small lobby gift shop is open seven days 8 A.M.–9 P.M. and there is an outdoor pool.

Shepler's, the largest seller of Western wear in the area, will send a van to pick you up for your shopping spree and return you to the hotel free of charge.

Business Services

This hotel has very fine business meeting and convention services. There are 14 large, nicely decorated meeting rooms with a spacious pre-function area surrounding them. Rooms, including a very attractive ballroom, can be designed to handle 10–1,000 persons. A unique facility is a 42-seat audiovisual room with built-in equipment that is excellent for slide presentations and can be rented separately at a daily rate. Photocopy machine is available for guest use weekdays during business hours, and secretarial and translation services can be arranged.

Eating and Drinking

The Red Apple, a casual restaurant serving Southwestern cuisine, is open seven days 7 A.M.–10 P.M. The Red Apple Lounge features Las Vegas-style entertainment Mon.–Sat. evenings. The Library Lounge is open Mon.–Sat. 4:30 P.M.–midnight.

GETTING AROUND TOWN

DALLAS, we have mentioned so many times, is growing at an almost unbelievable pace and the residents are justifiably proud of the solid economy and the forward-looking business and community leaders who have made this possible. The most noticeable problem resulting from this rapid growth is the lack of a mass transit system. As late as 1980, Dallasites rejected by a large plurality the concept of a mass transit system. This is even more complicated by the fact that business districts in Dallas are not clustered in the Downtown area alone. There are huge office complexes stretching along LBJ Freeway on the north, along North Central Expressway between LBJ and Downtown on the south and in a new area near the airport called Las Colinas. Each of these areas could be a separate city in itself. It is virtually impossible to walk from one appointment to another or from lunch to an office building even within one complex. Even though you can see where you need to be, the distances are usually much greater than you expect. Here are some tips we hope will help you to travel in and around Dallas by taxi, bus, limousine or rental car and occasionally even on foot.

HOW TO TRAVEL

Dallas is a city on wheels and the best advice we could give you is to rent a car if you have any travel to do within or around the city. For a major metropolitan area Dallas is woefully inadequate when it comes to mass transit or public transportation. The entire system consists of buses only—there are no trains, subways, trolleys or any other form of public transit. Taxis are available but they are expensive and you will have to find one at a hotel or other public building. There are very few floating cabs.

Hotels in Dallas are located in identifiable clusters. Restaurants, however, are even more closely clustered in groups because of the "wet" and "dry" areas designating the liquor sales policy in a given location. Restaurants are lumped in groups of five, six or ten along a short two or three block area where liquor sales are permitted. Texas is as sprawling as its reputation and you will generally find it impossible to walk from your hotel to a restaurant or a shopping area. You may be able to see where you are headed but the distances are deceiving and a car is a virtual necessity.

Driving around Dallas is generally easy with major north-south routes being North Central Expressway and Dallas North Tollway (25¢ exact change). The latter is an excellent choice if you must travel during rush hour into or out of Downtown. It is usually much less congested than North Central Expressway and just as direct (see map). Major east-west routes include Northwest Highway (Loop 12); LBJ Freeway (I-635), a circumferential highway with limited access which is particularly good in the north Dallas area and as a route from D/FW Airport; and R.L. Thornton Freeway (Route 30) which runs along the south of Downtown Dallas.

Certainly a map would be a sensible purchase if you are trying to traverse Dallas for the first time but in general, roads are perpendicular and easy to follow. Because the terrain is so flat and roads are wide the driving is much easier than in many other cities but you will log more miles than you realize just getting around town.

Roads in Dallas are clearly marked with major intersecting streets indicated by signs about two blocks prior to the intersection. Streets are wide and well-maintained but the speed could be intimidating—Texans universally ignore the 55 m.p.h speed limit. Be careful though because speed traps are set up daily along major routes and fines are stiff. A particularly hazardous part of driving in Dallas is school zones which are clearly marked with signs and often with blinkers. You must slow to 20 m.p.h. during the hours posted which generally are from 7:30 to 9:30 A.M. and from 2 to 4 P.M. The fine is $50 plus several dollars for each mile over the speed limit.

One special note of caution for first-time drivers in this area–when it rains or there is a shower which lightly covers the roadway with moisture the roads become as slick as snowy roads in the north. Slow up and turn carefully because the oily deposits mixed with light rain can cause you to spin out. In Texas a right turn on a red light is legal after coming to a complete stop. A few intersections are marked "No turn on red."

Parking is not a big problem in and around Dallas. For hotel guests parking is usually free and there are hundreds of parking facilities near office buildings and other public places. In the Downtown area you cannot park on the streets but there are plenty of indoor and outdoor lots usually with fees of $3 to $4 a day.

TIPS FOR PEDESTRIANS

When walking in downtown Dallas be sure to observe and obey the "Walk" and "Don't Walk" signs as well as the crosswalks marked on the corners. Jaywalking is no joke in Dallas, and $10 fines are imposed on the spot by policemen who monitor each intersection very carefully. If you are accustomed to the bustling corners and total disregard for pedestrians in other cities you will find Dallas very civilized. Pedestrians have the right of way over turning automobiles and in marked crosswalk areas. However, when the light is red or the signal indicates "Don't Walk" you cannot step off the curb. You must keep both feet on the sidewalk until the signal changes. It is no joke–"Forewarned is forearmed!"

BUSES

Dallas Transit System which operates within the city limits is comprised solely of buses and is the only form of mass transportation available in Dallas. Full schedule and route information is available at Dallas Transit System's Customer Assistance Center, Main & Akard Streets (Downtown) Mon.–

Fri. 7 A.M.–6 P.M. You can also call 826-2222 (Mon.–Fri. 6 A.M.–6:30 P.M., Sat., Sun. 8 A.M.–5 P.M.).

The bus system is essentially an in and out of downtown system; in other words, you cannot get from east to west on LBJ by public transportation, nor can you get from North Central Expressway to Stemmons Freeway and the Market Center area without going into town and then out. It is a very limited system and generally operates during daytime hours at full capacity and with severely restricted service after rush hour and on weekends. Generally service is provided 4:30 A.M.–1 A.M. weekdays on all routes and with limited schedules on Saturdays and Sundays. Many routes do not operate on weekends at all. It is important to remember that Dallas is a post-War city and was built with the premise that everyone owned a car; a central transportation system was not part of its conception. It is impossible to list all the routes and schedules so use the phone number listed herein and tell the operator where you are and where you need to go, and she will tell you if Dallas Transit can serve you.

The bus system is zoned in three concentric circles which correspond to the following: Region I—inside Loop 12 (Northwest Highway); Region II—between Loop 12 and LBJ Freeway; and Region III—beyond LBJ Freeway. Fares are subject to change but exact change is required and dollar bills are accepted in payment of fares.

Hop-A-Bus. For central downtown travel east and west, e.g., from Reunion Tower (Hyatt Regency) to uptown office buildings, you can use the Hop-A-Bus Mon.–Fri. 6:30 A.M.–7:30 P.M. Easily recognizable by its pointed ears attached to its vibrant pink body (yes, it's true), this service runs from Ross Avenue down Pearl Street and down Main Street to the Hyatt where it loops Reunion Arena area and returns uptown. It runs about every 15 minutes and is an inexpensive means of traveling the Downtown business corridor during workdays.

TAXIS

The taxi system in Dallas is metered and regulated by the Dallas Public Utilities Department. You will find cab drivers friendly and, on the whole, honest. There are three major cab companies licensed to operate in the city: Yellow

Cab, Terminal and State. Surtran taxis have limited operating rights in the Dallas business district and to and from the airport. A one-way trip to D/FW from Downtown costs about $18.

The meter in cabs currently starts at $1.30 with increments every mile thereafter. This is where you will really notice how sprawling Dallas is—it can often cost from $10 to $12 to travel one way from your hotel or office to the restaurant of your choice in another region. Because the roads are so straight and everything is so flat you may be amazed at the distances you travel in a brief time. Use the zones in our book to help you estimate what restaurant or hotel would be the best bet so you can save yourself unnecessary travel expense.

In summary, while you do not need to worry about circuitous routes or unscrupulous taxi drivers you may find your expenses mounting. A taxi from Downtown to a restaurant in the North Central zone can run $8–$10 each way, and from Downtown to LBJ about $12. Try to locate your business, entertainment and other activities in relatively central zones.

There are very few "floater" cabs in Dallas with the exception of the central Downtown area. You will find cabs at stands located in front of most hotels and some restaurants and you will be able to hail a taxi on the street Downtown. For all other zones you will find it easier to phone for a taxi. The dispatcher will give you a cab number and an approximate arrival time. If the cab does not show up you should report the number and tell the dispatcher you are waiting. There is no surcharge for ordering a cab.

YELLOW CAB, 426-6262

TERMINAL, 823-5120

STATE, 823 2161

SURTRAN D/FW, 251-1736

LIMOUSINE SERVICES

If you want to imitate "J.R." or just need to transport an important client around town you will find limousines of all sizes available as well as minibuses which can handle 14 to 17 passengers. Service is usually top-notch with uniformed chauffeurs, minibars, stereos, color TV and telephones. Rates vary but are generally $35–$40 per hour with a 3-hour minimum. Most companies prefer advance notice of 2–3 days and those we have chosen accept credit cards.

AARON LIMOUSINE SERVICE, 241-8258
All major credit cards.

CALIFORNIA LIMOUSINE SERVICE, 226-3743
AE.

CAREY LIMOUSINE OF DALLAS, 298-4619
All major credit cards.

DALLAS/FT. WORTH LIMOUSINES, 941-7800
AE.

DINO LIMOUSINE OF DALLAS, 692-5241
All major credit cards.

LIMOUSINES INCORPORATED, 827-7900
All major credit cards.

VIP LIMOUSINE SERVICE, 521-2837
All major credit cards.

CAR RENTALS

We have suggested, in fact strongly recommend, that you use a car to get around Dallas. There are numerous car-rental agencies in Dallas, many associated with auto dealerships. In our hotel listings we have indicated the auto rental facilities available at each hotel. The following will give you more sources. Most car-rental agencies are open from 7 A.M.–6 P.M. Monday through Friday and 8 A.M.–5 P.M. Saturday and Sunday. Companies at Love Airport are open seven days from 7 A.M. to midnight and most at D/FW are open 24 hours seven days.

One special note, since Dallas is a city on wheels and since conventions and meetings often take up many of the available rental cars you should reserve your car as early as possible. Especially during the "Markets" every few weeks in Dallas you will find cars scarce. All the companies we contacted suggested from three days to a week advance reservation to assure availability.

The following major agencies have outlets at D/FW Airport, Love Field and Downtown locations. We have provided their "800" listings so you can book a car in advance.

AVIS, (800) 331-2112
D/FW, 574-4100
Love Field, 357-0301
Downtown (Union Station), 748-8411
24-hour service available at D/FW only. All major credit cards.

BUDGET, (800) 228-9650
D/FW, 574-4141
Love Field, 357-0288
Downtown (1917 Commerce St.), 741-6843
LBJ at Preston Rd. 233-7609
24-hour service available at D/FW only. All major credit cards and Sears.

DOLLAR RENT A CAR, (800) 421-6868
D/FW, 256-4576
Love Field 357-8422
All major credit cards.

ECONO-CAR, (800) 228-1000
D/FW, 256-4551
Love Field, 350-5083
Downtown (1600 Jackson St.), 653-1801
All major credit cards.

HERTZ, (800) 654-3131
D/FW, 574-2000
Love Field, 350-7071
Downtown (1933 Commerce St.), 742-6814
24-hour service available at D/FW only. All major credit cards.

NATIONAL, (800) 328-4567
D/FW, 574-3400
Love Field, 357-0478
Downtown (2006 Bryan St.), 741-9356
24-hour service at D/FW Airport only. All major credit cards.

RESTAURANTS

DON'T come to Dallas looking for New York restaurants. There is neither the number nor variety here; what you do find are good restaurants, a few very good ones. There are a fair number of French and continental restaurants, many good Mexican restaurants, a surprising number of Japanese restaurants–and no Chinese restaurants of any note in our zones (strictly shopping-center Cantonese here). You will find good southern specialties in Dallas, from hush puppies to pecan pie, as well as Texas chili and barbecue–with some creole and Cajun cooking as well. Beef in Dallas is generally inferior to beef in the North–the cattle raised here are shipped to Kansas City to be rendered and never return! Few restaurants put much effort into side dishes–salads, vegetables, potatoes–and where there is a standout, we have mentioned it. Desserts too are less exciting in Dallas than elsewhere, and chocolate mousse, cheesecake, crème caramel and an occasional praline concoction are the mainstays here.

Dining in Dallas is less formal than in many other cities; you will often see men without tie and jacket in restaurants other than the most elegant and expensive ones. Because the city is growing so fast, Dallas hasn't had time to develop a true identity for fine dining; service is usually pleasant and courteous, but often uneven. Dining out in Dallas is fun, relatively reasonable, and a chance to catch a glimpse of an exciting, still growing city.

RATINGS

In this section we rate restaurants according to our own standards: food quality and preparation, efficiency of service from reservation through dessert, comfortable seating which allows privacy and quiet conversation. Remember that we are comparing *Dallas* restaurants; a four-star restaurant in Dallas may not rate four stars in New York or Los Angeles.

Restaurant reviews are always subjective and affected by circumstances of a particular visit, but we have rechecked and revisited when we felt our experience was not a typical one. We have attempted to highlight basic menu offerings or chef specialties where appropriate. This is not a gourmet's guide, but by reading each review you will have an overall view of the atmosphere and the cuisine. We have attempted to rate each restaurant in comparison to others of the same type. All visits were anonymous and no free meals or gratuities of any kind were offered or solicited. The following rating system was used:

★★★★ **Superb.** This indicates the best restaurants in Dallas which offer the finest in service, cuisine and atmosphere. They are usually expensive but have established themselves by reputation and experience to be the best in the Metroplex.

★★★ **Excellent.** Restaurants in this category are generally similar to the four-star listings, but have been reduced to three stars because of a specific deficiency such as high noise levels, less than superior service, etc.

★★ **Very Good.** Generally food in two-star restaurants is of fine quality but other criteria (table spacing, noise level) have been found wanting. We have attempted to identify what is good and what is lacking. You will find two-star restaurants very good but be prepared for shortcomings.

★ **Good.** Adequate food but poor business atmosphere usually places a restaurant in this category. Prices are generally good but either ambience or service has been found lacking. Some restaurants that we feel are not very good rate a star for tourist value.

OK. Restaurants in this category are exactly that, okay. They are generally not appropriate for business conversation. Food is adequate but not of gourmet quality. These listings are fine for a quick bite or when looking for an especially convenient location.

NR. Not Recommended. We have found these restaurants to have so many flaws that we do not feel you will be interested in trying them.

PRICES

Dallas/Fort Worth is still a relative bargain for diners. Our prices are based on meals for two people including: appetizer, salad, entree, dessert and coffee. They also include a 15% tip. A 5% sales tax is added to your bill and be sure to figure your tip on the basis of service provided—poor service should be recognized by a lesser tip and superior service rewarded. Tip should be based on price before sales tax is added.

PRICES FOR TWO		LUNCH	DINNER
$$$$	Very Expensive	$35 plus	$60 plus
$$$	Expensive	$20–35	$45–60
$$	Moderate	$12–20	$30–45
$	Inexpensive	Under $12	Under $30

LOCATION

We have used the same zones for restaurants that we use for hotels, since we feel that as a business traveler you won't have time to explore remote areas for restaurants, no matter how special. Do remember that the great distances in Dallas may add $10 or $20 to your meal in the form of cabfare, so you might prefer to stick to restaurants in your hotel's zone. At this writing, the Airport zone has no restaurants other than those located in the hotels we have reviewed. If you are staying at the airport you will want to sample other restaurants and will head Downtown (15–20 minutes), to the Market Center (10–15 minutes), or along LBJ (15–20 minutes). If restaurants are an important part of your trip to Dallas, you would be better off choosing a hotel in another section so you will be closer to a broader selection of restaurants.

You will notice that our reviews have included more restaurants in the North Central area than any other. This zone is the hub of night life in Dallas and the most complete dining area in town. If you crave good food, bustling crowds and night life after working hours, you should head for this zone.

Downtown has a number of fine restaurants and is the second busiest restaurant area in Dallas. The most active zone is located on the northern edge of Downtown along Cedar Springs, Routh and the Quadrangle, a recently restored shopping and dining area. This zone is easily accessible to the Market Center and to North Central as well.

There are, of course, restaurants in most hotels and they may prove convenient. It seems a shame, however, to miss out on some fine dining because you are timid about exploring new restaurants; we hope we can take the mystery—and the heartburn—out of restaurant testing in Dallas. There are a few hotel restaurants reviewed because we feel they are among the first-class dining establishments in the city.

HOURS AND RESERVATIONS

Restaurant hours in Dallas are the same as in most major American cities: lunch 11 A.M.–2 P.M., dinner 5:30–11 P.M. The Dallas area is growing at such a pace that in spite of the flurry of new restaurants opening weekly, there often seem to be more diners than space, and you will be more likely to have to wait in line here for your table than in other cities. Reservations are an absolute must on Thursday, Friday and Saturday nights at any restaurant worth a try. Unfortunately not all restaurants accept reservations and some that do are not too adept at honoring them. Believe us when we recommend you call ahead. Some excellent restaurants do not accept reservations, and it is not unusual, even in a top restaurant, to have a 10–20 minute wait. It's a fact of life here so you might as well accept it. So be patient, relax, and strike up a conversation with a local—people here are friendly and used to chatting while waiting. If you are in a hurry or have no patience, try dining at an early hour (5:30–6 P.M.).

DRINKING

Since Dallas is in the heart of what is commonly called the "Bible Belt," you will find liquor laws more restrictive than in most other cities. Liquor sales by the drink or bottle are determined according to precinct—wet or dry. This can be very confusing to an out-of-town visitor but the basic result is that restaurants and liquor stores are clustered along such familiar areas as the "Greenville Avenue Strip" as it is locally known. You will frequently find one side of a street wet and the other side of the same street dry.

Restaurants that are located in dry areas can serve liquor but will charge a membership fee. This means that you can order a drink but you must be a member, and fees for membership vary from $3 to $10. If you are in Dallas for one night or do not plan to visit the particular restaurant again you can inquire about a temporary membership which is cheaper and good for that night only. Otherwise, the fee is an annual membership and is good upon return visits. Only one member of each party need be a member and the fee is added to your bar bill. If you are a guest in a hotel in a dry area your room key serves as evidence of membership and you will not generally be charged a fee. Obviously, if you are not ordering drinks you will not be charged a membership fee.

LATE-NIGHT DINING

As you may have guessed, Dallas is not a late-night town and most restaurants serve only until 11 P.M. For service after that, refer to our listings in the "24 Hours a Day" chapter.

One hazard of restaurant reviewing, especially in Dallas, is that more restaurants go out of business each week than you can imagine. To avoid this pitfall we have reviewed established restaurants and have avoided most of the brand new ones. If you spy a nice-looking place we have not included, be sure to ask the hotel personnel or a business associate who lives here: Dallasites all have opinions about eating spots and are usually delighted to recommend a favorite. Meanwhile we will continue to update our guide and include those whose reputation seems to merit future reviews.

AIRPORT

★★★ **MISTER G's**
$$$ **Amfac–East Tower (D/FW Airport), 453-8400**
Open seven days, dinner only 6–11 P.M.
All major credit cards

A surprising find for this restaurant wasteland. The seating for this outstanding steak and seafood restaurant is reminiscent of the library in a turn of the century private home. Elegance and fine service are the key ingredients here with impeccable European waiters, silver breadbaskets and shelves of antique volumes. The dining room is small and might be noisy, but banquettes allow quiet dining. The only incongruous element–piped-in AM music complete with commercials. Victorian lighting fixtures and glass-shaded candle holders add to the glowing warmth of the surroundings. Cocktails are served in Waterford-type glasses.

Oysters are an excellent choice and they are served elegantly with lemon encased in a cheesecloth sack tied with a ribbon. The onion soup gratinée is also very good. The petit filet mignon was cooked to order and the side dish of Idaho skins fried with onions is more than enough for two people. They also serve an excellent rack of lamb and a fine salad of huge fresh tomatoes and Bermuda onions. Desserts are wonderfully fattening especially the creamy chocolate eclair or confetti cake. A complimentary cordial tops off a fine dining experience and is served from a large cart which holds desserts and cordials.

Reservations are a must here since this is such a small restaurant.

MARKET CENTER

★★ **EL TORITO**
$ **2701 Stemmons Freeway, 631-3050**
Open seven days
All major credit cards

Seven rooms with blue-tiled walls, terra-cotta tiled floors and Indian weave rugs, combined with ladderback wooden chairs under beamed ceilings, laden with handmade baskets and philodendron make you think you're South of the Border. The Mexican dishes are as good as you will find in any border town or in the best hotels. We tried the rellendo de res (marinated beef broiled with green peppers onions and topped with cheese), refried beans and pico de gallo. The combination platter is always a reliable selection for the novice diner. Service is fast and attentive and waiters pride themselves on remembering returning customers.

★★★ JAVIER'S GOURMET MEXICANO
$$ 4912 Cole St., 521-4211
Dinners seven days
All major credit cards

Javier's is one of the more famous Mexican restaurants in Dallas and the food is quite good. Its location makes it a steep cab fare from Downtown but it is worth the trip. White-washed walls, low lights, tile floors and other accouterments seem just the proper atmosphere for a Mexican meal.

Javier's serves the most authentic classical Mexican cuisine we know in Dallas and the menu has many grilled beef and pork dishes (with varying degrees of spiciness), huevos rancheros, and several combination platters with enchiladas, tortillas, tostadas and refried beans (excellent). The food is good so don't fill up on the chips as we always do. Waiters are friendly and willing to explain the menu items to those unfamiliar with the cuisine. When the restaurant is full the noise level is annoying.

★★ KOSTA'S
$$ 2755 Bachman Drive, 351-4592
Open seven days
All major credit cards

Located on the shore of Bachman Lake on the west side of Dallas slightly outside our Market Center zone, Kosta's is a Greek taverna complete with friendly waiters and strolling musicians playing authentic Greek instruments. The food is authentically Greek provincial. Luncheon is a real bargain with a complete meal including entree, salad, spanakipita and rice or potato costing under $6. Dinner is more expensive but still reasonable and includes gyros, sagnaki and kefalotiri. Helpful waiters will be glad to explain how each dish is cooked and make recommendations for the uninitiated. The restaurant is located in a restored Victorian lake house and is cozy and fun.

★★ LA TOSCA
$$ 7713 Inwood Road, 352-8373
Closed Monday
All major credit cards

This is a delightful restaurant serving excellent northern Italian food. The setting is simple: Wedgwood blue shutters, willow pattern dishes on the walls and black-and-white-tiled floors. Waiters wear black-and-white-striped sailor shirts.

Owners Antonio Capaccioli and Victor Mari join in serving the three dining rooms while Antonio's tall, blonde wife, Virginia, serves as hostess. Tables are comfortably spaced and service is very attentive, although at times it seemed as if our waiter had more tables than he could handle.

Fresh fish from the Mediterranean, including the octopus, mullet and sea bass, is flown in each day, we have been told. Portions of octopus salad are generous and surprisingly tender. All of the many pasta dishes are homemade, and the green and white noodles with cream sauce and the tagliolini la Tosca, thin noodles with a delicate salmon sauce, are both excellent. The vitello tonnato, however, was a disappointment because the roast veal was overcooked and the tuna sauce was too salty. A delicious house salad is served with freshly grated parmesan cheese.

There is a very good wine list, mainly Italian. There is a wide assortment of desserts, from chocolate-covered pastry with cream to strawberry tarts. We like the sliced oranges with caramel slivers in sweet liqueur.

★★ L'ENTRECOTE
$$$$ 2201 Stemmons Freeway (Loew's Anatole Hotel), 748-1200
Open seven days
All major credit cards

Enjoying the surroundings is a big part of the experience in this restaurant. Large windows look out onto the atrium, blue booths seclude diners while harp music gently envelops all in the small dining room. Waiters are extremely polite and women dining alone will receive special treatment and special attention.

The menu is traditional with a strong emphasis on beef. Most meals are prepared tableside with flamboyant skill although this attracts attention away from intimate conversations. As a recent addition to the menu (they change it every few months), we liked the 14-ounce baby salmon that came to the table filleted and stuffed with a scallop mousse. The waiter prepared a sauce of clam, lemon and orange juices to top the fish baked in fennel greens and dill. This came with wild rice and carrots, both good but not great.

The wine list at L'Entrecote is very good. Waiters are knowledgeable about different wines, many of which are kept in a glass case in the restaurant. There is a bar area, sunken and off to the side, where an after-dinner brandy is as enjoyable as a before-dinner cocktail. For dessert you can pass up the soufflé (not the best–or even near best–in town) and try the orange sherbet laced with liqueur and covered by a meringue and coconut crust. There is usually a dessert special not listed on the menu.

★★ OLD SAN FRANCISCO STEAK HOUSE
$$$ Stemmons Freeway at Walnut Hill, 357-0484
Open seven days, dinner only
All major credit cards

Here's a spot for out-of-towners anxious to capture the true feeling of an Old West saloon. You will dine on fine beef amid Gay Nineties decor with a piano player tickling the ivories and a dancehall girl swinging on a red velvet trapeze bar high above the main dining room. Reservations are recommended and you may have to wait even with a reservation.

A huge block of delicious Swiss cheese is brought to your table to slice away as you enjoy your cocktail. Lobster and steak are real winners here if you can concentrate on the eating amidst the circus atmosphere. Baked potatoes with all the toppings are excellent. Cheesecake is a good choice to finish off your meal.

Tables are rather closely spaced and there are often large parties which can make quiet conversation difficult at best.

★ **PELICAN'S**
$$ **10690 Composite (Stemmons at Walnut Hill), 357-0279**
Open seven days, Sat. and Sun. dinner only
All major credit cards

Although the seafood is usually good at Pelican's, the steaks are always outstanding. Located near what appears to be a sea of steakhouses, this rustic looking chain restaurant is a comfortable place for a meeting. Booths are secluded, although sometimes there is so much privacy that your waiter may forget about you. Service is generally friendly.

The shrimp peel, a large bowl of unshelled shrimp boiled in beer, oranges and cinnamon, is the only appetizer worth ordering. The house dressing is very tasty and at dinner the salad is all-you-can-eat. We are continually pleased with the New York strip steak because it is always large and tender. The fish offerings change daily and most are fresh and tasty. Small loaves of crusty brown bread are served with the meals.

NR **TRAIL DUST STEAK HOUSE**
$ **10841 Composite (Stemmons at Walnut Hill), 357-3862**
Open seven days, Saturday and Sunday dinner only.
Most major credit cards

This is a large, loud room filled with picnic tables. The menu: your favorite cut of steak broiled over desert mesquite wood. It comes with a salad, a bowl of red beans and a basket of white bread.

This is really a family place and at dinner the presence of small children running around makes business discussion difficult.

We found the service unforgivably poor. Despite an almost empty room, we had to wait for our order to be taken. After asking our waitress three times for a glass of wine we finally gave up, paid the bill and went home.

DOWNTOWN

★★ ANTARES
$$$ 300 Reunion Blvd. (Reunion Tower), 741-3663 or 651-1234
Open seven days
All major credit cards

Fifty stories above downtown Dallas, this revolving restaurant is as popular for its view as its food. Don't show up here without a reservation unless you're prepared to wait an hour. The atmosphere here (away from the crowded reservation desk) is quiet and formal, including waiters in black tie.

Steaks are the specialty here, but the restaurant does many other entrees equally well. The lobster and scallop St. Jacques appetizer is good, but we wish there were more pieces of lobster in the dish.

Beef tenderloin is one of the most popular items and justifiably so. Ours came with a side order of carrots and zucchini, shredded and tossed in a cheese dressing, and a baked potato. The chicken Caprice is a delightful combination of chicken, spinach and crabmeat stuffed in a flaky, homemade puff pastry.

The best dessert, we think, is the hot chocolate bread pudding made from rich, sweet chocolate with a hint of almond flavoring served with a warm whiskey and caramel sauce. From time to time, the Sacher torte will appear on the dessert table. When it does, order it for a blissful experience.

Service at Antares can be slow at any time of the day in spite of the large staff.

★★ BANNO BROS. SEAFOOD RESTAURANT
$ 1516 Greenville Ave., 821-1321
Closed Sundays
All major credit cards

The nautical setting is pleasant, if a bit too dark, and accented by homey things like a Christmas wreath made of shells, driftwood and pieces of coral. The service is casual beginning with a "Hi ya" greeting from one of the brothers and a "I'll be with ya in a minute, hon" note of recognition from the waitress. But the food is worth the experience.

Start with the seafood gumbo, a thick Cajun concoction that looks gooey but tastes wonderful, full of chunks of shrimp and fish. The sirloin steak covered in creole sauce was a little too spicy for our taste so we asked the waitress for help. She quickly returned from the kitchen with our steak, this time topped with a milder version of the pepper sauce. We were impressed. Shrimp in batter are large and plentiful and boiled lobster is unusually good. The broiled red snapper appears on the menu as the daily special from time to time and is always excellent. All dishes come with coleslaw, french fries and hush puppies (cornmeal cooked in oil like drop biscuits). The tartar sauce is the best we have ever had–rich and creamy, flavored slightly by onion and "old" pickles. Desserts here are the usual Dallas offerings.

★★★★ **CAFE ROYAL**

$$$$ **650 North Pearl St. (Plaza of the Americas Hotel), 747-7222**
Lunch weekdays, dinner Mon.-Sat.
All major credit cards

Behind the highly polished brass doors in the mall of the Plaza of the Americas is one of Dallas's newer and finer dining establishments. Do not come here if you are in a hurry; service is deliberate, if not downright slow. Do come ready to enjoy the beautiful surroundings and excellent French cuisine. The bar area is painted maroon with Oriental screens and all through the restaurant there are exceptionally beautiful antique pieces which lend the air of an opulent private home. Everything is classic from the formal service to the hushed tones which make conducting business a true pleasure. You will, of course, be paying handsomely for all this beauty.

There is a fixed-price luncheon menu which includes a daily suggestion from the chef, as well as an à la carte menu with an extensive list of main courses from duck with mustard sauce to veal steak with lime butter, and several varieties of seafood and steaks. Desserts are offered from the pastry cart or you may choose from an assortment of sherbets.

The dinner menu is in French with English translations. Hors d'oeuvres range from Scotch salmon (very expensive) to vegetable and chicken mousses with truffles. Our favorite soup is the creamed zucchini soup with crabmeat. Fish entrees are beautifully served (as is everything here) and each has a unique light sauce. One of the most unusual is fillet of sole with raspberry sauce and chantrelles. Other entrees, many prepared right at your table, include duckling with black current sauce, rack of lamb for two, chicken with sweetbread and lobster in lobster sauce and several beef offerings. All vegetables and salads vary with the best available market selections of the season and are very fresh.

As you might expect, desserts here are special and include deliciously light soufflés and flaming crepes or strawberries with Kirsch and Grand Marnier flambé.

All in all this is one of the finest and most expensive restaurants in Dallas.

★★★ CALLAUD'S
$$$ 2619 McKinney Avenue, 823-5380
Closed Sunday, Mon. and Sat. dinner only
All major credit cards

This is a graceful French restaurant where you will see business people engrossed in conversation and private thoughts. The service is very good; waiters are polite, attentive and well-trained in their art. The dining room is pleasant, with terra-cotta-colored suede walls, well-spaced tables, vases of fresh garden flowers, and formal sideboards from France. The midday sun beaming down through a central atrium can be overpowering at lunch, so choose your seat if you can.

The lunch menu is extensive. Tomato soup is light and delicious. Fillet of sole is our number one choice, except for the heavy amount of butter. The salmon in mustard sauce is an excellent alternative and both fish are fresh. A limited dessert tray offers light tarts and pastries.

Appetizers at dinner may include lobster soufflé (a must), red snapper pâté, duck pâté, smoked salmon, caviar and foie gras. Entrees are equally abundant ranging from quenelles to veal. A simple veal chop was a delight covered with a thin tomato sauce and sided by broccoli au gratin. The lamb, prepared under the direction of the Moroccan-born chef, Guy Callaud, is superb, encrusted in a pastry shell and covered with Madeira sauce flavored by truffles.

There is a tendency to linger over coffee, brandy or one of the many soufflés such as raspberry or chocolate.

★★ CHATEAUBRIAND
$$$ 2515 McKinney Avenue, 741-1223
Closed Sunday
All major credit cards

It's dark, mirrored and chandeliered inside this old building. You enter either into the dining room or the club. Meals are served in both and the club has better lighting. Many people consider this to be one of the finer restaurants in Dallas. We found the food to be above average (but expensive) and the service to be erratic. However, the atmosphere is lively and it is always fun to watch the people dressed elegantly at the well-spaced tables around the room.

The clubroom is the main dining room. It is decorated in red from the carpet to the peacock feathers on the wallpaper. Turquoise chairs and white linen tablecloths give a nightclub feeling to the two-tiered room.

The menu is extensive and includes everything from broiled steak, boiled lobster or veal prepared in one of four ways. The Chateaubriand was grilled to specifications but the broccoli was served in an oversalted sauce. The chicken Kiev was disappointing, though, with a tough crust covering a juicy breast. Crabmeat cocktail and oysters Rockefeller were both generously filled with fresh seafood.

The specialty of the house is the flaming dessert. Baked Alaska, Bananas Foster and Peaches Flambé are all good laced with brandy and set on fire at the table. We liked the rum pie, filled with ice cream, rum and a mixture of nuts.

Chateaubriand manages to be at once flamboyant and conservative. It's one of the only places women still show up for lunch in hats. One caveat: if the hostess doesn't know you, she may try to put you in the dining room away from the action. Request a seat in the club. You'll receive better service and a glimpse of Dallas glamour.

★ **CRACKER'S**
$ **2621 McKinney Avenue, 827-1660**
Open seven days.
All major credit cards.

This charming restaurant is located in an old house a few minutes from Downtown. The simple country French decor includes pale gray walls, framed vegetable prints and large porch windows. The seating is rather cramped but it is not noisy.

In addition to entrees such as beef burgundy and coq au vin, the menu includes several Greek specialties. The spanakopita, a mixture of spinach and cheese in a flaky pastry is delicious. We tried the souvlaki at dinner on our last visit and found it to be dry and lacking in seasoning.

Cracker's is well-known for the outstanding quality of desserts. Among the best are the bread pudding with brandy sauce and the homemade cheesecake and plum topping.

★ **CRAWDADDY'S**
$ **2614 McKinney Avenue, 748-2008**
Open seven days
Most major credit cards

It's all very informal in this cabin on McKinney. Seafood and Louisiana specialties are popular with the business folk as well as the local artists. At lunchtime it's hard to find a seat and impossible to have a conversation but, after all, there's only one reason to come here and that is the food.

The food includes an excellent prime steak and New Orleans dishes like barbecued shrimp and seafood gumbo. Large portions of shrimp and oysters (broiled or fried) include french fries, coleslaw and hush puppies. We like the deep-dish whole catfish which is always fresh. Dessert is a classic straight from the French Quarter, a light and sweet beignet, butter pecan ice cream with warm praline sauce.

★★★ FAUSTO'S
$$$$ 300 Reunion Blvd. (Hyatt Regency Hotel), 741-3663
Open seven days
All major credit cards

Located off the Atrium on the second floor of the Hyatt Regency this fine restaurant offers delectable seafood and other delicacies in a romantic setting. Tables are spaced for privacy and attentive waiters are quietly efficient.

Luncheon meetings over a light omelet topped with chicken and shrimp, or a spinach salad à la chef, are guaranteed to please a client or business associate. Try the shark gumbo and enjoy the marbled rye bread toasted with Parmesan cheese. Fausto's, which used to serve only seafood, now offers a wider variety of entrees. Dinner now also includes Rotisserie Duckling which is delicious. The choice for seafood lovers is more difficult. Our favorite is Scampi Cajun–shrimp sautéed with oil and garlic. There is a terrific oyster bar.

Desserts include Black Forest cake, apple struedel, chocolate chip cheese cake, and an unusual hot chocolate bread pudding that is delicious.

Be sure to have your parking ticket validated. When you finish you might want to use the underground walkway to Reunion Tower for a nightcap in the revolving lounge 50 stories above the gleaming city.

★★★★ THE FRENCH ROOM
$$$$ 1321 Commerce (Adolphus Hotel), 742-8200
Closed Sunday
All major credit cards

This brand new entry to the Dallas dining scene is part of the $45 million renovation of the Adolphus Hotel. It should become one of the finest dining spots in town if it maintains the excellence of our initial encounters–and it shows signs of doing just that.

The lovely surroundings–hand-painted murals on the walls and ceilings, silk-covered chairs, tapestry rugs–are dominated by one color. Pink. From the rosy hue on the cherubs' cheeks to the pastel strands of glass beads in the chandelier, the feeling is that of elegance, for business or pure pleasure. For all this, there is an expensive price tag. But the excellence of the cuisine is worth it.

From the appetizers, we selected the mussels, served with spinach in a white sauce, and the Royal Squab salad, which was excellent with a thinly sliced pigeon breast topped by truffles. The duck consommé was lightly spiced with ginger contained in a lion's-head tureen under a puffed crust.

The entrees listed on the menu are not numerous: one veal, one steak, several seafood and many game. The sea bass came to the table wrapped in lettuce leaves in a wine and lemon butter sauce. We ordered the quails (sometimes you get two, sometimes three); they were delicious glazed with honey and vinegar.

Desserts at the French room are outstanding to look at as well as to taste. The hot open apple tart and the hot puff pastry with fresh fruit and caramel sauce are prepared in the classic French manner and they are surprisingly light. The Grand Marnier soufflé, however, was the richest we've encountered. How appropriate for this room!

★ **HOFFBRAU**
$$ 3205 Knox Street, 559-2680
Open seven days, dinner only Saturday & Sunday
Most major credit cards

This down-to-earth restaurant serves some of Dallas's best steaks, and at lunch, booths and small tables fill up with bankers and lawyers doing business over cold longnecks: The narrow restaurant looks more like a saloon with its giant moosehead presiding over the long bar and a dark wooden staircase leading to a quiet balcony upstairs.

The service here is not in keeping with the excellence of the food. The steak-only menu is written on a chalkboard and displayed over the bar which makes it difficult to see. We ordered the 24-ounce T-bone and the rib-eye steaks; both are served with a salad of iceberg lettuce and gigantic french fries. In keeping with the basic no-frills style there are no desserts served here.

★★★★ **JEAN CLAUDE**
$$$ **2404 Cedar Springs; 653-1823**
Closed Sunday and Monday
All major credit cards

Devotees to this established eatery end up watching the chef. The dining room is small enough for sixty to dine near the center of activity–Jean Claude's exposed kitchen. Two seatings, one at six and one at nine, are sought-after affairs. Saturdays must be requested at least four weeks in advance. Is it all worth it? You bet.

The decor is subdued. Dark blue and orange paisley-print wall fabric, dark wood panels, brass chandeliers. The menu is fixed price, recited by the waiter each night at the table. Entrees vary and the waiters are quite articulate in discussing the ingredients, preparation, etc., of any unfamiliar dishes. During dinner, Jean Claude, an amiable young man, will stroll by and say hello. The overall effect is very elegant.

The best thing about dining at Jean Claude's is the food. This is a fact that continues to be substantiated by the slew of enticing meals prepared. In the tiny bar, diners converse on their past pleasures here while waiting to be admitted to their seating.

For appetizers, the escargots are among the sweetest we've tasted tossed in butter and garlic. A pâté foie gras was fresh served with crusty French bread. On our last visit, we were glad to find the lobster served steamed, split and covered with shrimp bisque. A dish of asparagus tips in béarnaise sauce was a perfect accouterment. The sweetbreads are always good, a reliable choice on any day. Our only complaint, and it is minor, concerns the salads which tend to be, for lack of another word, skimpy. And the house dressing never tastes of anything more than vinegar. However, the Caesar's salad is an exception. It is excellent.

Soufflés are one of Jean Claude's specialties and you can

tell by the amount of them that pass from the kitchen along with snifters of brandy and steamy coffee. Part of the fun is letting the waiter heap spoonfuls of sauce (Grand Marnier or vanilla) on to a piping hot soufflé. Homemade ice cream is another specialty that deserves sampling. For the price, Jean Claude's is worth a visit—at least once.

★★ JENNIVINE
$$$ 3605 McKinney Avenue, 528-6010
Closed Sunday
All major credit cards

Jennivine (pronounced Jenny Vine) is in a small, 100-year-old Cape Cod style cottage complete with window boxes. The inside resembles Edbury Street Wine Bar in London, after which it was modeled—a romantic setting of wood slat floors, green walls filled with Haitian primitive paintings and a few private coveys.

Dinners are very good, but perhaps not great value for the price. The menu changes daily on the blackboard. On one visit, a sole was served rolled around Alaskan salmon and covered by a light shrimp sauce, and a Duckling Queen Elizabeth consisted of thick slices of duck breast, served very attractively with an excellent peppercorn sauce. Side dishes were plopped down with such indifference we barely noticed them; the coldness did nothing to enhance their dull flavor.

Lunch and after-theater supper, when the menu is made up largely of wine, cheese and pâtés, may turn out to be a much better bet. Although the wine may cost as much as $5.50 a glass, the pâtés are done exceptionally well. Pâtés of note are the pâté maison made from chicken livers, cognac and herbs, and pâté Saxon, a creamy mixture of lamb, raisins and spices. Jennivine is convenient to the Dallas Theater Center and many business people drop in for lunch or dinner as well as late night pâté-ing.

★★★ JOZEF'S
$$$ 2719 McKinney Avenue, 826-5560
Lunch Mon.-Fri., dinner seven days
All major credit cards

The service at Jozef's is top quality and the seafood is outstanding. If there is any shortcoming to this posh Dallas eating establishment, it is that it's so popular that even with reservations you may have to wait to be seated. The small bar area is inadequate for diners waiting to be seated, particularly on weekend nights, but the bartender is pleasant.

The luncheon and dinner menus are practically identical with prices raised for evenings but service and quality still excellent. Though tables are too close together the carpeting keeps the noise level down.

Good fresh seafood is not easy to find in Dallas but you will find it here. Start with the delicious smoked trout with horseradish sauce, or fresh clams or oysters on the half shell. The gumbo is thick with seafood morsels. The sole with capers, the cold seafood platter, or the flounder stuffed with crabmeat are all outstanding. Salads are crisp and tasty and a side order of stuffed mushrooms is a good choice. The Praline Parfait here is *outstanding,* worth breaking a diet; other desserts are not unusual.

★★ L'AMBIANCE
$$$ 2408 Cedar Springs, 748-1291
Closed Sunday; dinner only on Saturday
All major credit cards

At the time of publication, L'Ambiance had just opened its doors for business. If the quality of food and service continues on the same level, we think this will become one of Dallas's most popular French restaurants. For now we are giving it two stars as a provisional rating.

The country-French decor includes French windows, blue patterned china and a wall covered with wine bottles. Tables are not close together, the room is large and elegant. Waiters are intelligent, pleasant and eager to point out the preparation, ingredients, etc., of some of the unusual items on the menu.

Our lunch entrees of salmon and a seafood casserole were too large for us to finish. At dinner, oddly enough, we found the portions smaller.

The Boston salad with roquefort dressing is wonderful—a generous bowl of crisp greens tossed with spicy vinegar and chunks of cheese. The loin of lamb with cucumbers sounded interesting but was a disappointment with a dry, ordinary tasting meat. The bay scallops, however, were sweet and delicious in a puree of mushrooms, wine and garlic.

Each entree is accompanied by small portions of scalloped potatoes, carrot soufflé and a third vegetable such as snow peas or creamed turnips.

Desserts are very rich and we suggest ordering raspberries or the fresh fruit with a small dollop of fresh whipped cream.

★★★ **LE RELAIS**

$$$ **650 North Pearl Street (Plaza of the Americas Hotel), 747-7222**
Open seven days
All major credit cards

The hotel calls this a coffee shop, but don't look for a counter or expect paper placemats. The Delft blue-and-white decor and comfortable banquette seating will make you want to linger over lunch or dinner. That might be fine since the service here is often very slow. The atmosphere however is most conducive to business entertaining and you will find many of Dallas's wheelers and dealers spending midday here.

The luncheon and dinner menus are similar in price and selection and each includes sandwiches, omelets, crepes, salads and full course meals of meat or fish. Service is continuous here so it is a good choice if you need to have lunch late or dinner early.

Appetizers include escargots, avocado with crabmeat and salmon with horseradish any of which is substantial enough for a lunch entree. The crepes with ham and mushrooms covered with a cream and cheese sauce are delicious. Omelets are full of fresh vegetables and meat in very different combinations. Our favorite is the Valencia omelet with spinach, peppers, tomatoes, onions and potatoes.

For a full dinner or heavier lunch you may choose from

fish offerings–prawns, scallops, red snapper or lobster or a full selection of meat entrees–veal, prime rib, steaks or loin of pork.

To assuage your sweet tooth try the attractive offerings from the pastry cart or one of six wonderful ice cream sundaes. Our favorite is the Jubilee which features black cherry vanilla ice cream, almonds and macaroons.

★★ **LE RENDEZ-VOUS**
$$ **3237 McKinney Avenue, 745-1985**
Open seven days
All major credit cards

This French restaurant has an atmosphere that is light and airy opened to the world by floor-to-ceiling windows. Natural wood, ficus trees and a stone fireplace add a measure of charm. Service is most courteous and efficient.

Each meal begins with a loaf of crusty bread and sweet homemade butter. We liked the seafood appetizer of cold salmon, shrimp and crabmeat in a vinaigrette dressing. The menu includes a wide selection of beef, veal and chicken dishes as well as fish. Veal medallions were sautéed in lemon butter and simmered in brandy. The broiled salmon was fresh and served with a béarnaise sauce. Both are simple and delicious. The creamed string beans, on the other hand, are bland. The house dressing for salads is wonderful and surpasses several others offered.

Fresh fruit for dessert includes blackberries, tangerines, kiwi and strawberries, perfect after a long meal. The Chocolate Rendez-Vous is a rich mousse in a heavy vanilla sauce. Either way, order the excellent coffee and linger awhile. This is the place to do it.

OK **THE LITTLE MUSHROOM**
$ **400 Decorative Center (Oak Lawn and HiLine), 747-4447**
Lunch only, closed Saturday and Sunday
No credit cards

This spot is popular with fabric buyers and senior citizens. The menu is limited to three entrees a day. We sampled the chicken breast in a wine and mushroom sauce. The mushrooms tasted like they had done some time in the can. The only other hot entree, salmon in a shrimp sauce, was disappointingly tasteless.

The charming French country decor includes terra-cotta tiled floors, ladderbacked chairs and a view of the patio garden. Three waiters service the small dining room and owner Marilyn Ronwebber often helps with the serving.

We think the corn muffins with tiny bits of jalpeno pepper are terrific but forgo the unremarkable chocolate mousse and peach cobbler desserts.

★★★ OLD WARSAW (LA VIELLE VARSOVIE)
$$$$ 2610 Maple Avenue, 528-0032
Open seven days for dinner only
All major credit cards

A Dallas landmark, Old Warsaw offers an elegant dining experience across the board. Executive chef John La Font is the main reason and the menus bear the official seal from when he served at President Reagan's inauguration.

Most of the guests seem to be absorbed in conversations about Dallas society and money. The waiters don't draw much attention; they give excellent unobtrusive service. Darkly upholstered walls and black leather chairs give the room a subdued feeling. Table settings are impeccable with silver, crystal and fresh flowers. In the lounge, photographs attest to the stream of celebrities who have dined here in the past.

The menu is French and includes over thirty entrees. For appetizers, we tried the terrine de canard, an exceptionally fine duck pâté. The mousse of frog legs prepared nouvelle cuisine was a rare delicacy we savored for days. The Old Warsaw salad, topped with nuts and a tangy dressing, was excellent. The poached salmon came with slivered cucumbers and mushrooms and was accompanied by a julienne of carrots and zucchini in a champagne sauce. Tournedos Rossini, (fillet of beef enlivened with goose liver and Madeira sauce) were wonderful.

The vegetables are top priority with the chef at Old Warsaw. Of them, the mushrooms sautéed with shallots and bordelaise sauce and the green beans are the best.

The extensive wine list is also an expensive wine list but everyone seems to have at least one bottle. The setting is conducive to lingering over business or the business of romance. Coffee is available flambéed with brandy and there is good espresso. We had the praline puff pastry filled with a light nutty cream from the cart for dessert. A wise decision.

★★★ PATRY'S
$$$ 2504 McKinney Avenue, 748-3754
Closed Mondays
All major credit cards

We think this family-owned French restaurant is one of the best in Dallas and so do many others. Reservations are strongly recommended for lunch and dinner.

Exposed brick walls painted in the colors of the earth dominate the decor and although the tables are a bit close, you can request a quiet one and have a good business conversation. Tables are elegantly appointed including a tiny silver service for garnishing the baked potato served with each entree. Tables are too close to each other, however, for private conversation in most cases. If you wish to be alone, request ahead of time and owner George Patry will reserve one of the quieter tables.

The food at Patry's is consistently excellent. For an appetizer, try poireaux farci, leeks stuffed with pork and veal and covered with a rich wine and cream sauce. The "regulars" we know are always touting the duck à l'orange. We tried it and were pleased with the crisp, tender bird and piquant citrus sauce. A side dish of broccoli was served with a lighter but no less delightful version of the hollandaise we were used to. The scallops meunière were delicious: tiny bay scallops cooked in butter with shallots and wine.

The desserts at Patry's, as good as you'll find at any French restaurant, tend to be loaded with sugar and range from pastry to chocolate mousse. The crème caramel and the L'ice Cake, a frozen confection laced with liqueur, are our suggestions.

The service is polished and refined. Many waiters have been here for years and know customers by name.

★★ PYRAMID ROOM
$$$ Ross and Akard Streets (Fairmont Hotel), 748-7258 or 748-5454
Closed Sundays except for brunch
All major credit cards

There was a time when Dallas oil magnates would gather at a table in the Pyramid Room and secretly determine the destiny of the city's economy. No more do those chieftains exchange wampum at such a rampant rate for such delicacies as fillet of sole en croûte and candy-coated strawberries. While the food is as worthy of praise as ever, the decor has gone decidedly down from year to year.

For a memorable meal it is still reliable–with tall chairs, the imposing inverted pyramid of gold overhead and a crew of attentive waiters. Fillet of sole comes wrapped in a flaky pastry shell and covered with lemon butter sauce and a lobster bisque dressing. Truly in a class by itself. But there are only a few entrees, in addition, worth mentioning. Filet mignon is good; béarnaise sauce accompanies it. A wine steward will climb the wall near the piano player to fetch your finest wine.

The pastry cart offers many French desserts baked in the hotel. Of the sweets, we liked the homemade ice cream the best.

★ RAPHAEL'S
$ 3701 McKinney Avenue, 521-9640
Closed Sundays
All major credit cards

This is the original and there is a second location at 6782 Greenville Avenue. The setting in this Mexican restaurant is casual and lively. Pine walls are covered with paper flowers, serapes and old photographs. Waiters bustle back and forth while soft folk music from across the border plays overhead.

The margaritas at Raphael's are delicious served in frosted beer mugs. There are many different appetizers to start with including queso flambedo chorizo, jack cheese melted at the table and rolled in a flour tortilla filled with spicy sausage. Nachos are excellent served on homemade tortilla chips.

Chicken enchiladas are the specialty of the house. They are excellent–mildly spiced and stuffed with marinated chicken. Other unusual entrees include shrimp enchiladas, topped with ranchero sauce and robalo veracruzano, fillet of flounder baked in a chili sauce. The menu includes all the traditional Mexican dishes and a few steak and seafood items as well. Service is friendly and fast but tables are very close together and most of the time the large restaurant is noisy.

★★ RATCLIFFE'S
$$$ 1901 McKinney Avenue, 748-7480
Open seven days, no reservations

For a little bit of San Francisco Ratcliffe's is the right place. On the main floor you can watch the chef at work in a kitchen that looks like a fish market while you wait to be seated.

The two dining rooms, upper and lower, are decorated tastefully with antique furniture, Oriental rugs and fresh lilies. Request a table upstairs for more quiet conversation.

We sampled the oysters Rockefeller which were delicious, plump and juicy, but the clam chowder tasted bland. We went a bit overboard on the tangy sourdough bread and almost sent the waiter back for thirds. Because the entrees are so generous, it is not a good idea to order a side dish. The mushrooms au gratin came laden with too much cheese.

We liked the seafood sauté, a tasty combination of scallops, shrimp and crab cooked in sweet butter, wine and garlic. But the daily special of broiled halibut was dry and unremarkable.

The Chinese gooseberry flan–a pastry shell topped with gooseberry custard and kiwi fruit–is superb.

★★ S & D OYSTER CO.
$$ 2701 McKinney Avenue, 823-6350
Closed Sundays; no reservations
MC, V

Devotées of this Dallas institution start lining up early for lunch and dinner since reservations are not accepted. Soft New Orleans jazz and ceiling fans hover over red-checkered tablecloths and canebacked chairs. The emphasis here is on seafood and the noise level is not conducive to quiet conversation.

The oysters are among the best in town, plump and delicious at a bargain price. The seafood gumbo is flavorful and hardly a spoonful goes by without a shrimp or oyster. Fried shrimp and oysters are always good. Most fish is offered in fillets but the whole flounder we sampled required the attentive waiter to debone it at our table. Stick with the fillets unless you have all day. Each dish is served with coleslaw, french fries and hush puppies. The lemon meringue pie is baked daily on the premises and is a refreshing ending.

★★★ SERGIO'S

$$ 2800 Routh (The Quadrangle), 742-3872
Closed Sunday
Most major credit cards

Located in the restored area of Downtown known as the Quadrangle, five minutes from Downtown, this fine Italian restaurant offers wonderful northern Italian cuisine. The restaurant has recently been enlarged to avoid turning away so many patrons (you may still have to wait to be seated however), but Sergio still keeps a watchful eye over all the proceedings. It is often noisy and bustling–especially at lunch and on weekends–but it has a wonderful family feel and it is a favorite of Dallasites.

All of the pasta is homemade and it is delicious. The lasagna is excellent and full of meat. Veal marsala is also a good choice. In fact, there is nothing on the menu to avoid. Salads are crisp and large and served with a tasty house dressing. Try cheesecake for dessert if you still have any room left.

This area is not particularly safe after dark so as a visitor to Dallas you might be more comfortable trying Sergio's for lunch.

NR **SUTHERLAND'S**
$$$ **2911 Routh St. at Cedar Springs, 698-0034**
Open Mon.-Sat., brunch Sunday
Most major credit cards

Located across the street from the Quadrangle this restaurant should steal the show with its extraordinary decor. Unfortunately, the cuisine is no match for the attractive surroundings. The atrium bar is one of the most attractive drinking spots we've seen. Antiques add a touch of elegance to the brick walls and the overall feeling of charm in this converted warehouse.

The flower-adorned dining rooms have adequate seating but quite closely spaced. Service could only be termed mediocre. The mushroom soup is tasteless and the onion soup gratinée inedible. The seafood special was trout with lemon and wine sauce—we never found the lemon! The chef's special changes daily but the veal cooked with light and clear melon and lemon sauce was the only highlight of the evening. The pastry cart consisted of five tired-looking selections, and Sutherland's coffee blends, which are expensive, were served lukewarm—inexcusable.

Without some improvements this will be another *former* Dallas spot.

NORTH CENTRAL

★★ **ANNIE'S SANTA FE**
$ **Greenville Avenue at Park Lane, 369-8600**
Open seven days
All major credit cards

For a casual restaurant with truly Mexican decor—from stucco walls to tile fireplaces—this may be the spot to try for lunch or dinner.

The menu for lunch and dinner is essentially the same with a slight increase in price at night. The numerous selections include burritos, chalupas and all kinds of familiar and unfamiliar Mexican offerings. If you are a novice at Mexican cuisine your waitress will be glad to make suggestions.

Tables are close together and Mexican music is played softly so this may not be the best place to close a major deal but the friendly atmosphere is typically Texan and the food authentic Mexican. You can order Sangria by the pitcher or glass and Mexican beer and California wine are also offered.

★★★ **ARTHUR'S**
$$$$ **8350 North Central (in Campbell Centre at Caruth Haven), 361-8833**
Open seven days
All major credit cards

You could almost overlook Arthur's as you drive out North Central Expressway. It is located next to the Doubletree Inn within an office complex. However, if you like good beef and excellent service and elegant dining—don't miss this one!

Do not be alarmed as you enter the main door to see hordes of people overflowing the busy bar area on the right of the entrance. This is the spot for "Happy Hour" (2 for 1 drinks). After working hours the place really jumps with music and chatter.

Almost the exact opposite is true of the dining room to the left which is very subdued and elegant. Reservations are recommended and are honored promptly. The decor is attractive with tartan carpet and tables set a comfortable distance apart. Quiet and efficient service is evident from the moment you enter and register with the hostess.

The thing to have at Arthur's is steak, and it is outstanding. It comes in all varieties and sizes, and is always tasty, tender and perfectly cooked to order. Though beef is Arthur's best bet we have found all the entrees delicious. Notably the chicken Arthur—a boneless breast of chicken with creamy white wine sauce, shallots and mushrooms—is wonderful. Shellfish is also good here. Desserts include Baked Alaska, chocolate mousse, Bavarian cream, strawberries flambé and Bananas Foster.

Throughout the meal the attentive maitre d' keeps his eye on the busboys to assure that each guest receives the finest service.

This spot, convenient to many office buildings and several hotels, is really worth a trip for lunch or dinner. Even the noisy, bustling bar is a fun place to check out the "Dallas scene."

★★ ASUKA
$$$ 7136 Greenville Avenue, 363-3537
Closed Monday
All major credit cards

Nestled among the few remaining trees along Greenville Avenue, Asuka is a tranquil haven in an area constantly under construction. The decor consists of antiques such as the yoroi, an ancient Japanese suit of armor, displayed in the entrance. The dining room is lit by six large white paper lanterns and the origami birds over the tempura bar reflect the delicacy of the decor.

Japanese businessmen visiting Dallas find this place very comfortable. For the uninitiated, a 12-page photograph album provides pictures of dishes such as sashimi (raw fish).

We tried the tonkatsu for lunch, a pork cutlet lightly battered and fried in a blend of oils. It was excellent. The tempura (shrimp and vegetable) was served crisp and piping hot. For those who love sushi, we found the dinner here to be above average. The various hibachi-cooked entrees include lobster, scallops, steak or chicken grilled lightly and full of flavor.

Save a little room for the delightful deep-fried ice cream balls.

★ BENNIGAN'S TAVERN
$ 8139 Park Lane, 696-2080
Open seven days
All major credit cards

While having a quiet conversation is not unheard of at Bennigan's, the emphasis is on drinking the latest promotional libations (the summer list is a 12-page drink menu) and people-watching. For a more relaxed meal and to take the din out of dinner ask for a seat along the windows–it is usually quieter.

The menu offers a good variety of dishes from salads to steaks. None of the dishes are outstanding but hamburgers are good and the portions are more than adequate. Try the fried cheese strips with marinara sauce for an interesting side dish. They also serve nachos and lighter fare. Try an ice cream sundae if you have enough room for dessert.

★ **BIFF'S**
$ **7402 Greenville Ave., 696-1952**
Open seven days; no reservations
Most major credit cards

Don't try to squeeze yourself into this swinging place on a Thursday, Friday or Saturday night! Better to try lunch or an early-week dinner when the lines are not quite so long and the tumult not quite so intimidating. Do not be alarmed by the masses at the bar toward the front. The decor is attractive and there is a two-tiered dining area. Tables are spaced for some privacy but ask to be seated in the rear if you want more quiet.

This is a nice spot for lighter dining; a variety of salads, hamburgers and omelets, as well as good soups. Try the zucchini strips—they're delicious. Desserts range from pecan pie to cheesecake and are not outstanding. The emphasis here is casual and that includes the service, but prices are reasonable.

★ **BIRRA PORETTI'S**
$ **9100 North Central (in Caruth Plaza at Park La.), 692-0565**
Open seven days until 2 A.M.
All major credit cards

This Dallas edition of a Houston restaurant offers a full array of Italian entrees at reasonable prices. Arrangements can be made for larger parties and the young staff is extremely accommodating. Tables and booths are well-spaced but the piped-in music is often too loud to allow conversation.

There is a large variety of pasta offerings as well as Italian appetizers, absolutely outstanding salads, Italian sandwiches and pizzas of any style. The house salad dressing is deliciously spicy. For dessert try a Birra Poretti Freeze! The wine list is adequate and a number of liqueur-based coffees are tasty.

All orders are available for take-out if you want to dine in your room and food is served until midnight. No need to dress up, just come and enjoy the forties atmosphere, complete with gas station signs and posters on the walls and Coca-Cola memorabilia.

★★ BOURBON ST. OYSTER CO.
$$ Caruth Plaza (Park Lane at N. Central), 363-2333
Open seven days, brunch Sunday
All major credit cards

This little bit of New England tucked into the attractive Caruth Plaza Shopping Center is good for lunch or dinner. With its tile floor and checkered tablecloths it offers a noisy but friendly atmosphere in which to enjoy a good variety of high-quality seafood–and seafood is all this restaurant offers. From oysters (baked, broiled, Rockefeller, etc.) to catfish (breaded and filleted) to shrimp (creole, boiled, fried or sautéed)–you will not be disappointed. Portions are so huge you will scarcely be able to finish. Traditional coleslaw is very good.

There is an attractive bar and the daily specials are quaintly listed on blackboards along the walls. The service is pleasant, the dress casual. Reservations are recommended for dinner and brunch.

★★ THE CHIMNEY
$$$ 9739 North Central (at Walnut Hill), 369-6466
Closed Monday
All major credit cards

Located in the Willow Creek Center on the northwest corner of North Central Expy. and Walnut Hill this little spot is rapidly becoming a favorite for lunch and dinner. This is a good place for business entertaining because it is close to numerous office complexes and because service is quietly efficient. Luncheon offerings include chicken and seafood entrees as well as salads, and a complimentary cup of clear broth is a refreshing opener.

The dinner menu is heavy on veal offerings, but offers delicious tournedos of venison as well as some beef dishes. The dinner salad is topped with delicious Italian dressing with bacon. Desserts include peach melba, chocolate mousse and cheesecake. Tables are close but afford private conversation and service is friendly.

★ **CORK 'N CLEAVER**
$$$ **8080 North Central (at Caruth Haven), 361-8808**
Lunch weekdays, dinner seven days
All major credit cards

This is a chain restaurant but the food is good and the service by young waiters is fine. The menu is brought to you on a meat cleaver and includes beef and seafood items. There is a nice salad bar in the center of the dining room from which you can serve yourself. Stick with the standard steak fare and you won't be disappointed, the portions are very generous. The mud pie (chocolate cookie crust, coffee ice cream covered with chocolate sauce, almonds and whipped cream) is especially good for dessert. If you want to linger after dinner you can adjourn to the stucco-walled lounge near the fireplace for some cordials or cocktails among the animal-head trophies which make the place feel like an old mountain retreat.

★★★ **ENCLAVE RESTAURANT**
$$$ **8325 Walnut Hill Lane, 363-7487**
Closed Sunday, no lunch Saturday
All major credit cards

Tucked away behind a series of garden-type office buildings this fine continental restaurant is a favorite of business people and locals. From the minute you enter you know this will be a special evening; the host will hand you matchbooks imprinted with the name of the person who made the reservation!

The decor is very European with flocked wallpaper and high-backed chairs in deep reds. Tables are comfortably placed for privacy and quiet conversation and the entire atmosphere is one of subdued elegance. Service is outstanding–waiters are all attired in black tie and are very attentive.

The menu is varied and from soup to dessert the food is well prepared, beautifully served and delicious. Vichyssoise is creamy and well chilled, oysters on the half shell or scallops with shrimp sauce are great appetizers. Main courses run the gamut from steaks to veal dishes to fish to fowl–at least five or six selections in each catagory. The Enclave's beef is always tender and served exactly as ordered. Veal Oscar or shrimp with lobster sauce are also good choices. All entrees are served with the vegetable of the day and there are several delicious à la carte vegetables including white asparagus. The dessert list is varied with crème caramel, strawberries in season, and they are justifiably proud of their chocolate mousse.

Dinner music is played quietly and there is a small dance floor. This is a great restaurant for business entertaining. You can arrange to have extra table space if needed and also can request to be seated in the back room which is a bit more private and a little quieter.

NR **HOULIHAN'S OLD PLACE**
$$ **4 NorthPark East (N. Central at Park Lane), 361-9426**
Open seven days
All major credit cards

The location of this restaurant right off North Central Expressway at Park Lane, surrounded by office buildings, should make it an ideal place for lunch or dinner. But the combination of crowds, too many tables placed too close together and poor food puts this on our Not Recommended list.

In its favor, Houlihan's does look attractive. There is an airy feeling to the dining room, with its plants and full glass side, which resembles a greenhouse. After that it is all downhill. An omelet was so leathery it was tasteless, rolls were not fresh and service was so casual as to be insulting. The final flaw was the condition of the restrooms which were absolutely unhealthy.

★★ IL SORRENTO
$$$ 8616 Turtle Creek Boulevard, 352-8759
Open seven days, dinner only
All major credit cards

Tucked away just a block north of Northwest Highway and two blocks from NorthPark Mall, this is a wonderfully outlandish dining spot. The ostentatious fountain in front is only a hint of the elaborate decor within; the interior has the air of a Roman or Venetian villa complete with statuary.

The menu is a potpourri of Italian goodies and the service is good. Tables are tightly spaced but they are adequate for privacy and the strolling musicians are pleasant and unobtrusive. There is an assortment of cold and hot antipasti, scampi and melon and prosciutto. The minestrone is laden with vegetables and quite tasty.

Italian specialties include fettucine, cannelloni and lasagna (all with homemade pasta) and deliciously seasoned. The excellent veal scallopino alla Genovese (one of many veal offerings) is sautéed in butter and white wine with shallots, mushrooms and artichokes. You can also order a good steak, pork chops, any number of beef dishes and any of several chicken dishes. Rum cake is the best dessert, but there is also cheesecake or ice cream. Service here is good.

★★ INDIA HOUSE
$ 5422 East Mockingbird Lane, 823-1000
Open seven days
All major credit cards

By day, young professionals and college students (SMU is right down the street) fill the booths of this dark restaurant for the lunch buffet. By night, the prices are higher but tables are covered with linen and candles, waiters seem taller and less surreptitious and a more formal, subdued atmosphere pervades. Even the miniature Taj Mahal glimmering on the counter seems brighter.

We liked the Thali service, a seemingly endless flow of silver platters of food. The Shahi dinner served in this manner included spiced lamb in yogurt, curried lentils and delicious fried saffron rice cooked with fresh peas. The dinner continued with plenty of warm kulcha, onion bread fresh from the oven, shish kebab, tandoori chicken and the essential chutney–mint, onion or fruit. The rasmalai was a surprisingly lightweight dessert with homemade cheese, milk and almond syrup for ingredients.

This small restaurant has about five tables and ten booths. Quiet conversations are going on and the noise level is usually low. Service is very personal but at times distracting as the waiters stand by and watch you eat.

★ **JUAN AND ONLY'S CANTINA**
$ **8021 Walnut Hill Lane (at N. Central), 739-6488**
Open seven days
Most major credit cards

From the people who brought us the Steak and Ale and Bennigan's chains, this theme restaurant serves very good food in a lively atmosphere.

The service is friendly and relaxed. The decor is eclectic ranging from colorful stuffed parrots and track lights to old photographs of Santayana, Tiffany-style lamps and an attractive cactus garden–all under one high corrugated roof.

The luncheon menu is imaginative. A chicken salad consisted of large chunks of chicken diced with jack cheese and vegetables topped with fresh guacamole. The fruit salad included large slices of melon, pineapple, bananas and oranges, orange sherbet, and a wonderful dressing of sour cream, honey and strawberries.

The soft, piped-in Latin music and wide spaces between tables make a business conversation quite possible.

OK KON TIKI PORTS
$$ 9100 North Central (Caruth Plaza at Park La.), 987-2333
Open seven days
All major credit cards

The elegant island decor of this quiet Polynesian restaurant is more impressive than the cuisine. There are the predictable island drink offerings which are large and potent. The menu includes beef, chicken, pork and seafood from chow mein and chop suey to egg rolls and egg Foo Yung.

There are two separate dining rooms, but tables are close. The upper room is available for private parties or larger groups of diners.

★★★ LE LOUVRE
$$$$ 9840 North Central Expy., 691-1177
Open seven days, no lunch on Saturday and Sunday
Most major credit cards

This formal and elegant restaurant is a newcomer to Dallas haute cuisine and, in two years, has acquired many loyal patrons.

The decor is dominated by a large crystal chandelier and booths covered in red leather along one wall. Service is very uneven; on one visit our waiter neglected to refill our wine glasses and never even looked at our drained water glasses.

The menu is French and continental. For an appetizer try the wonderful snail tart, a puff pastry shell filled with snails, diced tomatoes, ham, mushrooms, some herbs and almonds. A cup of lobster bisque is rich and flavorful.

The Beef Wellington we had heard so much about was served rare, the way we requested. But the layer of goose liver pâté was soggy and so was the pastry. On another visit we tried the red Spanish shrimp. They were large, juicy and lightly seasoned with garlic and pernod.

Finally, our dining experience had a happy ending. Desserts are truly grand here. Le Soufflé au Arlequin, half chocolate, half Grand Marnier, topped with two different sauces, was superb.

★ **MADISON'S**
$$ **8141 Walnut Hill Lane, 361-0644**
Open seven days, dinner only
All major credit cards

This is one of the more deceptive restaurants we've found. The polished brass nameplate on the outside and the valet parking led us to expect a private club atmosphere inside. To the contrary, the bar is a noisy gathering spot for singles and the decor of the place is early Salvation Army.

However, if you skip past the bar and sit down to dinner you can have a pretty fine meal for a reasonable price. The main dining area consists mostly of booths arranged around a huge salad bar, complete with large wooden crates full of lovely fresh vegetables. This "Italian Market" provides the backdrop for an excellent salad bar. The plates for salad are chilled in small refrigerated boxes, a nice touch.

Entrees of steak, poultry and seafood are good though not outstanding. Sticking with a good fillet or the simpler dishes is probably a good idea. This is not a gourmet restaurant but it is good. The valet parking seems a bit ostentatious for the rather casual atmosphere inside.

★ **NINFA'S**
$$ **5960 Greenville Avenue (at Southwestern), 369-8973**
Open seven days
All major credit cards

Mama Ninfa is a formidable woman who has a hand in every aspect of her growing chain of Mexican restaurants, from selecting the menu of homemade entrees to making the television commercials that remind viewers to eat at Ninfa's.

A nice touch is the guacamole sauce and salsa accompanying the traditional tostadas at no charge. We think the tacos al carbon are the best in Dallas. Our waiter suggested the pechugas, pieces of charcoal-broiled chicken, and an order of queso. The two made a delicious duo inside a warm flour tortilla. For dessert we liked the banana empiñada, a mixture of ripe bananas, raisins and pecans baked in a pocket bread.

This is a large complex of rooms and a quiet table can easily be acquired. Service is attentive but at peak hours reservations will help you avoid waiting in line.

★★ POMPANO SEAFOOD
$$ 6950 Greenville Avenue, 750-6728
Open seven days, dinner only
All major credit cards

Surrounded by nautical paraphernalia and red and blue decor you will enjoy delicious New England seafood and other fine cuisine. Certainly the seafood is the highlight here. The Dover sole and red snapper with mushrooms are especially good. Oysters Rockefeller and Louisiana seafood gumbo are great appetizers. If you choose to ignore the seafood entrees you might try the Veal Oscar or Chicken Kiev, but the seafood is really the best choice and some of the freshest in Dallas. Vegetables here are more interesting than in many other restaurants in town. Among the dessert choices are Bananas Foster and Cappuccino Pie.

Tables are comfortably spaced for conversation and the service is outstanding. If you dine here more than once the headwaiter will usually call you by name and the staff is exceptionally pleasant even when serving large groups. Retire to the piano bar for an after-dinner drink.

★★★ ROYAL TOKYO
$$$ 7525 Greenville Avenue, 368-3304
Open seven days, no lunch Saturday
All major credit cards

Among aficionados, Royal Tokyo is Dallas's most complete Japanese restaurant including screened tatami rooms, hibachi tables and a sushi bar. A Japanese architect designed the exterior as well as the interior to be authentic. Many wood panels are constructed without nails to fit together harmoniously.

The menu includes traditional entrees such as shrimp tempura and beef sukiyaki as well as shabu shabu, strips of beef and vegetables cooked at the table by dipping them into boiling broth. A novice will not feel intimidated here with all the special dinners such as the Shogun, named for the movie cast who visited the restaurant last year. This dinner includes a little bit of everything from sake to sashimi to tempura and more. Just don't depend on the waitresses for much more than pleasant delivery. There is a real problem with language when it comes to interpreting the menu.

The sushi bar is the best in town that we know of. Among the fresh fish (raw, of course) are tuna, salmon, shrimp, octopus, yellowtail and eel. An unusual variation is the California roll, rice filled with lobster, avocado, cucumber and homemade mayonnaise wrapped in seaweed. Delicious.

The decor of this restaurant is very nice. Over the entrance to the tatami rooms, hand-carved panels depict scenes from Japan's history. The feeling in these room is peaceful even though just a few feet away a chef vigorously prepares a meal for ten at a table.

In the bar, a piano player draws a crowd on weekends and occasionally a Japanese singer will take the microphone in hand and do a rendition of "I Left My Heart in San Francisco." It's all good fun.

★★★ SAHIB
$$$$ Caruth Plaza (Park Lane at N. Central), 987-2301
Open seven days
All major credit cards

When you enter this Indian restaurant you will genuinely feel you have entered British-occupied India around the turn of the century. The interior is opulently decorated with rattan chairs, wonderful photos of English military officers, a "chamiana" or gauze-covered bar area which is very dramatic and a veranda area available for small groups. Tables are well-spaced for quiet conversation.

This restaurant is definitely a dining experience. The unique Tandoori specialties are cooked in a clay oven (the tandoor) which is visible through a large glass window in the rear of the main dining room. The breads and entrees are baked in these 600° ovens and the meats come out with a remarkable barbecue flavor.

There is an appetizing buffet offered at lunch and at dinner for a fixed fee which is reasonable. However, the rest of the menu is à la carte and unless you are on an unlimited expense account you will find it one of the most expensive restaurants in Dallas.

Lamb, chicken and seafood entrees are varied and plentiful and are carefully described on the menu. Most of the cuisine is prepared with mild seasonings but if you wish to try spicier dishes ask for assistance from the Captain. If you decide on an appetizer, salad, bread (à la carte also!) and vegetables to complete your entree, you will be running up quite a tab.

This is a northern Indian restaurant distinguished by the use of less curry and more chutney. Try this restaurant once on the expense account because the food is very good but you may not want a return engagement because of the very steep bill.

★★ **THREE VIKINGS**
$$$ **2831 Greenville Avenue, 827-6770**
Dinner only, closed Sunday
Most major credit cards

The owner of this restaurant greets guests at the front door with a charming Swedish accent and her husband often taxis out-of-town guests back to local hotels. Local diners enjoy the casual atmosphere with antique tables covered in blue cloths and simple folk art paintings lending a country air.

Head chef, Anders Edman, son of the owners, works hard to maintain a loyal following with his original creations. The Finnish shrimp chowder is superb (and too much to finish). The highlight here is the entrees. Roast duck is very tender and glazed in a delicious almond sauce. Any of the three veal entrees is simply prepared and delicious. Our favorite is veal medallions stuffed with fresh mushrooms and cheese. All dinners include salad and potato or vegetable. The asparagus was overcooked and tasted bland on our last visit. Desserts here are not outstanding.

Service is gracious and several tables are secluded just enough for quiet conversation.

LBJ-NORTH

★★ BENIHANA OF TOKYO
$$ LBJ at Coit Road, 387-4404
Lunch Sun.-Fri., dinner seven days
All major credit cards

This is part of the well-known chain by the same name and it offers the same dining experience which is as much acrobatic as it is culinary. The setting is on a man-made lake and each of the ten separate dining rooms has windows overlooking waterfalls, rock formations and Japanese gardens.

Conversation can be difficult if you are easily distracted by the Japanese chefs who prepare the seafood, beef and chicken with oriental vegetables right at your table. The food is tasty and the experience is fun but not the perfect setting for every kind of serious conversation–especially when you must share a table with others watching your chef perform.

OK CAPPUCCINO'S RESTAURANT AND CLUB
$$$ 12801 Midway Road (at LBJ), 241-1417
Closed Sunday, lunch weekdays only
All major credit cards

There are three separate dining rooms in this restaurant with ceiling fans and wood paneling and arrangements of dogwood blossoms. It has a clubby atmosphere but the red-coated waiters are not as attentive as one would like and the food is merely adequate.

Sautéed scallops arrived in a creamy sauce (which was good) but the cauliflower soup tasted like they dipped a head of cauliflower in watered-down milk and had precious little cauliflower. The best entree was the veal Cappuccino served with crabmeat and tomato sauce. The crème caramel was leathery and served with a stale strawberry on the top.

This restaurant seems to attract an older crowd than many other Dallas restaurants and loud conversations at too-close tables can be disturbing. All in all not the best in town but food is adequate.

★★★★ FARFALLO
$$$$ 12900 Preston Road (at LBJ), 387-0369
Lunch weekdays, dinner Mon.–Sat.
All major credit cards

Located at one of the busiest intersections in the LBJ-North area and hidden in the bottom floors of the North Dallas Bank Building, this is one of Dallas's finest restaurants. The service is outstanding and the continental cuisine very fine. The Victorian decor with round tables for six is elegant and allows diners to converse in privacy. There are also booths for two or four people.

The Brochette de Fruits de Mer included lobster, shrimp, scallops and mushrooms in a delicate sauce. The crepe with chicken, ham and mushroom is also light and tasty. All appetizers are generous and there are both hot and cold offerings.

We found the Brie soup with sherry and mushrooms delicious. The list of entrees is equally divided among fish, steaks, veal and lamb dishes and all are outstanding. Red snapper with sauce Bretonne was particularly tasty. Salads are crisp and sizable and everything is served beautifully. Desserts include Bananas Foster, Cherries Jubilee and Cappuccino Pie, each excellent and beautifully served.

There is a membership fee for liquor service since this is a dry area but one membership per table is all you need. Ask for a temporary membership if you won't be visiting here frequently; it is less expensive than the annual membership fee and is good for a shorter time. The owner is friendly and concerned that his patrons be treated well. Reservations are recommended and honored.

★★★★ **GABRIEL'S**
$$$ **The Summit Hotel, 243-3363**
Open seven days
All major credit cards

We have not reviewed all the restaurants in hotels in Dallas but Gabriel's is special and has quickly become one of the favorite dining spots in town. Because of this you should be sure to make a reservation, especially on weekends when even with a reservation you might have a wait–without a reservation you won't get in.

Located right off the lobby of the Summit behind the greenery this restaurant has two large dining areas, each pleasant with well-spaced tables. The main room is dominated by the most lavish sideboard packed with salad makings and all-you-can-eat hot and cold hors d'oeuvres. There is a gigantic bowl of fresh shrimp which could fill you up even before you order dinner. The specialty of the house is Long Island duckling that is cooked to perfection. Service is extremely efficient and waiters are adept at clearing away promptly but not rushing your meal.

If your waistline can handle it you should certainly save room for the ice cream sundae bar which is a potpourri of flavors with any topping you can imagine. Scrumptious!

★★ **MARIO & ALBERTO**
$ **Preston Road at LBJ, 980-7296**
Closed Sunday
AE, MC, V

As you enter this Mexican restaurant tucked away in the shopping center on the southwest corner of LBJ and Preston Road you will immediately feel a festive air. The decor is bright and colorful with huge baskets of paper flowers and a Mexican ambience which is unmistakable.

The lunch and dinner menus are identical and the food is very good. Burritos, chalupas, guacamole–all are deliciously different treats for people from other parts of the country and you can sample many varieties at a very reasonable price. Margaritas, as you might expect, are the drink of choice for most diners and iced tea is profuse for those who prefer it.

Tables are close but you are able to chat in relative privacy and the generally happy feel of the surroundings should make any conversation enjoyable. Mexican waiters are more than eager to assist you in choosing menu items.

★★ VINCENT'S SEAFOOD
$$ 13327 Midway Road (at LBJ), 387-3690;
2742 Bachman Blvd., 352-2691;
900 Six Flags Drive, 265-9171
Open seven days, Saturday dinner only
All major credit cards

Serving Dallas since 1898 Vincent's now has several locations where you can dine on top-quality seafood in attractive surroundings. Seating for two to 10 or more is well-arranged with planters dividing small sections of each room and cutting down on noise levels.

Begin with the Louisiana seafood gumbo or fresh New Orleans oysters on the half shell. Though you can order a sirloin or shish kebab the real treats here are seafood. Shrimp à la Vincent's in a light creamy cheese sauce with mushrooms is delicious. Stuffed flounder with crabmeat dressing is so rich you will hardly have room for Vincent's famous coleslaw. There are usually two daily specials created from the freshest catch—red snapper is always a good bet.

Service is friendly and the restaurant feels like it still has a family behind it—even as it grows in number of locations.

NOT IN OUR ZONES BUT WORTH IT

★★★★ THE MANSION ON TURTLE CREEK
$$$$ 2821 Turtle Creek Blvd., 526-2121
Open seven days
All major credit cards

Managed by the "21" Management Company, famous for its New York establishment, this new addition to the Dallas restaurant scene is one of the most elegant dining experiences in town. The restaurant is located in a restored mansion with a spiral stairway in the entry foyer, a huge breakfront with "21" memorabilia and a gigantic urn of fresh-cut flowers. It is a hotel restaurant but has the definite feeling of a private club and the service and ambience are in keeping with the formal setting. The interior of the mansion has been totally restored to its original beauty with enameled and inlaid wood ceilings, carved granite fireplace mantles and oak paneling. The three public dining areas include the beautiful library which still has its secret panel; the main dining room with fireplace and beautiful inlaid ceiling; and a gorgeous plant-bedecked enclosed porch. There are also several private dining rooms available on the first and second floors. The bar is reminiscent of New York's original "21" with a dark wood floor and forest green velvet wall coverings and English hunting prints.

The food here is equal in quality to the surroundings and service which are outstanding. The lunch menu includes five soups (we loved the vichyssoise), salads and hot and cold entrees. Poached salmon with sauce verte, mixed grill with lamb chops, kidney, bacon and sausage or swordfish steak with capers are all delicious and served impeccably. There are also egg dishes and a variety of salads and lunch specials daily.

Dinner at the Mansion is a royal feast offering everything from Beluga caviar to tortilla soup for openers. Roast quail Farcis in potato nest or rack of lamb for two are specialties worth a try. The Red Snapper with herbs is very tasty. If your tastebuds want a cold entree try the shrimp & crabmeat Louis with avocado and papaya. Vegetables, all à la carte, are unusual too and include french fried zucchini and interesting casseroles.

Desserts include a nice coconut macaroon with chocolate sauce and crème caramel, which on one visit was dull and dry.

In summary, this is the high spot for elegant dining in Dallas. It is extremely expensive but worth the time and expense if you want a truly fine meal in beautiful surroundings. Coat and tie are de rigueur.

★★★★ MARIO'S
$$$ Turtle Creek Village (Oak Lawn & Blackburn), 521-1135
Dinner only, seven days
All major credit cards

This is probably the most formal of Italian restaurants in town. Located in the exclusive Turtle Creek Shopping Village and surrounded by designer shops the atmosphere both inside and outside is lovely. Tables are very well-spaced for privacy of conversation and the waiters are well trained and efficient.

Start with the antipasto, which has more than a dozen offerings from artichoke stuffed with shrimp and scallops to Manicotto—a crepe stuffed with ricotta cheese and covered with fresh tomato sauce. There is a wide choice of salads as well, most topped with a deliciously seasoned house dressing. The Minestrone alla Genovese is full of fresh vegetables and thin pasta strips. The main courses here are certainly not limited to pasta though the pasta is delicious. The linguine with fresh clams, garlic and herbs is terrific and so is the fettucine alla carbonara with ham, onion, white wine, heavy cream and parmesan cheese. If you are hungry for fish you can choose from several red snapper dishes, scallops, lemon sole and even lobster. The menu is literally pages long and includes numerous veal dishes and beef and lamb as well. Of course, when you select an Italian restaurant you are usually better off sticking to the more traditional Italian specialties but at Mario's you will probably not be disappointed with any selection.

Desserts are specialties at Mario's also. Try the chocolate mousse or apricots flambé with pistachio ice cream for two.

Mario's is located north of Downtown but it is not too long a trek from any of our selected zones and it is well worth the time.

QUICK SNACKS AND LUNCHES

You will not starve in Dallas; there are at least three or four fast food stands at every major intersection, from McDonald's to Taco Bell. But there are not many small, pleasant non-chain snack restaurants with interesting food. Most of the shopping malls have a section of side-by-side stands offering everything from New York deli sandwiches to baked potatoes with toppings of all sorts. If you are close to any of the malls, this may be your best bet for a quick snack.

In the Airport and Market Center zones you will probably do best to eat in the hotel coffee shop or one of the other more casual eating spots in your own or a neighboring hotel. There are very few places open in the Market Center zone at night and the area is not particularly safe anyway. Along LBJ and North Central Expressway there are restaurants and quick snack shops every 10 feet so we have chosen a few favorites. Downtown presents the most difficulty because the few quick-eating places are always crowded and not easy to locate. Most of the Downtown sandwich shops are only open weekdays during business hours. Many of these shops will not accept credit cards.

MARKET CENTER

SONNY BRYAN'S, 2202 Inwood, 357-7120. Mon.–Fri. 7A.M. –5 P.M., Sat. 7 A.M.–3 P.M., Sun. 11 A.M.–2 P.M. This spot is a Dallas institution and serves about the best barbecue in town with the largest helpings at the best prices. Don't let the outside shabbiness deceive you—the inside is equally bad! You will be joined in line by busy executives in three-piece suits and truckers who always know a good spot to eat. No credit cards.

DOWNTOWN

THE ATRIUM, 1404 Main, 651-8414. Mon.–Fri. 11 A.M.–2:30 P.M. Beer, cheese, soup, quiche and sandwiches served in a small and always crowded shop in the heart of Downtown. No credit cards.

BELL'S BETTER BURGERS, 913 Ross, 651-0225. Mon. Fri. 10:30 A.M.–3 P.M. Not only good burgers but some of the tastiest Chinese food around. Egg rolls, pork dishes as well as standard burger fare. No credit cards.

EIGHT-O BAR, 2800 Routh (The Quadrangle), 741-0817. Open seven days 11:30 A.M.–2 A.M. Burgers and sandwiches in an atmosphere so gaudy it is distracting but food is good and cheap. AE, MC, V.

EL TAXCO, 2126 St. Paul, 742-0747. Closed Tuesday. 11 A.M.–3 P.M. Lunch specials (six per day) and a great Tex-Mex menu. Nachos are terrific. No credit cards.

GREAT GATTI'S, Plaza of the Americas, 749-0107. Open seven days. Mon.–Fri. 6:30 A.M.–9 P.M., Sat. & Sun. 11 A.M.–7 P.M. Sandwiches, pizza, soup and salad and the busiest spot in the Plaza at lunch hour. Most major credit cards.

GREAT OUTDOORS, 1914 Main, 741-1609. Mon.–Fri. 7 A.M.–6 P.M. Soup, salad, sandwiches in endless varieties. Food is good and service is friendly even though it is cafeteria-style. No credit cards.

HIP POCKET SANDWICH SHOP, 115 W. Main, 285-8044. Mon.–Fri. 11 A.M.–8 P.M., Sat. 11 A.M.–3 P.M. For a quick sandwich or takeout service this conveniently located shop will serve your needs. No credit cards.

PICKLE BARREL, 1715 Commerce, 741-0241. Mon.–Fri. 7 A.M.–3:30 P.M. Counter service for sandwiches, soup and general luncheon fare. No credit cards.

ZODIAC RESTAURANT, Neiman-Marcus, 1618 Main, 749-7343. Mon.–Sat. 11 A.M.–4 P.M. Full and formal service with widely spaced tables and a complete luncheon menu. Perfect spot for a business lunch in the heart of Downtown. Reservations accepted. No credit cards.

NORTH CENTRAL

CHURCHILL'S POLO TAVERN, NorthPark Center, 368-2861. Mon.–Thurs. 11 A.M.–9:30 P.M., Fri. & Sat. 11 A.M.–10:30 P.M. Closed Sunday. An English pub atmosphere with a good hamburger and salad menu at lunch. Great spot to eat before or after shopping in the Mall or between meetings along North Central Expressway. Most major credit cards.

JUDGE BEAN'S, Park Lane & Greenville (1 block east of N. Central), 363-8322. Open seven days. Tues.–Sat. 11 A.M.–2 A.M., Sun. & Mon. 11 A.M.–11 P.M. Burgers and nachos in a rustic setting. Crowded but a fun taste of the Old West. All major credit cards.

LUBY'S ROMANO CAFETERIA, 10425 N. Central (at Meadow), 361-9024. Open seven days Mon.–Thurs. 11 A.M.–2:30 P.M. and 4 P.M.–8 P.M., Fri.–Sun. 11 A.M.–8 P.M. Full line of hot and cold foods in a cafeteria setting. Home-baked pastries and service to go. No credit cards.

MAGIC PAN, NorthPark Center, 692-7574. Open seven days 11 A.M.–midnight. Crepes of all kinds in an atrium setting right in the Mall. AE, MC, V.

WYATT'S CAFETERIA, NorthPark Center, 368-3371. Open seven days 11 A.M.–8:30 P.M. A great place to catch a quick, nourishing meal. Reminiscent of your old college cafeteria but the food is good and you cannot beat the prices. No credit cards.

LBJ-NORTH

DENNY'S, 6061 LBJ, 387-2779. Open seven days 24 hours. From a full breakfast menu at any hour to terrific fried clams for dinner or lunch, this is a clean and convenient spot for a quick meal. No credit cards.

FRESH APPROACH, LBJ & Preston (southwest corner), 934-8065. It may surprise you to find this grocery store in our list of quick snack shops but they have the best deli counters in town and their own bakery on the premises. It may lack a little in decor (the floor is bare concrete) but the food is great. No credit cards.

WYATT'S CAFETERIA, Valley View Mall (northwest corner of LBJ & Preston), 233-4874. The same wonderful prices and down-home cooking found in the other Wyatt's around town. You can act like a kid in a candy store picking out your favorites, such as cornbread with jalapeno pepper and chicken-fried steak. No credit cards.

WEEKEND BRUNCH

Brunch means different things to different people and can include everything from Eggs Benedict to roast beef. In Dallas Sunday brunch (there is only one on Saturday) is a big event and the best spots in the city are some of the larger hotels who pride themselves on a lavish culinary extravaganza.

Service is generally from 11 A.M.–2:30 P.M.; most brunches are fixed price and range from about $9 to $15 per person; and the buffet brunch is standard. Here are some of the better spots—we hope you will try one if you are in Dallas over a weekend. Other restaurants advertise brunch, but frequently this is just the usual breakfast menu and does not compare to the variety and quality of brunches in the following places. All listed hotels accept all major credit cards for brunch.

AIRPORT

AMFAC HOTEL, Branding Iron Restaurant, Penthouse Level, West Tower, 453-8400
Sunday 10:30 A.M.–2:30 P.M. Reservations a must. Full buffet with salads, Eggs Benedict, roast beef and wonderful desserts.

MARKET CENTER

LOEW'S ANATOLE, Atrium I, 748-1200
Sunday 11 A.M.–2:30 P.M. Reservations recommended. This is *the* brunch spot with reputedly the most lavish buffet in the entire Southwest. It boasts 50 entrees from Belgian waffles to

seafood specialties and everything in between. The ice and bread carvings used as decorations are a sight in themselves. Worth the trip from your own hotel to the Market Center area.

LOEW'S ANATOLE, La Esquina, 748-1200
Saturday 11 A.M.–2:30 P.M. The only Saturday brunch in town and also the best Mexican brunch. This is a terrific spot to try a full buffet of Mexican cuisine sampling everything from guacamole to papaya. A real bargain, too.

DOWNTOWN

FAIRMONT HOTEL, Venetian Room, 748-5454
Sunday, two seatings 11 A.M. and 1 P.M. Reservations a must. Lovely buffet brunch featuring salmon, salads, beef and ham and a full array of pastries.

HYATT REGENCY, Fausto's Restaurant, 651-1234
Sunday 10:30 A.M.–2:30 P.M. No reservations required. Full-range brunch buffet served in the atrium area, with seating in Fausto's and the open coffee shop surrounding the fountain.

PLAZA OF THE AMERICAS, LeRelais Coffee Shop, 747-7422
Sunday 11 A.M.–2:30 P.M. Sumptuous brunch buffet served in this most elegant of coffee shops overlooking the lovely Plaza atrium area. Reservations not required.

NORTH CENTRAL

DALLAS HILTON INN (at Mockingbird), 827-4100
Sunday 11 A.M.–2 P.M. Brunch buffet is set up in the flower-bedecked lobby and seating is in the quaint French Market restaurant right off the main lobby. No reservations required. Champagne is complimentary.

DOUBLETREE INN, 691-8700
Sunday 10 A.M.–2 P.M. Named the Food Festival, this is another lavish display of food and features the widest variety of

cuisines including Cajun, kosher, Texas and Mexican fare. Reservations are required and seating is in the Peter B Restaurant off the lobby.

LBJ-NORTH

CENTRE PLAZA-HOLIDAY INN, Cafe in the Court, 385-9000
Sunday 11:30 A.M.–2:30 P.M. Free champagne accompanies the buffet which features 12 hot entrees and numerous salads and individually prepared omelets. No reservations accepted.

MARRIOTT INN-PARK CENTRAL, Currency Club Restaurant, 233-4421
Sunday 10 A.M.–2 P.M. This brunch buffet features a full line of kosher offerings as well as traditional entrees. There is music from strolling musicians and the price is very reasonable. Reservations are not accepted.

SUMMIT HOTEL, served around the indoor pool, 243-3363
Sunday 11 A.M.–2 P.M. Full brunch buffet set up in beautiful atrium surroundings. Reservations not required except for large groups over 12 people.

BUSINESS SERVICES

YOU cannot carry your entire office and staff with you as you travel around the country conducting business. In Dallas you will find a full range of business services provided by local firms. We have researched some major categories of services which seem to be needed by traveling business people—translators, office machine rentals, meeting planning services.

General office hours in Dallas are somewhat staggered to try to relieve some of the congestion and spread out the rush hour traffic. Generally, however, offices are open from 8:30 A.M. to 5 P.M. When in doubt it is probably best to call ahead to check out the particular office you will be visiting.

We have listed those companies that have a full range of service in a particular line, will accept credit cards or arrange company billing, provide delivery and set-up service where necessary and are easily accessible by telephone for information and fee data. Those companies where your personal visit is required were also chosen for safety and convenience of location. (We checked them in person.) Once again there are no listings for business services in the Airport area because D/FW Airport is simply that, an airport. It has no nearby office complexes—yet! In the next two years a major expansion around the airport will alter this dramatically.

We have not received, nor have we given, any fees or guarantees to the companies we have listed. If you are dissatisfied with the service of any of our recommended companies, please let us know. We are continually updating and checking services but companies do change ownership, hours, and services provided. This is an ongoing problem for guidebooks but we have attempted to give you the very latest information from the companies themselves. We hope you will find this section valuable.

AUDIOVISUAL EQUIPMENT AND RENTAL

Most of the large hotels that have meeting facilities will provide you with basic audiovisual equipment or they will rent it for you. We have listed outside companies to serve you. In all cases they will pick up and deliver, set up and operate equipment if necessary. In most instances, equipment is available with short notice but all prefer advance reservations when possible.

AV-BAUER AUDIO VIDEO, INC., 2911 N. Haskell (at N. Central), 528-3800
24-hour service. C.O.D. only. No credit cards.

AVW AUDIO-VISUAL, INC., 2241 Irving, 634-9060
24-hour service. No security deposit. All major credit cards.

HOOVER BROTHERS, INC., 2930 Canton, 741-4527
24-hour service. No security deposit. All major credit cards.

SIBONEY COMMUNICATIONS, INC., 1133 Empire Central, 631-1318
No security deposit. No credit cards; direct billing can be arranged or will accept company check.

CATERERS

Most major hotels are able and eager to cater anything from a small reception to a large formal dinner. There are also some facilities available should you wish to entertain away from your hotel. We have listed a few companies that will provide everything from the place to have your party to a complete variety of foods. Most require deposits for larger groups and generally all bills must be paid on the day of the affair. Be sure to be specific about what you want—they can do almost anything from the locally favored barbecue to elegant hors d'oeuvres. Credit arrangements and advanced notice requirements are indicated.

CARR'S OF DALLAS, 7621 Village Trail, 387-1929
Carr's has a northeast Dallas location on a private lake for outdoor parties, as well as an apartment for smaller parties. They will set up tents for a large group and are able to cater to as few as two people! At least 24 hours notice needed for small groups and several weeks for larger ones. Deposit not generally required. No credit cards.

THE CATERING COMPANY, 2008 Bryan, 742-9975
Facilities available for 50 to 4,000 people. Three to four days' notice is required for small groups but larger groups should allow two weeks. Deposit required. All major credit cards.

DALLAS INTERNATIONAL CATERING, 3716 Bowser, 521-4374
This company will arrange for the facilities and provide any kind of food for parties of one to thousands. Ice sculptures are a specialty and sure to delight your guests. Advance notice is required–24 hours for small groups and longer for large groups. Deposit is not usually required for business groups but is required for personal entertaining. No credit cards.

ERNIE'S OF DALLAS, 4412 Lovers Lane, 368-6151
There is no group too large for this company to handle both facility and food (they have served 7,000 at Texas Stadium). One week to six months' notice is required depending on the size of the group and the availability of space. Deposit required for large groups. No credit cards.

FRED'S BARBECUE, 2917 Expressway Tower, 368 1489
Informal facilities available at several locations accommodating 50 to 300 people. With 3 to 5 days' notice they will provide corporate lunches–delivered but not served. Large parties require a 10% deposit. No credit cards.

VANCE GODBEY'S, 8601 Jackson Highway, Ft. Worth, 498-5005
This is a popular catering service for both Dallas and Fort Worth. There is a facility for 500 people located in Fort Worth but they will cater anywhere for groups of 50 to a mob in Texas Stadium. They require advance notice of 30 days to six months depending on the affair. No deposit required. No credit cards.

CONVENTION SERVICES

More than 1,600 conventions, meetings, trade shows and expositions are held in Dallas annually with more than two million attendees. If you are here for one of these meetings we have investigated some services which you might find useful when organizing, setting-up, or running your meeting or show.

CONVENTION FACILITIES

DALLAS CONVENTION CENTER, 650 S. Griffin, 658-7000
Contact the Convention Services Department for any activity you are planning within the current year. For longer term projects you will need to contact the Dallas Convention and Visitors Bureau which handles arrangements more than twelve months in advance.

DALLAS EXHIBITION BUILDING, 11210 Harry Hines, 484-4190
Located near the Market Center area. Several months' advance notice required.

CONVENTION SERVICES

Here are some local companies that will make all the arrangements for your meeting in Dallas from setting-up meetings, scheduling speakers, guiding tours and providing parties for your business associates. All work under company billing arrangements and all work regular Mon.–Fri. 9 A.M.–5 P.M. hours except during meetings.

DESTINATION DALLAS, 1341 W. Mockingbird, 528-7916

KALEIDOSCOPE, 3131 Turtle Creek Blvd., Suite 1118, 522-5930

UNITED EXPOSITION SERVICE CO., 3191 Commonwealth, 631-4848

DISPLAY SERVICES

Check out these companies if you need a display set up or dismantled. They all arrange company billing.

BILL REED DECORATIONS, INC., 333 First Ave., 823-3154

DALLAS DISPLAY CO., 2724 Taylor, 747-9642

FREEMAN DECORATING CO., 1300 Wycliff, 741-1463

NOVELTIES

If you need badges, pens and pencils with your company logo, flags, bumper stickers or any other novelty item or table gifts, here are some suppliers who will make what you need and most will deliver to the local site of your meeting. Most companies require between 2 and 3 weeks' advance notice but all have some items in stock. None accept credit cards but all will arrange company billing.

AAA ADVERTISING SPECIALTIES, 3616 Bryce, 263-6363
Pens, pencils, T-shirts, etc. Three weeks' advance notice required. Local delivery.

DALLAS SPECIALTIES, 11126 Shady Trail, 243-5922
Name badges, plaques, awards, engraving on brass. At least 7–10 days' advance notice required.

HUGH CAMPBELL CO., 2116 N. Haskell, 821-2321
"Ashtrays to Umbrellas" and everything in-between is what this company offers. Anything at all you wish to have imprinted with your company name. Large selection of flags in stock and also table favors. Two to four weeks' notice for imprinting.

WEAVER BADGE & NOVELTY, 2909 McKinney, 748-4059
Badges, ribbons, trophies, pens and pencils. Allow two weeks for imprint.

CONVENTION PERSONNEL

A large number of temporary-help agencies in Dallas can provide convention personnel–models, demonstrators, exhibitors, trade show personnel and hostesses. All have a 4-hour minimum rate and all will arrange company billing or accept company checks.

COURTESY PERSONNEL, 5740 E. Mockingbird, 827-8631
Models, hostesses, demonstrators. Only company with no minimum hourly requirement.

GREYHOUND TEMPORARIES, 6440 N. Central, 369-8281
Marketing people, hostesses, trade show personnel.

HARTMAN TEMPORARY PERSONNEL, 6116 N. Central, 691-7660
Convention personnel, demonstrators, models.

KELLY SERVICES
2424 One Main Place, 742-1721
LBJ & Hillcrest, 233-9093
Demonstrators, models, hostesses.

COPYING AND OFFSET PRINTING

Most of the hotels we have investigated in Dallas provide a copy machine for guest use during regular office hours and while it is not being used by the hotel itself. If you need a copy or several hundred copies, here are some places convenient to the hotels.

In general, you should use photocopying for fewer than 50 copies. For more extensive copying–over 50 copies of the same page–you should select offset printing. This sometimes takes longer but is much more economical. Photocopy machines charge anywhere from 6¢ to 20¢ per copy. Offset printing service can provide you with a full range of paper colors, weights and sizes; prices obviously vary greatly, but they are generally less per page.

We have noted delivery service where available as well

as credit information. Unless noted, all do offset and photocopy. None of our listings accept credit cards.

MARKET CENTER

CLARKE & COURTS, 2929 N. Stemmons, 638-4400
Mon.–Fri. 8 A.M.–5 P.M. Pickup and delivery. No credit cards.

ECONOMY PRINTING & LITHOGRAPHING,
11070 Stemmons, 247-1234
Mon.–Fri. 8 A.M.–6 P.M. Pickup and delivery. No credit cards.

QUIK PRINT
2600 Stemmons (between Inwood & Motor), 638-0750
3131 Stemmons (between Mockingbird & Inwood), 688-0341
Mon.–Fri. 8 A.M.–5:30 P.M., Sat. 9 A.M.–1 P.M. Free pickup and delivery. No credit cards.

RED-E PRINT, 8383 Stemmons, 637-2532
Mon.–Fri. 8 A.M.–5 P.M. No credit cards.

DOWNTOWN

ALLIED PRINTING, 501 N. Good-Latimer, 827-5151
Mon.–Fri. 8:30 A.M.–5 P.M. Free delivery and pickup. No credit cards.

CENTURY PRINTING CO., 701 N. St.Paul, 741-3191
Mon.–Fri. 8 A.M.–5 P.M. Free pickup and delivery on $6 minimum order. No credit cards.

PDQ PRESS, 902 Commerce, 748-0268
Mon.–Fri. 8 A.M.–4:30 P.M. Commercial printing only, no copying. Free pickup and delivery. No credit cards.

PIP (POSTAL INSTANT PRESS)
904 N. Hawkins (behind Plaza of Americas), 741-6209
2012 Commerce, 741-9091
1326 Elm, 745-1171
Mon.–Fri. 8 A.M.–5 P.M. Delivery and pickup service on $15 minimum order. No credit cards.

QUIK PRINT
1 Main Place, 741-1425
513 N. Ervay, 748-6711
Mon.–Fri. 8 A.M.–5:30 P.M., Sat. 9 A.M.–1 P.M. Free pickup and delivery. Telecopier services. No credit cards.

SIR SPEEDY, 1 Dallas Centre, 744-3266
Mon.–Fri. 8:30 A.M.–5:30 P.M. Delivery Downtown area. No credit cards.

NORTH CENTRAL

CLIFF'S PRINTING & INSTANT COPY SHOP,
5307 E. Mockingbird, 826-8911
Mon.–Fri. 8 A.M.–5 P.M., Sat. 10 A.M.–3 P.M. Free delivery on minimum $20 order. They are willing to work all night if necessary to complete large orders (over $100) in 24 hours. No credit cards.

MINUTEMAN PRESS, 11617 N. Central (at Forest),
363-2876
Mon.–Fri. 8:30 A.M.–5 P.M. Delivery service on $25 order or more. No credit cards.

QUIK PRINT, 11111 N. Central (above Royal Lane),
368-8933
Mon.–Fri. 8 A.M.–5:30 P.M., Sat. 9 A.M.–1 P.M. Free pickup and delivery. Telecopier service. No credit cards.

THRIFTY INSTANT PRINTING, 4516 N. Central,
821-5283
Mon.–Fri. 8:30 A.M.–5:30 P.M., Sat. 9 A.M.–1 P.M. Free city delivery. No credit cards.

LBJ-NORTH

CLIFF'S PRINTING & INSTANT COPY SHOP
LBJ & Dallas North Tollway, 398-8124
12810 Hillcrest (at LBJ), 980-4714
Mon.–Fri. 8 A.M.–5 P.M. Pickup and delivery on orders over $20. Orders over $100 completed in 24 hours. No credit cards.

LIGHTNING PRESS, 3001 LBJ (at Webbs Chapel), 620-1031
Mon.–Fri. 9 A.M.–4 P.M. Pickup and delivery service. No credit cards.

QUIK PRINT, 2877 LBJ (at Josey), 243-2831
Mon.–Fri. 8 A.M.–5:30 P.M., Sat. 9 A.M.–1 P.M. Free pickup and delivery. Telecopier service. No credit cards.

GRAPHIC ARTISTS & DESIGNERS

Whether you need posters or signs or logo work or some other design work to complete your meeting these folks will be able to help you. Be advised however that they require advance notice, do not accept credit cards (though some will bill your company) and not all of them pick up and deliver. Here's our selection of the best available in town.

THE ART BOARD, 2636 Walnut Hill, Suite 330 (North Central), 351-3245
Small jobs in 24 hours. All work done on premises so one to three days' notice is sufficient. Pickup and delivery on jobs over $50. Estimates by phone. Payment on completion. Will accept company check.

DESIGN GROUP - DALLAS, 11500 Stemmons (Market Center), 241-4085
Printed material only (photo, art, etc.). Company billing.

HILLSIDE GRAPHICS, 7540 LBJ (LBJ-North), 980-1004
Typesetting and pasting, design work. No printing. Cash only.

RAINBOW, Carillon Tower (Preston above LBJ, LBJ-North), 233-2932
Complete design studio. All work prepaid. Will work weekends on special assignments.

UNIGRAPHICS, INC., 2700 Oak Lawn (Downtown), 526-0930
All types of graphics. Delivery by arrangement. Company billing or cash only.

OFFICE AND DESK SPACE RENTAL

We were unable to locate any fully furnished offices which were available for rent by the week or by the day, but we did find some conference rooms that could double as offices. We also suggest that the business traveler who needs an office or interview room call any of the hotels we have listed and request a "parlor" or "sitting room." These rooms are available by the day and while they do not have the ambience of a true office, they are not bedrooms with desks but rather sitting areas with a desk and comfortable chairs. The locations are those of the companies.

GOLD KEY SERVICES, 4455 LBJ (between Midway & Welsh, LBJ-North), 233-9139
One conference room available which holds 10 people. It has a phone, and secretarial and copying services can be arranged. Company billing.

TLC EXECUTIVE SUITES, 8585 Stemmons (at Regal Row, Market Center), 638-7230
Conference room available by the hour or day with secretarial services available. No credit cards.

OFFICE SUPPLIES

Whether hunting for a legal pad or carbon paper or in dire need of major stationery items, there should be a full-line office supply shop near your hotel. These are our choices based on hours of operation, complete stock of supplies and credit card acceptance policy.

MARKET CENTER

BROOKHOLLOW OFFICE PRODUCTS, 8383 Stemmons, 630-8232
Mon.–Fri. 8:30 A.M.–5 P.M. Free delivery on minimum order of $10. MC, V.

DRAWING BOARD, 256 Regal Row, 637-0390
Mon.–Fri. 8:30 A.M.–5 P.M. No delivery. MC, V.

DOWNTOWN

CLARK & COURTS, INC., 120 Main Tower, 742-8074
Mon.–Fri. 8 A.M.–5 P.M. Free delivery downtown for $5 order or more. No credit cards.

COE PRINTING & STATIONERY, 600 N. St. Paul, 747-0811
Mon.–Fri. 9:30 A.M.–4 P.M. No delivery. No credit cards.

DRAWING BOARD
First National Bank Mall, 1401 Elm, 741-7471
Mon.–Fri. 8:30 A.M.–5 P.M. No delivery. AE, MC, V.
Plaza of the Americas, 742-9251
Mon.–Fri. 8:30 A.M.–6 P.M., Sat. 10 A.M.–3 P.M. MC, V.

OAK CLIFF OFFICE SUPPLY, 242 W. Jefferson, 943-7421
Mon.–Fri. 8 A.M.–5 P.M. Free city-wide delivery. MC, V.

NORTH CENTRAL

CROSSROADS OFFICE PRODUCTS, 5111 Greenville (at Lovers Lane), 361-8292
Mon.–Fri. 8 A.M.–5 P.M., Sat. 9 A.M.–4 P.M. Free delivery with no minimum. MC, V.

HILLCREST OFFICE PRODUCTS, 3026 Mockingbird (1 block west of N. Central), 363-4479
Mon.–Fri. 8:30 A.M.–6 P.M., Sat. 9 A.M.–5 P.M. No delivery. Most major credit cards.

LBJ-NORTH

ALPHA OFFICE SUPPLY, 11335 Harry Hines (just south of LBJ), 241-3436
Mon.–Fri. 9 A.M.–5 P.M. Delivery on orders of $15 or more. MC, V.

BRISTOL OFFICE SUPPLY SERVICE, 13327 Montfort (just north of LBJ), 387-3933
Mon.–Sat. 8:30 A.M.–5:30 P.M. Delivery charge. AE, MC, V.

CONTINENTAL OFFICE SUPPLY, 13830 Harry Hines (just north of LBJ & I-35), 247-9668
Mon.–Fri. 8 A.M.–5:30 P.M. Free delivery with no minimum. MC, V.

PAGING SERVICES

Local paging services will not rent to individuals on a daily basis but the fees for the usually required minimum monthly rental are reasonable and should you need a beeper while in Dallas you could contact one of the companies listed below. Page America Communications will arrange for a pager in advance if you call them at their toll-free number (800) 223-1260 and tell them which hotel you will be staying at in Dallas. They are currently providing contract service to a number of Dallas hotels (they can arrange for billing to your hotel also) but can furnish this service virtually anywhere in Dallas.

FORESTER RADIOTELEPHONE, 2700 Flora (Ross & N. Central), 263-0004
Mon.–Fri. 8:30 A.M.–5 P.M. One month fee in advance plus insurance fee. MC, V.

PAGE-A-FONE CORP., 12810 Hillcrest, 385-2390
Mon.–Fri. 9 A.M.–5 P.M. Deposit of $50 is refundable. Monthly fee and an additional connection fee. Cash only.

RAM BROADCASTING, 1330 N. Industrial, 747-1852
Mon.–Fri. 8:30 A.M.–5 P.M. Monthly fee; no deposit required. Free delivery. Company billing arranged.

REPORTING SERVICES

The following reporting services will provide someone to sit in on your meeting, take notes, and transcribe a record of the session for you. They all require some advance notice and most will arrange company billing. Most are open only during normal business hours, but can provide a recorder for whatever time you require.

CROSS WALDIE & ASSOC., 1309 Main, 521-8480
Mon.–Fri. 8:30 A.M.–4:30 P.M. Company billing.

DALLAS COURT REPORTING, 2920 Stemmons, 630-3571
Mon., Tues. & Thurs. 8 A.M.–10 P.M., Wed. & Fri. 8 A.M.–6 P.M. Cash only.

SHELBY J. MORGAN REPORTERS, 810 Main, 651-9919
Mon.–Fri. 8:30 A.M.–5 P.M. Phone answered 24 hours. Company billing.

WAKEFIELD & ASSOC., 810 Main, 651-7334
Mon.–Fri. 9 A.M.–5 P.M. Company billing arranged.

WARD STROUD & ASSOC., One Main Place, 748-6661
Mon.–Fri. 9 A.M.–5 P.M. No credit cards.

TEMPORARY HELP

When you are away from your own office you may find yourself in need of secretarial help or a demonstrator to display your product at a convention. The following temporary help agencies provide personnel for basic office work, convention and trade show personnel, laborers and trained accountants and data processing people. There is generally a four-hour minimum workday required. Company billing can be arranged but none accept credit cards. Most companies would prefer advance notice but they have all indicated the ability to fill your needs promptly if not immediately. None of these firms, for obvious reasons, will send temporary help to a hotel room to work so you will need to arrange for space and equipment to be available before calling for help. Most companies are open weekdays during business hours only, but they can provide help at almost any time that you need someone.

ACCOUNT ABILITIES PERSONNEL, 5529 LBJ, 980-4184
Accounting, bookkeeping, data and word processing, secretarial, general office personnel. One-day notice.

ACCOUNTEMPS, 2 NorthPark East, 363-3300
Accounting, bookkeeping and computer personnel.

ADIA TEMPORARY SERVICES
1802 Main, 742-4721
13601 Preston, 661-1356
Clerical, light industrial personnel. No advance notice.

CDI TEMPORARY SERVICES, 4255 LBJ, 233-0046
Marketing, office clerical and light industrial help.

COURTESY TEMPORARY SERVICE, INC.,
5740 E. Mockingbird, 827-8631
General office, laborers, convention models and hostesses. No minimum hours required.

DURHAM TEMPORARIES, INC., 806 Main, 747-3612
Office, clerical, laborers, key punch, bookkeeping personnel.

GREYHOUND TEMPORARY PERSONNEL,
6440 N. Central, 369-8281
Marketing, convention and trade show workers, secretaries, bookkeepers and general office personnel, light industrial.

KELLY SERVICES
2424 One Main Place, 742-1721
12820 Hillcrest (at LBJ), 233-9093
Convention personnel (demonstrators, models, hostesses), general office and secretarial personnel.

MHA TEMPORARY SERVICES, 7515 Greenville Bank
Tower, 691-3430
Accounting, programming, bookkeeping, clerical, secretarial and word processing personnel.

NORRELL SERVICES
5580 LBJ, 980-4205
2001 Bryan Tower, 742-8831
General office, secretarial, typists, data processing, survey workers, hostesses.

OLSTEN TEMPORARY SERVICES, 1525 Elm, 748-0531
General office, clerical, bookkeeping, data processing and light industrial. Convention models and demonstrators.

TEMPORARIES, INC.
First International Bldg., 742-1315
Hillcrest & LBJ, 233-2568
Secretarial, clerical and word processing personnel.

TEMPORARIES OF DALLAS
717 N. Harwood, 745-8850
1125 Campbell Centre, 691-8415
LBJ & Dallas Parkway, 661-8620
Convention personnel including models, hostesses and marketing people, general office bookkeeping, accounting, data and word processing personnel.

TOD SERVICES, 7540 LBJ, 661-5396
Bookkeeping, secretarial, typing and accounting personnel.

VOLT TEMPORARY SERVICES
8383 N. Stemmons, 638-5650
1509 Main, 741-5052
Clerical, bookkeeping and technical personnel.

TRANSCRIPTION SERVICES

If you need to have material typed the following firms can provide transcribing service from both tape and written material and most offer 24-hour service. Most operate on normal business-hour schedules but they can provide you with help at other times by arrangement.

ADAMS SECRETARIAL SERVICE, 8350 N. Central (at Campbell Centre), 691-3011
24-hour service on small orders. No delivery. Cash only.

ESP, 1341 W. Mockingbird (at Stemmons), 233-6797
24-hour service available. Dictation by phone. Secretarial services. Delivery service available. No credit cards.

EXECUTIVE EXCHANGE, 4924 Greenville, 368-5801
24-hour service. Cash only.

HERITAGE SECRETARIAL, 4825 LBJ (behind LBJ Hilton), 233-4513
One-day service on smaller items. Cash only.

HILLCREST GREEN SECRETARIAL SERVICES, 12700 Hillcrest (at LBJ), 385-1188
Notary public also available. No credit cards.

LIAISON ENTERPRISES INTERNATIONAL, 3131 Turtle Creek, Suite 606, 528-2731
Complete secretarial services, notary public, Telex services in English and foreign languages. Typewriters with foreign characters. All major credit cards.

MS SECRETARIAL SERVICE, 701 Commerce, 698-1123
24-hour service. Cash only.

TRANSLATORS & INTERPRETERS

With business becoming more and more international in scope, the business traveler often finds a need for the services of a translator or interpreter. The following companies are able to provide both translators and interpreters. Western languages are readily available but Oriental and other less familiar languages are a little harder to locate. Most firms operate during normal business hours but can provide a translator or interpreter whenever you need one. All will provide 24-hour service for short translations. Pickup and delivery is provided for large jobs but not for short translations. Advance notice is preferred especially for difficult languages. Company billing will be arranged for well-known firms. One outstanding service provided free in Dallas is the Language Bank sponsored by the Dallas Council on World Affairs at the World Trade Center, 744-3109. Volunteers who can speak over a hundred different languages are on file.

AMERICAN INSTITUTE OF LANGUAGES, 2829 W. Northwest Hwy., 351-3032
Translators and interpreters. Two weeks' advance notice required. MC, V.

BERLITZ, 15340 Dallas Parkway, 387-4454
Translators and interpreters.

ESCOBAR TRANSLATION SERVICE, World Trade Center, 698-9889
Translators and interpreters.

INTERNATIONAL TRANSLATING & TYPESETTING, Stemmons Tower West, 630-0840
Translators and interpreters.

LIAISON SERVICES INTERNATIONAL, 3131 Turtle Creek, Suite 606, 528-2731
Translators and interpreters. Notary public and secretarial services in most Western languages. One-day notice requested. All major credit cards.

TYPEWRITER & OFFICE MACHINE RENTAL

There is no service that we could locate in Dallas that would rent a typewriter on a one-day basis. Due to the cost of maintenance and repair as well as the risk of loss this may be understandable. The following firms will rent typewriters, adding machines and other light office machines for three days or more. Cash prepayment is required but not a security deposit. There are many others that will rent for a month and their fees are not too steep. However, we feel you can find what you need from the following companies.

ABC BUSINESS MACHINE, 3626 Maple, 741-5349
Mon.–Fri. 9 A.M.–6 P.M., Sat. 9 A.M.–1 P.M. Three day minimum rental. $12.50 delivery fee. Typewriters, adding machines and cash registers. No credit cards.

AIRPORT BUSINESS MACHINES, 317 W. Airport, 252-5515
Mon.–Sat. 8 A.M.–5 P.M. Typewriters and other business machines. Minimum one week rental. Pickup and delivery from Airport and Market Center hotels. No credit cards.

BANKING SERVICES

SOME hotels in our listings offer foreign currency exchange and cashier services but the following local banks will be able to help you during normal banking hours (Mon.–Fri. 9 A.M.–3 P.M., Fri. until 6 P.M.) with your other banking needs including cash advances on credit cards. There is, by law, no branch banking in Texas so we have listed a selection of the larger full service banks which are convenient to hotels. Only large Downtown banks and a few hotels offer foreign currency exchange—you will have trouble finding this service in our other zones. Check the hotel listing for availability of exchange services.

AIRPORT

DALLAS/FORT WORTH AIRPORT BANK, South Gate Exit (next to admin. bldg.), 574-3666
Mon.–Fri. 9 A.M.–3 P.M., Thurs. till 6 P.M. Cash advance on MasterCard and Visa.

MARKET CENTER

DALLAS BANK & TRUST COMPANY, 1825 N. Industrial (just west of Stemmons), 741-5881
Mon.–Thurs. 9 A.M.–3 P.M., Fri. 9 A.M.–6 P.M. Cash advance on American Express, MasterCard and Visa.

FIRST CITY BANK, 2525 Stemmons, 631-1721
Mon.–Thurs. 9 A.M.–3 P.M., Fri. 9 A.M.–6 P.M. Cash advance on MasterCard and Visa.

TEXAS AMERICAN BANK, Harry Hines & Mockingbird (just north of the Market Center complex), 353-8100
Mon.–Thurs. 9 A.M.–3 P.M., Fri. 9 A.M.–6 P.M. Cash advance on MasterCard and Visa.

DOWNTOWN

FIRST NATIONAL BANK, Pacific at Akard, 744-8000
Mon.–Thurs. 9 A.M.–3 P.M., Fri. till 4 P.M. Cash advance on MasterCard and Visa. Foreign currency exchanged.

MERCANTILE BANK, Main at Ervay, 698-6000
Mon.–Fri. 8:30 A.M.–3 P.M. Cash advance on MasterCard and Visa. Will cash foreign travelers checks and foreign currency.

NATIONAL BANK OF COMMERCE, 1525 Elm, 658-6111
Mon.–Fri. 8 A.M.–4:30 P.M. Cash advance on American Express, MasterCard and Visa. Will cash foreign travelers checks and foreign currency.

REPUBLIC NATIONAL BANK, Pacific at Ervay, 653-5000
Mon.–Thurs. 9 A.M.–3 P.M., Fri. till 4 P.M. Cash advance on MasterCard and Visa. Foreign currency exchange.

NORTH CENTRAL

LIBERTY NATIONAL BANK, 10501 N. Central (above Meadow), 369-6200
Mon.–Thurs. 9 A.M.–3 P.M., Fri. till 6 P.M., Sat. 9 A.M.–1 P.M. Cash advance on MasterCard and Visa.

REPUBLIC BANK, Greenville Avenue, Walnut Hill & Greenville (3 blocks east of N. Central), 369-8400
Mon.–Thurs. 8:30 A.M.–3 P.M., Fri. till 6 P.M. Cash advance on American Express, MasterCard and Visa.

TEXAS COMMERCE BANK, 8150 N. Central (at Caruth), 691-6001
Mon.–Thurs. 8:30 A.M.–5 P.M., Fri. till 6 P.M. Cash advance on MasterCard and Visa.

LBJ-NORTH

COMMONWEALTH BANK, 2964 LBJ (between Webbs Chapel & Josey), 247-3141
Mon.–Thurs. 9 A.M.–3 P.M., Fri. till 6 P.M. Cash advance on MasterCard and Visa.

LINCOLN CENTRE BANK, 5400 LBJ (between Montfort & Inwood), 385-7400
Mon.–Thurs. 9 A.M.–3 P.M., Fri. till 6 P.M. Cash advance on MasterCard and Visa.

TEXAS COMMERCE BANK, LBJ & Coit, 231-1406
Mon.–Fri. 7:30 A.M.–5:30 P.M. Cash advance on MasterCard and Visa.

TOWN NORTH NATIONAL BANK, LBJ at Midway, 980-6800
Mon.–Thurs. 9 A.M.–3 P.M., Fri. till 6 P.M. Cash advance on MasterCard and Visa.

FOREIGN CURRENCY EXCHANGE

You will have trouble getting foreign currency exchanged except at the D/FW Airport and the larger Downtown banks. There is a Deak-Perera office in the Amfac Hotel at D/FW, but it is not always staffed. A few hotels offer foreign currency exchange, but this is usually as a courtesy for their own guests only. As we said in our introduction to Dallas, we would advise foreign visitors to buy travelers checks in U.S. dollars before leaving home.

D/FW AIRPORT

AMERICAN AIRLINES TERMINAL, Sect. A, 574-4754
Open seven days, 9 A.M.–7 P.M.

BRANIFF TERMINAL, Gate 13-14, 574-2814
Open seven days, 9 A.M.–7 P.M.

DOWNTOWN

AMERICAN EXPRESS, 1201 Elm, 748-8606
Mon.–Fri. 9 A.M.–5 P.M.

FIRST CITY BANK, 1 Main Place, 655-8000
Mon.–Thurs. 9 A.M.–3 P.M., Fri. till 6 P.M.

FIRST NATIONAL BANK, Pacific at Akard, 744-8000
Mon.–Thurs. 9 A.M.–3 P.M., Fri. till 4 P.M.

MERCANTILE BANK, Main at Ervay, 698-6000
Mon.–Fri. 8:30 A.M.–3 P.M.

NATIONAL BANK OF COMMERCE, 1525 Elm, 658-6111
Mon.–Fri. 8 A.M.–4:30 P.M.

REPUBLIC NATIONAL BANK, Pacific at Ervay, 653-5000
Mon.–Thurs. 9 A.M.–3 P.M., Fri. till 4 P.M.

TRAVELERS CHECK DISPENSING MACHINES

American Express Travelers Check Dispensers are available seven days, 24 hours, at the following locations for customers enrolled in their program.

DALLAS/FORT WORTH AIRPORT
- Braniff (Gate 9)
- American (Lounge)
- Delta (Departure Level)
- Texas International (Departure Level)
- Amfac Hotel (Lobby)

LOVE FIELD (next to coffee shop)

MARRIOTT HOTEL (Market Center) Lobby

INFORMATION: (800) 528-1000

LOST OR STOLEN CHECKS: (800) 221-7282

DELIVERY AND POSTAL SERVICES

PAPERS, parts, packages—all need to be moved from one city to another or within the same city. Finding a dependable delivery service in a strange city can be confusing and frustrating. Here are our choices.

AIR FREIGHT

Most airlines provide cargo and freight services. The following companies also deliver nationwide and worldwide by air. Most will not accept credit cards and operate seven days, 24 hours.

EMERY AIR FREIGHT, 574-6300
Mon. 6 A.M.–1 A.M., Tues.–Fri. 5 A.M.–1 A.M., Sat. 6 A.M.–8 P.M., Sun. 9 A.M.–5:30 P.M. Nationwide and worldwide. No credit cards. Company billing and COD.

PUROLATOR, 438-4713
Mon.–Fri. 8 A.M.–5 P.M. Overnight delivery by air and ground, domestic and overseas. Call before 3 P.M. for next day delivery to most major cities.

SKY COURIER, (800) 336-3344
Seven days, 24 hours. Same-day service if called in by 4 P.M. National and international service. AE, MC, V.

SMITTY'S AIR FREIGHT, 351-3796
Seven days, 24 hours. Radio dispatched local pickup and delivery. Nationwide and worldwide service. No credit cards. Company billing and COD.

TEXAS AIR COURIERS, 630-2930
Seven days, 24 hours. Call in early A.M. for delivery before 5 P.M. locally. AE.

SURFACE LONG-DISTANCE DELIVERY

GREYHOUND BUS LINES, Commerce at Lamar (Downtown), 747-8856
Seven days, 24 hours. Bring package to terminal. There is a 100 lb. limit and package must not exceed 24″x24″x45″. MC, V.

TRAILWAYS, 1500 Jackson (Downtown), 655-7000
Seven days, 24 hours. Pickup arranged Mon.–Fri. 8 A.M.–5:30 P.M. Maximum weight 150 lbs. MC, V.

UNITED PARCEL SERVICE, 10155 Monroe (Walnut Hill near Market Center), 350-3341
Pickup service Mon.–Fri. 8 A.M.–5 P.M. No credit cards.

LOCAL DELIVERY SERVICES

All firms listed offer citywide pickup and delivery and some provide all-night service. Only a few accept credit cards.

CORPORATE EXPRESS, INC., 637-3131
Mon.–Fri. 8 A.M.–5 P.M. No credit cards. Company billing arranged.

ONE HOUR DELIVERY SERVICE, 352-1732
Open seven days, 24 hours. MC, V.

SECURITY COURIERS, 688-0031
Mon.–Fri. 9 A.M.–11 P.M. No credit cards. Company billing arranged.

UNITED MESSENGERS, INC., 980-8272
Open seven days, 24 hours. Also nationwide and worldwide. No credit cards. Company billing arranged.

PUROLATOR, Dallas Terminal, 3225 Century Circle, Irving, 438-4713
Open seven days, 24 hours. No credit cards. Company billing.

POST OFFICES

Post offices in Dallas are few and very far between. You will recognize one only by the American flag flying overhead. They are located in small shopping centers and in very out-of-the-way locations so if you cannot see one ask for help. Even the natives have trouble finding them. Most post offices in Dallas are only open weekdays from 8 A.M.–5 P.M. The only stations with Saturday hours (8:30 A.M.–noon) are in the suburbs. The following branches have Express Mail Service.

AIRPORT

D/FW AIRPORT (at SW end, far from terminals), 574-2685
Mon.–Fri. 8 A.M.–5 P.M. 24-hour service available for sending and receiving express mail.

MARKET CENTER

MERCHANDISE MART, 500 S. Ervay, 767-5251
Mon.–Fri. 8 A.M.–5 P.M.

WORLD TRADE CENTER, 2050 Stemmons, 741-1935
Mon.–Fri. 8 A.M.–5 P.M.

DOWNTOWN

MAIN POST OFFICE, 400 N. Ervay, 767-5648
Mon.–Fri. 8 A.M.–5 P.M.

ONE MAIN PLACE, 767-0797
Mon.–Fri. 8 A.M.–5 P.M.

LBJ-NORTH

ROYAL LANE STATION, Preston & Royal, 361-2922
Mon.–Fri. 8 A.M.–5 P.M., Sat. 8:30 A.M.–noon

FARMER'S BRANCH, 13904 Josey, 247-3546
Mon.–Fri. 8 A.M.–5 P.M., Sat. 8:30 A.M.–5 P.M., Sat. 8:30 A.M.–noon.

PERSONAL SERVICES

LIFE on the road as a business traveler has its ups and downs but trying to cope with the downs in an unfamiliar city can be most discouraging. What if the lift on your shoe falls off and you have three meetings in a row? What if the heat makes your hairdo wilt just before the company banquet? And what if your annual migraine strikes in the middle of the night?

To help you resolve a few of these "what if's" we have listed businesses in Dallas which are convenient to hotels, take credit cards, keep late hours and/or have delivery service. We have checked all shops listed to make sure they are pleasant and clean. It is not an all-inclusive listing but it should give you some hints on how to solve those nettling personal emergency situations.

There are no services outside of hotels in the D/FW Airport zone so you will need to check the hotel listing carefully to determine whether the service is available in-house. For the Market Center zone we have very limited listings because this area is comprised mainly of hotels, the Market Center complex and industrial buildings. The surrounding areas are generally unsafe to wander around. If there is no listing in a particular category it indicates we found no suitable service in that area and we recommend you use a Downtown service (about 10 minutes away) or an LBJ-North listing (10–15 minutes away). You will find hotels in the Market Center area tend to provide more complete in-house services and you can always ask hotel personnel for suggestions when in doubt.

None of these stores was told it would be included in our

book and no fees were paid to us. We would like to know if any store listed did not provide acceptable service.

BAKERIES

Like post offices and a few other services in Dallas, bakeries are not very numerous and are frequently tucked away in little local shopping centers. There are bakeries in many of the large supermarkets which sell everything from fresh Danish to birthday cakes personalized and decorated. Here are a few independent bakeries where you can stock up on supplies for your sweet tooth. None of them deliver.

DOWNTOWN

PASTRY BOUTIQUE, located in the Brasserie Restaurant of the Fairmont Hotel, Ross & Akard, 748-5454
Open seven days, 24 hours. French pastries, croissants, breakfast Danish, cakes. Special orders on one-day notice. All major credit cards.

NORTH CENTRAL

BLACK FOREST BAKERY, 5819 Blackwell (one block north of N. Central & Northwest Hwy.), 368-4490
Mon.–Fri. 8 A.M.–6 P.M., Sat. 8 A.M.–5 P.M. Breakfast cakes, European specialty cakes and pastries. One-day notice for special orders. MC, V.

LBJ-NORTH

MCGLYNN BAKERY, 13131 Montfort (at LBJ), 239-4941
Mon.–Sat. 9 A.M.–10 P.M. Breakfast cakes, pastries, cookies, cakes. One-day notice for special orders. AE, MC, V.

CLEANERS

Most of our hotels have same-day dry cleaning and laundry service, but operate Monday through Friday only. Here is some help for those Saturday-night-important-dinner-Friday-night-clam-chowder-on-the-lapel-emergencies. We have chosen only cleaners located near our hotels.

MARKET CENTER

ONE HOUR MARTINIZING, 4422 Maple, 521-1297
Mon.–Fri. 7 A.M.–6 P.M., Sat. 7:30 A.M.–3 P.M. Laundry and alteration service available in one hour if in by 11 A.M. No delivery. MC, V.

SUNSHINE LAUNDRY & DRY CLEANERS,
4011 Maple, 521-9921
Mon.–Fri. 6:30 A.M.–7 P.M., Sat. 6:30 A.M.–5 P.M. One-day service if in by 10 A.M. weekdays and 8:30 A.M. Saturdays. No delivery and no credit cards.

DOWNTOWN

RED'S ONE HOUR CLEANERS & LAUNDRY,
1320 Patterson (across from Fairmont Hotel), 742-3317
Mon.–Fri. 7 A.M.–7 P.M., Sat. 8 A.M.–2:30 P.M. One-day service on laundry and dry cleaning (Sat. on cleaning only). Delivery service. AE, MC, V.

ZIP SIXTY MINUTE CLEANERS
1212 Main, 748-1081
104 S. Pearl, 747-0516
Mon.–Fri. 7 A.M.–5:30 P.M., Sat. 8 A.M.–2 P.M. Drop off by 9:30 A.M., ready by afternoon. Minor alterations. No delivery. No credit cards.

NORTH CENTRAL

FISHBURN CLEANING & LAUNDRY, 5521 Greenville,
361-6510
Mon.–Fri. 7:30 A.M.–6 P.M., Sat. 8:30 A.M.–3 P.M. One-day service if in by 8:15 A.M. This is the finest in town and can save anything, from silk to cashmere. Specialists in suede and leather. No delivery. No credit cards.

UNIVERSITY CLEANERS, 3034 Mockingbird (just west of N. Central), 368-9002
Mon.–Fri. 7 A.M.–7 P.M., Sat. 7 A.M.–6 P.M. One-day service is available if in by 9 A.M. on cleaning and alterations. No delivery. No credit cards.

LBJ-NORTH

ONE HOUR MARTINIZING, 13347 Preston, 239-5884
Mon.–Sat. 7 A.M.–6 P.M. Cleaning ready in one hour if in by 1 P.M. (Mon., Tues., Thurs., & Fri.); by 11 A.M. Wed. and by noon Sat. Laundry in by 8 A.M. out by 5 P.M. No delivery. MC, V.

COMET 1-HOUR CLEANERS, 5441 Alpha (between Preston and Dallas North Parkway), 239-4371
Mon.–Fri. 7 A.M.–6:30 P.M., Sat. 8 A.M.–5 P.M. Cleaning ready in one hour if in by 1 P.M. Mon.–Fri. and 11 A.M. Sat. Laundry ready in one day at an additional charge. No credit cards.

DRUGSTORES AND PHARMACIES

Most hotels carry aspirin, deodorant, suntan oil and toothpaste but frequently you need a name brand drug, vitamins or a personal hygiene product which isn't on the shelf. All listed stores accept credit cards and have safe and convenient locations. Those with pharmacists on duty are noted. For best local advice you should inquire at the front desk of your hotel.

MARKET CENTER

This area really has no drugstores—hotel newsstands here are very well stocked with drug items to compensate for the lack of services outside—but we have listed one drugstore fairly close to this zone.

REVCO, 4125 Cedar Springs, 522-0460
Mon.–Sat. 9 A.M.–9 P.M., Sun. 10 A.M.–6 P.M. No delivery. MC, V.

DOWNTOWN

COMPLETE PHARMACY, 1711 Pacific, 742-2231
Mon.–Fri. 8 A.M.–5:30 P.M. Free delivery. MC, V.

REVCO
1029 Elm, 747-9366
Mon.–Fri. 9 A.M.–6 P.M., Sat. 9 A.M.–1 P.M. No delivery. MC, V.
Main & Commerce, 742-6211
Mon.–Sat. 7 A.M.–6 P.M. No delivery. MC, V.

SUN REXALL DRUG, 4101 Bryan (at Haskell), 824-4539
Seven days, 24 hours. Pharmacist on duty 9 A.M.–midnight. Delivery Mon.–Sat. until 9 P.M. MC, V.

NORTH CENTRAL

ECKERD'S DRUG, 3012 Mockingbird (at N. Central), 363-5525
Seven days, 24 hours. Pharmacist on duty at all times. No delivery. MC, V.

NORTHPARK PHARMACY, NorthPark Mall (N. Central at Park La.), 691-3565
Mon.–Sat. 9:30 A.M.–9 P.M., Sun. 11:30 A.M.–3 P.M. MC, V.

PAGE DRUGS, Meadow Creek Mall, Meadow at N. Central, 369-3872
Open seven days, 24 hours. Pharmacist on duty at all times. MC, V.

REVCO, 5500 Greenville (just east of N. Central), 691-0861
Mon.–Sat. 9 A.M.–9 P.M., Sun. 9 A.M.–6 P.M. No delivery. MC, V.

LBJ-NORTH

REVCO, 236 Preston Forest Shopping Center (just south of LBJ & Preston), 363-2583
Seven days, 24 hours. Pharmacist on duty at all times. No delivery. MC, V.

REVCO, 9035 Forest, 234-4126
Mon.–Sat. 9 A.M.–9 P.M., Sun. 10 A.M.–6 P.M. No delivery. MC, V.

FILM PROCESSING

Fast photo service is easy to locate in Dallas. There are chain stores and professional photography shops in almost every shopping area. Those listed below have rapid service, are easily accessible to hotels, and some take credit cards. None offer delivery service. It is also good to know that most large chain grocery stores in Dallas offer one-day photo service, but they do not accept credit cards.

DOWNTOWN

FOTOMAT, 501 N. Harwood (at Bryan), 745-1856
Mon.–Fri. 8 A.M.–5 P.M. One-day service if in by 1 P.M. but there is a fast-service fee. No credit cards.

FOX PHOTO
1414 Main (at Eckerd's Drugs), 651-1129
1901 Live Oak Drive-In (across from Republic Bank), 741-5857
Mon.–Fri. 8 A.M.–5:30 P.M. Full service camera stores for supplies and film processing. Seven-hour service if in by 9 A.M. for an extra charge. One-day service if in by 2:30 P.M. MC, V.

NORTH CENTRAL

FOTOMAT, 3070 W. Mockingbird, 691-0575
Mon.–Fri. 10 A.M.–7 P.M., Sat. 10 A.M.–3 P.M. See listing under Downtown.

FOX PHOTO, 1055 W. Mockingbird, 631-6783
Mon.–Fri. 8 A.M.–5:30 P.M. See listing under Downtown.

LBJ-NORTH

DOC MILLER & SONS, Preston at Forest (south of LBJ), 369-7971
Mon.–Sat. 9:30 A.M.–6 P.M., Thurs. till 8 P.M. Full photography service including rental equipment. Fast service on standard color film (in by 11 A.M. out by 5 P.M.). MC, V.

FOTOMAT, 13231 Montfort (at LBJ), 233-3535
Mon.–Fri. 10 A.M.–7 P.M., Sat. 10 A.M.–3 P.M. See listing under Downtown.

FOX PHOTO, 12821 Preston, Drive-In, 239-7612
Mon.–Fri. 8:30 A.M.–6:30 P.M., Sat. 10 A.M.–2 P.M. See listing under Downtown.

FLORISTS

There are many good flower shops throughout Dallas with local delivery, wire service, telephone charge service and good hours. If you've forgotten your wedding anniversary or just want to say thank you to a good client while on the run you should find this list helpful. Many offer a selection of other gift items as well.

MARKET CENTER

FLOWERS BY MARY, 4238 Maple, 526-8453
Mon.–Fri. 8:30 A.M.–5 P.M., Sat. 8 A.M.–1 P.M. Phone orders, national wire service. Gifts and dried flower arrangements. All major credit cards.

FRIDAY'S FLORIST, 4319 Lemmon (at Wycliff), 521-2002
Mon. Sat. 9 A.M.–6 P.M. Gifts, dried and silk flower arrangements. Worldwide delivery, FTD, Florafax, Telaflora, AFS. AE, MC, V.

MY FLORIST, 5342 Lemmon, 528-0287
Open seven days, 8 a.m.–7 P.M. Phone orders, no wire service, delivery in Dallas only. MC, V.

DOWNTOWN

HALE-GERALDINE, 1706 Main, 748-1226
Mon.–Fri. 8 A.M.–5:30 P.M., Sat. 8 A.M.–noon. Gifts and all types of flowers (silk and dried arrangements). Citywide delivery, phone orders, FTD. AE, MC, V.

MCKAY'S FLORIST, 1923 Commerce, 741-1706
Mon.–Fri. 8 A.M.–4:30 P.M., Sat. 8 A.M.–noon. Phone orders, citywide deliveries. All major credit cards.

ONE MAIN PLACE FLOWER & GIFT SHOP,
One Main Place, 742-8674
Mon.–Thurs. 9 A.M.–5 P.M., Fri. 8:30 A.M.–5:30 P.M. Silk and dried flower arrangements. Phone orders, AFS, citywide delivery. MC, V.

PETALS & STEMS
Fairmont Hotel (Ross at Akard), 653-1625
Mon.–Sat. 9 A.M.–5 P.M.
Plaza of the Americas (North Pearl Blvd.), Mon.–Sat. 10 A.M.–6 P.M.
Gift items, dried and silk flower arrangements. Phone orders, Florafax, Teleflora, AFS. Citywide delivery. All major credit cards.

REPUBLIC FLOWERS & GIFTS, Republic National Bank Bldg. (Pacific at Ervay), 741-5071
Mon.–Fri. 8 A.M.–5 P.M. Phone orders, FTD, delivery. AE, MC, V.

NORTH CENTRAL

BILGER FLORIST & GREENHOUSE, 3525 Greenville (between Mockingbird & McCommas), 824-3637
Mon.–Fri. 7:30 a.m.–5 P.M., Sat. till noon. Phone orders, city and suburban delivery, FTD. AE, MC, V.

HOLT'S FLORIST, INC., 2017 Greenville, 827-3221
Mon.–Fri. 8:30 A.M.–5:30 P.M., Sat. 8:30 A.M.–1 P.M. FTD and AFS service. AE, MC, V.

MEADOW CENTRAL FLORIST, 10203 N. Central (at Meadow), 363-2732
Mon.–Fri. 8:30 A.M.–5:30 P.M., Sat. 8:30 A.M.–1 P.M. Phone orders, AFS and FTD. AE, MC, V.

LBJ-NORTH

A TOUCH OF CLASS, 13410 Preston (just north of LBJ), 386-5010
Mon.–Sat. 8:30 A.M.–5:30 P.M., Thurs. till 9 P.M. Specializing in dry flowers, silk flower arrangements and fresh flowers and plants. Phone orders, FTD. AE, MC, V.

FARMER'S BRANCH FLORIST, 2901 Valley View (at LBJ), 241-2177
Mon.–Sat. 8 A.M.–6 P.M. Citywide delivery, phone orders, FTD, Florafax, AFS, Teleflora. All major credit cards.

PETALS & STEMS, LBJ at Montfort, 233-9037
Mon.–Sat. 8:30 A.M.–5:30 P.M. Citywide delivery, phone orders, Florafax, Teleflora, AFS. All major credit cards.

YOUR FLORIST, LBJ at Inwood, 233-9666
Mon.–Fri. 8 A.M.–9 P.M., Sat. till 7 P.M., Sun. 8:30 A.M.–5:30 P.M. Also open holidays. Discount prices. Orders by phone, delivery, AFS. All major credit cards.

FORMAL WEAR

In case you arrive in Dallas to find the banquet is a Black Tie affair or if your old tuxedo just won't stretch around your middle one more time, you will find the following outlets can supply you with formal wear. You should try to plan ahead so fittings and reservations for your attire can be done properly. There are no women's formal wear rentals in the city. None of the companies offer pickup or delivery service.

DOWNTOWN

AL'S FORMAL WEAR, 2207 Commerce, 651-1331
Mon.–Sat. 9 A.M.–6 P.M. Full line of formal wear and all accessories. Order by 11:30 A.M., ready by 3:30 P.M. DC, MC, V.

NORTH CENTRAL

SKEFFINGTON'S, 5500 Greenville (Old Town Shopping Village), 361-6866
Mon.–Sat. 9:30 A.M.–6 P.M., Thurs. till 8 P.M. Can be ready on several hours' notice. MC, V.

LBJ-NORTH

AL'S FORMAL WEAR, INC., LBJ & Preston (Preston Valley Shopping Center), 233-7739
Mon. & Thurs. 9:30 A.M.–8 P.M., Tues., Wed. & Fri. 9:30 A.M.–6 P.M., Sat. 9:30 A.M.–5:30 P.M. Also by appointment. Order by 11:30 A.M., ready by 3:30 P.M. DC, MC, V.

GROCERIES & GOURMET SHOPS

Sitting watching late night TV after a long day of meetings you may find yourself yearning for a little snack. You can stock up at any of the stores listed below, some are even open 24 hours. Gourmet shops are not numerous in Dallas and there are few "Mom & Pop" or independent markets. Larger chain groceries are a way of life here and often they have a surprisingly complete gourmet section, some even deliver. The very best idea is to shop while you are out and around during the day so your munchies will be ready when you return after a hard day. There are supermarkets in nearly every shopping center, sometimes even two on opposite corners. There are also 7-Elevens, Magic Markets and other quick stop markets located near most of the hotels. Here are a few special gourmet shops which Dallasites use.

MARKET CENTER

SIMON DAVID (Tom Thumb Grocery), 7117 Inwood, 352-1781
Open seven days 8 A.M.–10 P.M. Specialties, liquors and fruit baskets. Citywide delivery. No credit cards.

DOWNTOWN

FISHER FOOD STORE, 4260 Oak Lawn, 526-7251
Mon.–Sat. 8 A.M.–6 P.M. Fruit and cheese baskets, prime beef, liquor. Delivery service in Downtown area with minimum $15 purchase (good idea to use this since the area is not one of the better ones in Dallas). MC, V.

NEIMAN-MARCUS, 1618 Main, 741-6911
Mon.–Sat. 9:30 A.M.–5:30 P.M., Thurs. till 8 P.M. Wonderful baked goods, nuts, popcorn, teas, chocolates—a treat any way you slice it! Try their own Red River brand gourmet selections. Delivery available with advance notice.

NORTH CENTRAL

ANTONE'S IMPORT CO. OF DALLAS, 9100 N. Central, 369-6982
Open seven days 8:30 A.M.–9:30 P.M. A tempting world of foreign foods, imported beers and wines. Great Poor Boy sandwiches, too.

SPIRITS, Caruth Plaza (Park Lane at N. Central), 696-3535
Mon.–Sat. 10 A.M.–9 P.M. Everything you need to have a great cocktail party in your room. Cheese trays made to order, complete spread for small groups. This store also has about the best wine selection in the city and sells all other kinds of liquor and beer as well. Delivery service. All major credit cards.

LBJ-NORTH

GOODIES FROM GOODMAN, 12102 Inwood. (just south of LBJ), 387-4804
Mon.–Sat. 9 A.M.–6 P.M. Imported foods and gifts, top quality meats, candy, fruit baskets, cookbooks. Deliveries within the city. AE, MC, V.

HAIRDRESSERS & BARBER SHOPS

Unlike the Hollywood starlets who bring their own hairdressers with them when they travel, most business travelers must rely on local barbers and beauticians when in need of a fresh hairdo or neat haircut. Some hotels and office buildings have barber shops and beauty salons but here are some other suggestions.

DOWNTOWN

MERCANTILE BARBERS & STYLISTS, Main & Commerce, 741-4489
Mon.–Fri. 8 A.M.–5 P.M. No appointment necessary. No credit cards.

MERCANTILE DALLAS BEAUTY SALON, 1807 Commerce, 748-7677
Mon. & Sat. 7 A.M.–1 P.M., Tues.–Thurs. 7 A.M.–5 P.M. Appointments preferred. MC, V.

V-ANN'S BEAUTY SALON, 511 N. Akard, 748-8604
Mon.–Sat. 7 A.M.–4:30 P.M., Tues. & Thurs. till 6:30 P.M. Evenings by appointment. Appointments preferred. No credit cards.

NORTH CENTRAL

CREATIVE IMAGES, 5230 Greenville (at Lovers Lane), 369-4344
Mon.–Sat. 9 A.M.–9 P.M. Unisex hairstylists. MC, V.

DESIGNER'S LOFT, 5500 Greenville (Old Town), 692-7605
Tues.–Sat. 10 A.M.–5 P.M., Thurs. till 8 P.M. Appointments preferred. MC, V.

THE HAIR COMPANY, 8842 N. Central (NorthPark East), 361-7826
Mon.–Sat. 9 A.M.–6 P.M. Thurs. evening by appointment. Full

service salon including facials, manicures, pedicures and his and her hairstyling. Appointments preferred. MC, V.

LBJ-NORTH

MAKING WAVES, Valley View Mall (Dillard's Department Store), 387-5757
Mon.–Sat. 9 A.M.–9 P.M. No appointment necessary. Manicurist. Unicuts. MC, V.

SAMSON & DELILAH HAIRSTYLING STUDIO, 2038 Valley View Center (LBJ at Preston), 233-7735
Mon.–Sat. 9 A.M.–9 P.M. No appointment necessary. Men's and women's haircuts. No credit cards.

LIQUOR STORES

As we have indicated several times in our guide, the sale of liquor by the bottle or by the drink in and around Dallas is based on a quiltlike pattern of wet and dry areas which roughly align with voting precincts. In general, LBJ-North is dry which means you will have to buy liquor in another zone (Market Center or North Central) or further north of LBJ in Addison (about a 10-minute ride). Liquor stores are lined up like ducks in a row along those streets which are in wet areas—one side of the street is often wet while directly across the street is dry. No sense in trying to figure out where the lines are drawn, just use this list as a source of libations convenient to hotels. Operating hours of all liquor stores in Dallas are restricted by law—Monday–Saturday 9 A.M.–10 P.M. There are no exceptions and all stores listed here take full advantage of these hours. A few hotels frown on delivery of liquor so be sure to check with the front desk if you plan to use a delivery service. Also, they cannot deliver to a hotel in a dry area.

MARKET CENTER

EAGLE LIQUOR, 4703 Maple, 559-3870
Some snacks and cold drinks. No credit cards.

TEXAS LIQUORS, 4321 Maple, 526-9752
Local deliveries. All major credit cards.

DOWNTOWN

ARCADIA LIQUOR STORE, 1629 Elm, 747-5933
Party snacks and ice. Free downtown delivery. No credit cards.

DALLAS LIQUOR STORE, 918 Commerce, 747-0563
Snacks. No delivery and no credit cards.

CENTENNIAL LIQUOR STORE, 969 S. Lamar, 565-1659
Snacks and delivery service. AE, MC, V.

RED COLEMAN'S LIQUORS, 1226 S. Lamar, 565-9229
Snacks. All major credit cards.

WAREHOUSE LIQUOR STORES, 730 Young (across from Dallas Morning News), 748-7931
Snacks. AE, MC, V.

NORTH CENTRAL

CENTENNIAL LIQUOR STORE, 1501 North Park Center, 368-0589
Snacks and delivery service. AE, MC, V.

RED COLEMAN'S LIQUORS, 7735 Greenville, 363-1025
Snacks. All major credit cards.

WAREHOUSE LIQUOR STORES
9810 N. Central, 691-0673
7735 Greenville, 363-1025
Snacks. AE, MC, V.

LBJ-NORTH

This is a dry area so you cannot have liquor delivered to your hotel and you cannot buy it in the immediate vicinity of your hotel. The following liquor stores are a quick ride away, but are in wet areas north of this zone.

CENTENNIAL LIQUOR STORE, 10967 Stemmons (near LBJ), 556-0641
Snacks. AE, MC, V.

WAREHOUSE LIQUOR STORE, 14825 Inwood (north of LBJ), 233-6392
Snacks. AE, MC, V.

LOCKSMITHS

Nothing is more frustrating than forgetting your luggage keys, locking your car keys inside your car, or having a key break off in a lock. In the unhappy event you find yourself in this predicament, here are some people willing and able to help. All have 24-hour emergency service.

A-A AAACE KEY & LOCK, 13342 Preston (at LBJ), 233-2442
24-hour service. MC, V.

A-A LOCK & SAFE CO.
4815 Ross (at Fitzhugh), 826-1020
6015 Royal Lane (at Preston) 368-2331
24-hour service. MC, V.

AARON'S, 1401½ N. Zang, 943-3381
Mon.–Sat. 7 A.M.–6 P.M. 24-hour emergency service. MC.

A-WEBB LOCK & SAFE, 11425 Harry Hines, 241-8866
24-hour mobile service. MC, V.

CHIEF'S LOCK SHOPS
4131 Gaston, 821-3501
5122 Greenville, 692-1444
24-hour service. MC, V.

GREENVILLE AVE. LOCK & KEY, 2375 Gus Thomasson, 750-5912
24-hour mobile service. MC, V.

LUGGAGE & HANDBAG REPAIR

Should your briefcase handle fall off or your suitcase be abused (heaven forbid!) by the airlines, you will need a speedy leather repair shop and here are some good ones. None of them deliver.

DOWNTOWN

BROOKS HANDBAG & LUGGAGE REPAIR,
921 N. Haskell (near Baylor Hospital), 824-7010
Mon.–Fri. 9:30 A.M.–5 P.M. Quick service, one-day service where possible. All leather goods repaired, zippers. No credit cards.

MAIN STREET SHOE REPAIR, 1809 Main, 741-5950
Mon.–Sat. 7 A.M.–5 P.M. Will do most minor repairs on any leather goods while you wait or one-day service depending on extent of repairs needed. No credit cards.

NORTH CENTRAL

THE SHOEMAKER, 10455 N. Central (at Meadow),
363-2042
Mon.–Fri. 8 A.M.–6:30 P.M., Sat. 9 A.M.–6 P.M. Leather repairs, zippers. No locks repaired. All major credit cards.

LBJ-NORTH

PRESTON SHOE & TAILOR SERVICE, 11608 Preston,
361-7054
Mon.–Fri. 8 A.M.–5:30 P.M., Sat. 8 A.M.–3 P.M. Shoe and luggage repair. Emergency service on minor repairs. MC, V.

PRESTON LUGGAGE & GIFTS, Preston Center,
361-4931
Mon.–Sat. 9:30 A.M.–5:30 P.M. Minor leather repairs done. No zippers or locks. AE, MC, V.

VALLEY VIEW SHOE REPAIR, 13370 Preston, 386-8783
Mon.–Sat. 8 A.M.–6 P.M. Luggage and handbag repairs take two days. No credit cards.

FOREIGN AND OUT-OF-TOWN NEWSPAPERS

Don't get homesick in Dallas. Not only are there very few out-of-town newspapers available—you won't even see corner newsstands selling local papers (those are sold in coin-operated boxes). Most hotel lobby shops do carry the daily and Sunday *New York Times* and *Wall Street Journal.* The best selection of other newspapers can be found at two major news dealers downtown.

COMMERCE STREET NEWSSTAND, 1513 Commerce (Akard), 741-0062
Mon.–Sat. 5:45 A.M.–10:30 P.M., Sun. 6 A.M.–9 P.M. Carries most major city newspapers (although most of them two to five days late), *Wall Street Journal, New York Times* and all types of other publications including London newspapers and some foreign magazines. Try to get here during daylight hours; after business hours it is often a hang-out for people wandering the streets and some of its magazine offerings draw a tough crowd. Cash only.

MAIN TOWER NEWS, 1200 Main, 742-4886
Mon.–Fri. 6 A.M.–6 P.M. Major business publications and *New York Times.* No credit cards.

OPTICIANS

If you need your glasses to find your glasses life can come to a grinding halt with an accidentally broken lens or frame. Here are some suggestions for emergency assistance.

MARKET CENTER

THE OPTICAL CENTER, 9101 Carpenter (1 block from the LeBaron Hotel), 637-3501
Mon.–Fri. 9 A.M.–5 P.M. MC, V.

OPTICAL CLINIC, 3098 Stemmons, 638-1320
Mon.–Fri. 8:30 A.M.–5:30 P.M., Sat. 8 A.M.–1 P.M. Optometrist located next door Mon.–Fri. 9 A.M.–5 P.M., Sat. 9 A.M.–noon. MC, V.

DOWNTOWN

BOERGER OPTICAL CO., 608 N. St. Paul, 742-8314
Mon.–Fri. 8:30 A.M.–5 P.M., Sat. 8:30 A.M.–11:30 A.M. MC.

LEE VISION CENTER, 1705 Elm, 741-6771
Mon.–Sat. 9 A.M.–5:30 P.M. Emergency repair service available for frames. MC, V.

TEXAS STATE OPTICAL, 1525 Main, 741-3514
Mon.–Fri. 9 A.M.–5:30 P.M., Sat. 9 a.m.–1 P.M. MC, V.

NORTH CENTRAL

OPTICAL CLINIC, 2727 N. Central, 521-5775
Mon.–Fri. 8:30 A.M.–5:30 P.M., Sat. 8:30 A.M.–5 P.M. MC, V.

SAN FRANCISCO OPTICAL CO., 5521 Greenville, 361-6130
Mon.–Fri. 10 A.M.–6 P.M., Sat. 10 A.M.–4 P.M. Emergency contact lens and eyeglass repair. MC, V.

TEXAS STATE OPTICAL, 638 NorthPark Center, 363-7864
Mon.–Fri. 10 A.M.–8:30 P.M., Sat. 10 A.M.–6 P.M. MC, V.

LBJ-NORTH

EYECARE CENTERS OPTICIANS, 7750 Forest (at N. Central), 987-2220
Mon.–Fri. 10 A.M.–5:30 P.M., Sat. 10 A.M.–noon. Emergency service and repair. One-day service. MC, V.

OPTICAL CLINIC, 2877 LBJ (at Josey), 214-9055
Mon.–Fri. 8:30 A.M.–5:30 P.M., Sat. till 1 P.M. MC, V.

PEARLE VISION CENTER, 13534 Preston (across from Valley View Mall), 696-4614
Mon.–Fri. 9 A.M.–9 P.M., Sat. till 6 P.M. Emergency service. MC, V.

SHOE REPAIR

As you step off the airplane the lift on your heel falls off or you just had to bring that pair of brown shoes you keep meaning to take to the shoemaker and never seem to find time. Where do you find the "Lil' Ol' Shoemaker?" Don't look in the airport, we can't find one there. In fact they're hard to find anywhere near hotels; most are in local shopping areas.

MARKET CENTER

AIRWAY SHOE SHOP, 8110 Denton (near Love Field), 352-0025
Mon.–Fri. 8 A.M.–5:30 P.M., Sat. 8 A.M.–2 P.M. No credit cards.

DOWNTOWN

DALLAS SHOE SHOP, 1407 Main, 748-1584
Mon.–Fri. 8 A.M.–5:30 P.M. One-day service. No credit cards.

MAIN STREET SHOE REPAIR, 1809 Main, 741-5950
Mon.–Sat. 7 A.M.–5 P.M. One-day and while-u-wait service. Shoe shines. Will also do handbag and luggage repairs on premises if minor. No credit cards.

STANDARD SHOE REPAIR, 1821 Main, 741-0425
Mon.–Fri. 7 A.M.–5:30 P.M., Sat. 10 A.M.–4 P.M. Minor handbag repair. One-day or while-u-wait service. No credit cards.

NORTH CENTRAL

NICK'S, 5521 Greenville, 363-3621
Mon.–Sat. 8 A.M.–6 P.M., Thurs. till 8 P.M. Emergency repairs while-u-wait. All major credit cards.

LBJ-NORTH

NICK'S, 10305 Coit (1 block north of LBJ), 231-6657
Mon.–Sat. 8 A.M.–6 P.M., Thurs. until 8 P.M. All major credit cards.

PRESTON SHOE & TAILOR SERVICE, 11608 Preston, 361-7054
Mon.–Fri. 8 A.M.–5:30 P.M., Sat. 8 A.M.–3 P.M. Shoe and luggage repair. Emergency service. MC, V.

VALLEY VIEW SHOE REPAIR, 13370 Preston, 386-8783
Mon.–Sat. 8 A.M.–6 P.M. One-day and while-u-wait service. Luggage and handbag repairs take two days. No credit cards.

TAILORS

When you pull a string and the hem of your dress or jacket comes out completely or you catch your pocket on a nail and need a hole repaired in a hurry you might find these shops useful to know about.

DOWNTOWN

MANUEL'S & FRANK'S REWEAVING AND TAILORING SHOP, 608 N. St. Paul, 747-2330
Mon.–Fri. 8 A.M.–5:30 P.M., Sat. 9 A.M.–12:30 P.M. One-day service. MC, V.

NORTH CENTRAL

FANTASTIC TAILORS, 2023 Greenville, 823-9111
Tues.–Fri. 9 A.M.–7 P.M., Sat. 9 A.M.–6 P.M. Men's and ladies' custom alterations, minor repairs done immediately. No credit cards.

FISHBURN CLEANING & LAUNDRY, 5521 Greenville, 361-6510
Mon.–Fri. 7:30 A.M.–6 P.M., Sat. 8:30 A.M.–3 P.M. Probably the best tailor in town. No delivery. No credit cards.

LBJ-NORTH

NICK THE TAILOR, 605 Preston-Forest Shopping Center (just south of LBJ), 361-5698

Mon.–Fri. 8 A.M.–5:30 P.M., Sat. 8 A.M.–3 P.M. Men's and women's clothing. MC, V.

TAILORS UNLIMITED, 11617 N. Central (at Forest), 363-7031

Mon.–Sat. 8:30 A.M.–5:30 P.M. Same-day service on alterations. MC, V.

THE TAILOR SHOP, 12938 Midway (at LBJ), 233-4184

Mon.–Sat. 10 A.M.–6 P.M., Tues. & Thurs. until 9 P.M. One-day service available. No credit cards.

ZOLTAN TAILOR SHOP, 12801 Midway (at LBJ), 247-0718

Mon.–Fri. 9 A.M.–6 P.M., Sat. until 5:30 P.M. No credit cards.

24 HOURS A DAY

UNLIKE "The Big Apple," Dallas is not a city whose lights never dim and where no one ever sleeps. Here are a few places for those insomniac business travelers who need to find food, fun, or pharmacy items in the middle of the night.

RESTAURANTS

BRASSERIE, Fairmont Hotel (Downtown), 748-5454
Includes bar service and all meals in a nice setting. All major credit cards.

DENNY'S
8954 Stemmons (Market Center), 630-5666
4400 N. Central (North Central), 824-1269
6061 LBJ (at Preston), 387-2779
Everything from breakfast to a full course dinner. Try the French Dip (thin slices of roast beef au jus on a roll!) No credit cards.

HOWARD JOHNSON'S
3111 Stemmons (Market Center), 634-8242
10323 N. Central (North Central), 369-7119
Just like its counterparts in other parts of the country—passable food, mediocre service but their ice cream is great. No credit cards.

JOJO'S
1415 Motor at Stemmons (Market Center), 630-9949
10011 N. Central (North Central), 369-8972
8059 LBJ at Coit (LBJ), 231-5536
Extensive menu all day and night for breakfast, lunch, dinner or just a snack. MC, V.

KIP'S, 5706 E. Mockingbird (just east of N. Central), 827-3798
Open Fri. & Sat. all night but other nights till 1 A.M. Hamburgers, breakfast, anytime, soup and salad and some of the best coffee in town. No credit cards.

MIRAGE KIOSK, Loew's Anatole, 2201 Stemmons, 262-8298
If you are staying in another hotel this may give you a good chance to see this beautiful hotel while the crowds are smaller. Lovely setting and good food. All major credit cards.

DRUGSTORES AND PHARMACIES

ECKERD'S, 3012 Mockingbird (at N. Central), 363-5525
Pharmacist on duty at all times. MC, V.

PAGE DRUGS, Meadow Creek Mall, Meadow & N. Central, 369-3872
Pharmacist on duty at all times. MC, V.

REVCO, 236 Preston-Forest Shopping Center (3 min. south of LBJ & Preston), 363-2583
Pharmacist on duty at all times. MC, V.

SUN REXALL, 4101 Bryan (Downtown), 824-4539
Pharmacy open 9 A.M. to midnight but drugstore is open 24 hours. Delivery service available until approximately 9 P.M.

GROCERY STORES

Groceries are what these are. None are interesting enough to have been listed in our gourmet section in the personal services chapter, and none accept credit cards.

KROGER
4760 W. Mockingbird (near Tollway), 350-4939
6120 E. Mockingbird (east of N. Central), 826-8221
8081 Walnut Hill (east of N. Central), 692-7415

SKAGGS ALPHA-BETA
13100 Josey (just north of LBJ), 241-0531
6464 E. Mockingbird (east of N. Central), 692-7415

TOM THUMB
9310 Forest (just south of LBJ), 341-8666
5500 Greenville (Old Town), 691-0571
10455 N. Central (at Meadow), 369-9694

DELIVERY SERVICE

ONE HOUR DELIVERY SERVICE, 352-1732
MC, V.

SJY COURIERS, (800) 336-3344
AE, MC, V.

SMITTY'S AIR FREIGHT, 351-3796
No credit cards.

TEXAS AIR COURIERS, 630-2921
AE.

UNITED MESSENGERS, INC., 980-8272
No credit cards.

BOWLING

DON CARTER'S ALL STAR LANES
East–6343 E. Northwest Highway, 363-9418
West–Stemmons at Walnut Hill, 358-1382

EXPRESSWAY LANES, 5910 N. Central, 826-6930

SPORTS AND ENTERTAINMENT

DALLAS IS the Dallas Cowboys and vice versa. Everyone has heard about them, watched them play in the Super Bowl and if you happen to come to Dallas during the season you will find the entire town preoccupied with its team. There are, however, other sports in Dallas and a variety of cultural and other entertainment features. We have limited this section to an overview of available attractions after business hours. All work and no play . . . .

For more complete and up-to-date listings check the *Dallas Morning News* or the *Dallas Times Herald,* both of which do an excellent job of highlighting activities in and around town. Their "Weekend" sections are most informative. There are also several magazines published monthly which offer entertainment information including *"D"* magazine and *Texas Monthly.*

TICKETS

There are numerous ways of purchasing tickets to major sporting and entertainment events in town. Many of the newer hotels are including concierge services in the lobby which include ticket and reservation services. You can also pick up tickets at the gate but this is risky since the best seats are sold out early for most programs. The following general ticket agencies sell tickets to a variety of events and many accept credit cards. You may find these the handiest for your needs as a busy business traveler, and unlike agencies in many other major cities, their service charges are very small.

CENTRAL TICKET OFFICE, 1007 Commerce, 429-1181
Mon.–Fri. 9 A.M.–5:30 P.M., Sat. 10 A.M.–3 P.M. Tickets to the opera, ballet, symphony and major entertainment events. Service charge. AE, MC, V.

NORTHPARK BOX OFFICE (located in Joske's department store, lower level—NorthPark Mall), 692-0203
Mon.–Sat. 10 A.M.–6 P.M. Tickets to the Dallas Symphony, Starfest and Jazzfest only. AE, MC, V.

PRESTON TICKET AGENCY, 8111 Preston (at Loop 12), 363-9311
Mon.–Fri. 9 A.M.–4:30 P.M., Sat. 10 A.M.–2 P.M. Tickets to major concerts, theater, rodeo, some sporting events. This is the only service where you can order tickets by phone and pick them up at the gate. Service charge. MC, V.

RAINBOW TICKETS, Sears in Valley View Mall (LBJ), 565-5281 and 6225 Hillcrest (between University & Mockingbird), 521-3670
Mon.–Fri. 10 A.M.–6 P.M., Sat. 10 A.M.–3 P.M. Tickets for plays, concerts and sporting events. Service charge. Cash only.

SPORTS

Dallas fields teams in every major sport and Dallasites are fanatic sports fans. With beautiful weather most of the year and excellent arenas and stadium facilities Dallas is the ideal place to indulge your spectator-sport urges.

BASEBALL

TEXAS RANGERS, 273-5100
Play their games at Arlington Stadium on Rt. 30 (Dallas/Fort Worth Turnpike) 20 minutes west of downtown. There is ample parking but traffic does jam up before and after games.

BASKETBALL

DALLAS MAVERICKS, 988-0117
This NBA team plays in Reunion Arena Downtown adjacent

to the Hyatt Regency Hotel complex. The season runs from October to April.

DALLAS DIAMONDS, 350-5586
One of the more successful of the women's basketball franchises. Their home games are played at Moody Coliseum on the SMU campus (Mockingbird west of N. Central). They were title contenders last year and always draw a good crowd.

FOOTBALL

DALLAS COWBOYS, 369-3211
Football fever runs in the blood of most Dallasites. You will not find an impartial observer during the season—everyone loves the COWBOYS! Games are played at Texas Stadium west of Downtown. You can order single game tickets by mail if you expect to be in town on a game day but order early—tickets are scarce as hen's teeth and nearly every home game is a sellout. Send money order or cashier's check for the number of tickets plus $1 for postage and handling to Dallas Cowboys, 6116 North Central Expy., Dallas, 75206. If you like football you will love the flair of a Dallas Cowboys game—it is a real "happening."

ICE HOCKEY

DALLAS BLACK HAWKS, 565-0362
This team plays at Fair Park just to the east of Downtown. The season runs from October through March. This area of town is not safe especially at night so either take a taxi or be sure you know where you are going.

RODEO

MESQUITE RODEO, 285-8777
Contrary to public opinion cowboys do not ride through the streets of Dallas but they certainly do ride every weekend from April through September at the Mesquite Rodeo located on the LBJ Freeway about 20 minutes east of Downtown. Shows are at 8:30 and 10:30 P.M. This is a full-fledged outdoor rodeo with calf ropin', bronc bustin' and all the trappings.

Reunion Arena (745-1540) hosts many other events both sports and general entertainment all through the year. Major concerts, the circus, ice shows—all are presented in this fabulous new arena.

Southern Methodist University (SMU) and North Texas State University and Bishop College all field football teams and a variety of other sports in intercollegiate competition. In Texas high school football is a regular Friday night must. Some of the local high school stadiums would rival major league stadiums of other cities. Check the papers for schedules and other information.

ARTS IN DALLAS

If you have time and enjoy music and theater you will find first-rate entertainment in Dallas but not in the variety or volume you find in some other major cities like New York, Philadelphia, or Washington. Dallas's cultural development has come rather slowly but will be immeasurably improved with the addition of a Fine Arts Center in central Downtown within the next year or so. Meanwhile, here are some of the best bets for a cultural shot in the arm.

MUSIC

DALLAS SYMPHONY ORCHESTRA, Music Hall at Fair Park (east of Downtown), 565-9100

Symphony season runs from September through May with Eduardo Mata conducting. Tickets are available at the door and at Joske's NorthPark (lower level). You can even arrange to have supper before the concert and there is a bar open before concerts and during intermission.

STAR FEST, Electronic Data Systems (Hillcrest & Forest)

Summer entertainment featuring outdoor concerts by the Dallas Symphony and other well-known popular artists. Bring a picnic supper, a bottle of wine and a blanket to sit on the grassy slopes under the beautiful Texas sky. Tickets are available at the gate or through the Dallas Times Herald which sponsors the concerts.

DANCE

DALLAS BALLET, Majestic Theater, 1925 Elm, 744-4398
The Ballet performs at McFarland Auditorium on the campus of Southern Methodist University (SMU) and tickets are available two weeks prior to performances which run from October to March.

DINNER THEATER

COUNTRY DINNER PLAYHOUSE, 11829 Abrams (just south of LBJ), 231-9457
Reservations required. Fixed price includes dinner, show and tax. Shows Tuesday through Sunday evening (doors open at 6 P.M.; showtime 8:30 P.M.) and Sunday matinee (doors open at noon; showtime 2:30 P.M.). All major credit cards.

GRANNY'S DINNER PLAYHOUSE, 12205 Coit (south of LBJ, one block west of N. Central), 239-0153
Reservations required. Shows Tuesday through Sunday evening (doors open 6 P.M.; showtime 8:15 P.M.). All major credit cards.

THEATER

DALLAS REPERTORY THEATRE, NorthPark Community Hall (NorthPark Mall), 369-8966
Reservations by phone Tues.–Fri. 1–6 P.M. Major Broadway shows and repertory productions, September through July. All major credit cards.

DALLAS THEATER CENTER, 3636 Turtle Creek (between Downtown and North Central zones), 526-8857
Drama, comedy, Broadway shows, October to August. Most major credit cards.

HAYMARKET THEATRE, Olla Podrida Mall (Coit just south of LBJ), 233-1958
A marionette show offered Thurs.–Sat at 10:30 A.M., 1 P.M.

and 4 P.M. Tickets are available at the box office 15 minutes prior to each show.

THEATRE THREE, 2800 Routh (the Quadrangle), 748-5191
Legitimate theater, musical comedies, drama, Broadway shows, children's shows. Reservations made by telephone with major credit card. Box office is open seven days 10:30 A.M.– 6 P.M. Show times are Tues.–Thurs. 8 P.M., Fri. & Sat. 8:30 P.M. and Sun. 2:30 P.M. and 7 P.M. MC, V.

MOVIE THEATERS

Texas always does things in a big way and Dallas movie theaters are no exception. There are numerous multitheater movie houses showing five or six of the latest films all under one roof. Dallas always has first-run movies and bargain rates are available for shows before 6 P.M. weekdays and for the the first matinee weekends. Rather than list all the theaters here we refer you to the daily newspapers which not only list the theaters but provide you with a wonderful map divided into zones so you can easily locate the theaters nearest to your hotel. The following movie houses are clean, comfortable, safe and conveniently located. There are no movie theaters at the airport or Downtown.

MARKET CENTER

WALNUT HILL 6, I-35 at Walnut Hill

NORTH CENTRAL

NORTHPARK I & II, NorthPark Shopping Center

NORTHPARK III & IV, Park Lane & N. Central (across from NorthPark Shopping Center)

UA CINEMA, N. Central at Yale

LBJ-NORTH

VALLEY VIEW, LBJ & Preston

LOEW'S QUAD, LBJ & Coit

NORTHTOWN 6, LBJ & Webbs Chapel

NIGHT LIFE

Nighttime activities in Dallas are legion but you need to know where the best spots are. As we mentioned in the restaurant section of our guide, the North Central zone and specifically Greenville Avenue Strip are indisputably the kings of the after-hours crowds. Major hotels, however, all have live music and hopping cocktail lounges so be sure to check out the scene where you are staying.

If you decide to venture out, here are some of the fun spots which sell drinks, ooze Texas hospitality and display some of the best talent in "Big D."

AGORA BALLROOM, 6532 E. Northwest Highway (North Central), 696-3720
Rock and roll, New Wave and jazz.

BELLE STAR, 7724 N. Central (North Central), 750-4787
Country and Western dancing (C&W to insiders) in its purest form. They'll teach you the Cotton-Eyed Joe and the two-step.

BILLY BOB'S TEXAS, 2520 Commerce, downtown Ft. Worth, 625-6491
Legendary throughout the country for performers like Willie Nelson and some lesser known Western stars, this is reputedly the largest night club in the country with 40 bars, its own rodeo—an unbelievable place. See our Sightseeing chapter for a tour package which includes a visit to Billy Bob's. Otherwise you will have to allow a complete evening since it is about 40 miles from Dallas. Worth the trip if you just have to see the latest in "Texas Huge."

CIRRUS LOUNGE, Doubletree Inn, N. Central at Northwest Hwy. (Loop 12), 691-8700
Dancing and listening to music seems like more fun with the full view of nighttime Dallas through the top floor windows. Jazz on Sundays is terrific.

COMEDY CORNER, 8202 Park Lane, at Greenville (North Central), 361-7461
A steady stream of Texas and transplanted comedians trying for the big break. This new spot has really caught on with the locals.

COTTON-EYED JOE'S, 2711 Storey, near Northwest Hwy. and Harry Hines (Market Center), 358-1771
Tues.–Sat. 7 P.M.–2 A.M. Live band most nights and some of the best "cowboy" watching in Dallas.

COWBOY, 5201 Matilda (North Central), 369-6969
The epitome of Dallas C&W disco, this place is always crowded, very noisy and often rowdy. Nonetheless, it is a great spot to catch "urban cowboys" strutting their stuff.

EIGHT-O, 2800 Routh (the Quadrangle, Downtown), 741-1817
High-tech artists' cafe. Jazz is live at lunch. Jukebox is the main source of entertainment, other than people-watching at night.

GRAN CRYSTAL PALACE, 2424 Swiss at N. Central (North Central), 824-1263
This supper club was formerly an old warehouse and now houses some of the best musical shows in Dallas.

GREENVILLE AVENUE BAR & GRILL, 2821 Greenville (North Central), 823-6691
One of Dallas's oldest bars features Dixieland jazz Tuesday and Thursday. Plenty of local color.

ISADORA, Center Plaza Holiday Inn, LBJ at Valley View, 385-9000
This is one of the newer "in" spots in Dallas. Cozy spot for dancing–disco, rock, C&W–anything that is au courant.

LONGHORN BALLROOM, 216 Corinth (Market Center), 428-3128

Wed.–Sun. 7 P.M.–2 A.M. This is one of the favorite spots to see and be seen doing the latest Texas dances—the two-step or the Cotton-Eyed Joe. Free dance lessons.

STRICTLY TABU, 4111 LomoAlto (Dallas North Tollway and Lemmon, near Love Field), 522-8101

Jazz at its finest in an intimate and often crowded room. Excellent Italian cuisine upstairs.

TOP OF THE DOME, Hyatt Regency Hotel complex, Reunion Tower, 651-1234

A bona fide tourist attraction. You can enjoy a drink in the revolving cocktail lounge which even has the directions conveniently marked on the windows so you know when you are looking at North Dallas.

VENETIAN ROOM, Fairmont Hotel, Ross & Akard, 748-5454

This is Dallas's most famous Downtown supper club—the great and near-great—and not just on the stage.

SHOPPING

A FAMILIAR sight at D/FW Airport is the departing visitor carrying a big Stetson hat box and wearing a pair of brand new cowboy boots. Shopping in Dallas, however, goes well beyond just Western goodies. Downtown at Neiman-Marcus you can purchase everything from an oriental vase of the Ming dynasty for $120,000 to a drop of oil encased in acrylic or a set of bar glasses depicting, of all things, the weeds of Texas for a scant $20. There is also more to the market place than Neiman's.

Because your main purpose in coming to Dallas is business and not shopping we have not attempted to give you a complete guide to shopping. However, shopping in Dallas is a real treat and we have tried to list some of the outstanding stores in selective categories. Store hours vary but in general stores open between 9 and 10 A.M. and Downtown stores close about 6 P.M. Malls are open until 9 P.M. but many of the smaller shops close earlier. Thursday night is generally a late shopping night. Because of stringent blue laws in Texas all stores are closed on Sunday but the malls are usually open for browsing and window shopping. Be sure to wear comfortable shoes because you can log a lot of kilometers in a Texas mall–they are huge!

If you are looking for toys to take home to the kids, Texas trivia, tobacco, or tacos you will find a fine selection in any of the malls we have listed. We have highlighted a few individual items which most travelers to Dallas covet but for literally anything else you need just head for one of the malls–if they don't have what you need you probably won't find it in Dallas.

SHOPPING MALLS

Dallas has more than its share of shopping malls and we have selected several for this section because of their proximity to the hotels. There are also several collections of shops which do not fit the standard definition of a mall but, rather, take on a character all their own. For example, the Quadrangle, located just a few minutes from Downtown, is a little bit of Olde World Europe with a harmonious blend of shops dealing mainly in apparel, art and antiques.

DOWNTOWN

PLAZA OF THE AMERICAS
Two levels of specialty stores and restaurants. Clothiers include Jas. K. Wilson and Sakowitz for men; Courreges, St. Denise, Sakowitz Boutique and Rodeo for women. Other shops include David-Anderson of Norway, selling fine jewelry, crystal and porcelain from Europe, B. Dalton Bookstore, Coffee & Tea Trading Co., Bag n Baggage for leather goods and a wine and cheese store.

THE QUADRANGLE, 2800 Routh, 742-8679
This is one of the trendiest locations for shopping after-shopping activities. Begin with a drink at the Eight-O Bar. There are 47 shops including sellers of military miniatures and one store that only sells books on architecture. The Afterimage Gallery has changing exhibits, sells books and represents some of the Southwest's finest photographers. Pick up an embroidered Mexican dress at LaMariposa or a lacy camisole from James' Lingerie. You can find exclusive designs in women's apparel at Handel's or a brass bell at The Nautical Wheeler. Did we leave anyone out? There is Crabtree & Evelyn for soaps, the Coffee Co. for java and Godiva chocolates, Sergio's restaurant for homemade cannelloni and plenty more.

NORTH CENTRAL

NORTHPARK CENTER, N. Central between Park & Northwest Hwy., 363-7441
Occupying 95 acres almost exactly in the center of the Dallas city limits, NorthPark was the brain child of one man, Ray Nasher, owner and developer. There are 135 stores in the complex with fountains, changing flower displays and a host

of seasonal decorating extravaganzas. At Christmas, every bit as breathtaking as Fifth Avenue in New York, this is complete with mechanically moving displays and famous pecan-covered reindeer suspended from the ceilings. The mall is perfect for a walking tour even if you don't intend to spend a dime.

Neiman-Marcus opened its first branch store here and it is the cornerstone of the mall. Lord & Taylor and Penney's are the major national stores and Joske's department store is the local chain representative. Included in the many other stores are leather goods from Gucci, silk dresses at the fashionable Carriage Shop and Lester Melnick's and collector's records at the Melody Shop. There are several restaurants including The Magic Pan and Churchill's Polo Tavern and even an Orange Julius stand reminiscent of New York. You could survive here for a week and never starve–just go broke!

OLD TOWN VILLAGE, Greenville at Lovers Lane, 750-1517

Catering to the many young, single people in the area this is probably one of the most unique malls. It stretches for several blocks along Greenville Avenue and includes lots of restaurants (some are here today, gone tomorrow) and a variety of shops. You can find women's designer clothing at Barbara Robertson's, men's famous-label clothes (Givenchy, Yves St. Laurent) and Johnston Murphy shoes at L. O. Hammond's and custom-made perfumes from the Scent Shop. Two favorite restaurants are T.G.I. Friday's and Mariano's, but the crowds are huge. Other shops sell children's clothes, crystal, cameras, kitchenware and stereo equipment. You can find practically anything here and its convenient to any of the North Central hotels.

LBJ NORTH

OLLA PODRIDA, 12215 Colt (just south of LBJ), 239-8541

This unique mall is an old barn housing fine local artisans and their crafts. Quilts, quills, custom silver jewelry, antiques, jellybeans, modern graphics, nuts and bolts sculpture, wicker, kites–just about anything in the arts and crafts line is sold here. There is a puppet theater for the children with two shows daily and you can even munch on Greek food at the Upper Crust restaurant.

PRESTONWOOD TOWN CENTER, Belt Line at Dallas North Tollway extension (3 miles north of LBJ), 980-4275

One of the newest malls in Dallas, this gigantic center includes an ice skating rink and a full selection of fast food stands serving everything from New York deli food to pizza to foot-long hot dogs—all overlooking the skaters. The central feature of the mall is a two story open-works clock which helps you tally the hours you will want to spend wandering in and out of the hundreds of small and large stores in the mall. Plush and beautiful with plants and sculptures, this shopping center is the last word for fashion: both expensive (Neiman-Marcus, Lord & Taylor), and moderately-priced (Joske's, Penney's and Montgomery Ward). You can buy Italian imports at Carrugi-Santi, precious jewels from Linz, or spend the day at the exclusive salon, The Nailery. A bit north of our northern boundary but worth the extra time and travel because you can spend the day and do all your shopping under this one roof.

SAKOWITZ VILLAGE, Belt Line at Dallas North Tollway extension (north of LBJ), 934-8300

At this writing the newest of the new when it comes to elegant shopping centers. Be sure to bring your fat wallet to this exclusive spot and when you get wornout spending your money stop for a drink at the Palm Court in Sakowitz. Some of the outstanding stores in the Village include: Haltom's Jewelers, Magigue for fine furniture, L'Image for facials and make-overs and any number of merchants selling oriental rugs, caviar, stuffed animals and monograms. Take in the Highland Park Cafeteria if you get hungry.

VALLEY VIEW CENTER, LBJ at Preston, 661-2424

While this is one of the older (for Dallas) malls it is still attractive, convenient and fun to spend a few hours wandering through. Sanger Harris is the major local department store and Sears has a large department store in the center. Dillard's is a moderately priced department store at the other end of the complex. In between these major stores you can shop at The Limited or Casual Corner for women's clothes,

Oshman's for sporting goods, Linz for jewelry and any of over 125 other nice stores. There are three restaurants and 14 fast-food places in the mall.

OUT OF THE WAY–BUT WORTH IT

HIGHLAND PARK VILLAGE, Preston at Mockingbird, 521-5285
With the Dallas Country Club, the most exclusive in Dallas, across the street the local Highland Park crowd can play a set of tennis, amble over to see the latest Ralph Lauren in the Polo Shop and be back at the Club in time to tee off.

Not precisely in one of our zones, but in the residential area between Downtown and North Central, this is really not so far out of the way. This mall is known for its Mexican architecture and the high quality (and prices) of the merchandise sold here. Some of the exclusive shops here include: Sanger Harris, Jas. K. Wilson, Bond Jewelers, Harold's, Courreges, Guy Laroche, Pierre Deux, Kron Chocolatiers and the Collector's Covey, specializing in wildlife artifacts. This is truly a preppy's home away from home!

ART AND ANTIQUES

Art dealers and galleries line McKinney Avenue and Routh Street near Downtown and create a little village all their own in converted old houses and small store fronts. Another area, known as the Vineyard, is bounded by McKinney, Oak Lawn, and Maple avenues and is just five minutes from Downtown. There are 96 antique dealers and art galleries in this district–perfect for browsing on Saturday afternoon. A few blocks to the west of the Vineyard on Sale Street there are several more shops specializing in American and English antiques. If you have more money than you know what to do with, try a trip to the East & Orient Company at 2901 Henderson nearby–it is an experience worth the trip.

Since Dallas is a creature of this century you won't find the numbers or the quality of antiques that you might expect to find in the Northeast but people in the Southwest crave antiquities and are willing to pay the price. You will find numerous small shops in the shopping malls which carry a limited line of older objects which while not authentically antique may be fun to have.

BOOKS

Once again, bookstores are staples in most of the malls here in Dallas. Most of the large chains of bookstores have shops conveniently located near hotels and major business areas. The following are a few more specialized book sellers we think might help you while away an hour or three between meetings.

AIA DALLAS BOOK SHOP, 2800 Routh (the Quadrangle Downtown), 651-1490
Want to read the latest ideas on city planning or pick out some plans for a passive solar house? This architect's book store has a large selection of beautiful and unique books on subjects ranging from interior decorating to furniture design and restoration.

COKESBURY, 1910 Main (Downtown), 748-8711
This is predominantly a religious bookstore but they also carry a good selection of general reference books, business books and beautiful volumes on art.

HALF-PRICE BOOKS, 4528 McKinney (Downtown), 526-8440
Open seven days a week this used bookstore is a bibliophile's paradise. Over one million books and records are neatly categorized. Find a favorite issue of *Life* magazine or an out-of-print novel or put together a library of classics for under $20.

TAYLOR'S, 4001 Northwest (North Central), 363-1500
A supermarket bookstore carrying everything from paperbacks to valuable art books. Large selection of how-to books, guides, biographies and books about the great state of Texas.

CANDY

CANDY DANDIES, 8108 Spring Valley (just north of Coit & LBJ), 783-4138
Mon.–Thurs. 10 A.M.–6 P.M., Fri. & Sat., 10 A.M.–9 P.M. Specialty chocolates molded into figures, e.g., Snoopy, Big

Bird. All types of other candies and candy jars. You can also buy X-rated chocolates if you are over 19 years of age (they are displayed in the back room). No credit cards.

CANDY MAN, Olla Podrida, 661-8415
Mon.-Sat. 10 A.M.-5:30 P.M. Nostalgic candies from your childhood memories of the neighborhood candy store. Special candy containers. Will also mail anywhere. MC, V.

KRON CHOCOLATIERS, Highland Park Village, 526-4722
Mon.-Sat. 10 A.M.-5:30 P.M. Famous Kron (N.Y.) chocolates. Will mail anywhere. MC, V.

RUSSELL STOVER, NorthPark Center, 361-2550
Mon.-Sat. 10 A.M.-9 P.M. Candies and nuts. No credit cards.

CLOTHING FOR MEN & WOMEN

In our listings of shopping malls we have indicated some of the fine apparel stores in Dallas. There are, of course, hundreds of smaller stores and you will notice that Dallasites are very well dressed. Here are a few of the shops favored by local residents and by visitors to Dallas including movie stars and other people in the public eye who seek the best in fashion.

BROOKS BROTHERS, First International Bldg. (Downtown), 748-4700
"Does eat oats and mares eat oats and little rams eat Ivy Leaguers!" The little ram insignia is popping up on everything from T-shirts to wallets. This national clothing chain continues to be the bastion of tasteful clothing.

HAROLD'S, 88 Highland Park Village (between Downtown and North Central zones), 521-4770
The *only* place to go for Ralph Lauren Polo shirts and Nipon dresses. This store is packed to its grosgrain gills with preppy clothes–khakis, Lanz nightgowns, Burberry raincoats and Shurka luggage as well as a good selection of tailored suits and dresses. An institution in Highland Park and a chance to see the in-crowd of Dallas.

LOU LATTIMORE, 4320 Lovers Lane (Highland Park), 369-8585

Exclusive women's store with labels from Chloe, Giorgio Armani, Adolpho, Claude Montana (leather), Christian Dior (Paris), Lanvin and many new European couturiers. Lingerie by Montenapoleone of Milan. Posh hair salon called Show Biz, Orlane Institut de Beaute. You will be rubbing elbows with national newsmakers, Hollywood starlets and other "Beautiful People."

MARIE LEAVELL, Inwood at Lovers Lane (Market Center), 357-6441

This elegant collection of boutiques carries classic European and American couture, cosmetics, shoes, lingerie, precious jewels and other fine gifts such as china and crystal. For over 50 years Marie Leavell has had a reputation for rare and unusual merchandise.

WOOLF BROS., NorthPark Center (North Central), 747-8811

Very fine men's suits are the specialty here. Major labels include Hickey Freeman, Ralph Lauren and Chaps. Good selection of women's clothing from Evan Piccone, Dalton, Anne Klein and Charlotte Ford. Salvatore Ferragamo shoes and handbags in a wide selection of styles.

TOBACCO

ALFRED DUNHILL, NorthPark Center (North Central), 691-0191

Mon.–Fri. 10 A.M.–9 P.M., Sat. 9 A.M.–6 P.M. Pipes, cigars and special tobacco mixes. AE, MC, V.

LACY'S PIPE & TOBACCO, Preston at Royal (LBJ), 363-9838

Mon.–Sat. 9 A.M.–6 P.M. Hand-rolled cigars, pipes and all types of smokers' supplies. AE, MC, V.

WORLD TRADE TOBACCONIST, 2050 Stemmons (Market Center), 744-1759

Mon.–Fri. 7 A.M.–4:30 P.M. All types of smokers' supplies. No credit cards.

WESTERN WEAR

You probably will not want to leave town without at least looking into cowboy boots or the purchase of a 10-gallon hat. It used to be hokey to strut your stuff in a cowboy outfit but with the advent of the Urban Cowboy, this stuff is really in demand and Dallas is definitely the place to find the latest in Western wear. Here are some of the best spots to find what you need. They offer the best selection and are delighted to assist you in your search for the perfect boots or hat.

CUTTER BILL'S WESTERN WORLD, 5818 LBJ, 239-3742
The most exclusive store for everything Western—from crocodile boots to a 1952 Rolls-Royce pickup. This is the place for the finest skins in Texas anaconda, ostrich, you name it they have it! Don't be surprised to see Mick Jagger or Larry "J.R." Hagman lining up their wardrobes nearby—everyone knows Cutter Bill's.

LONGHORN RANCHWEAR, 121 Walnut Hill Village (Market Center), 358-5463
A large selection of boots from Larry Mahan, Justin, Dan Post, for both men and women. English riding bridles and clothing, Western shirts in silk and plaids, jeans, belts, hats, etc.

MASTER HATTERS, 2365 Forest (LBJ), 276-4114
This is a great place to find a bargain straight from the hat factory next door. They offer a full selection of straws, felts in all sizes and shapes at outlet prices.

SHEPLERS, 2500 Centennial Drive (Arlington), 461-0191
This is a spot that is worth the drive if you are really sincere about wanting the best selection of boots in all styles, riding tack, clothing, hats, etc. They also have a terrific gift department with belt buckles, collar tips, books and hat pins. You can also price out a set of Texas longhorns as a hood ornament for your car!

WELLS BOOT CENTER, 857 W. Pipeline (Hurst), 268-2621
The largest boot store in the Dallas area has 50,000 sq. ft. of space. Every name is represented including Tony Lucchesi, Nocona, Larry Mahan, in every size and width possible. Take the Airport Freeway to Precinct Line exit, turn left to Pipeline then go right ¼ mile.

DON'T MISS

NEIMAN-MARCUS, 1618 Main (Downtown), 741-6911
A trip to Dallas is not complete without a trip to N-M even if you hate shopping. We recommend you take a few minutes out of your busy schedule and browse through the Downtown store. In the past few years Neiman's has opened stores in the outlying malls but we feel those stores just do not have the same ambience as the original store Downtown. It has the aura of opulence from the time you enter the doors near the jewelry department or by the cosmetics department with the best-known names in makeup offering the latest scents and colors. Clothing and housewares are chic and expensive but you can find bargains if you are in town during one of N-M's famous sales. Stop for lunch in the beautiful dining room upstairs–it is one of the better Downtown lunch spots. If you want to order a catalog (the Christmas one featured "his and her" ostrich eggs last year) you can get information at the credit office. There is just no place to match Neiman-Marcus and it is definitely a "must see."

KEEPING FIT

IF your normal at-home schedule includes jogging before breakfast or a game of tennis after work, you won't need to alter your lifestyle while visiting Dallas. With an annual mean temperature of 65°, this is an outdoor town and youthful Dallasites are evident throughout the city playing softball or soccer, jogging or playing tennis–all on marvelously well-maintained public facilities. There are, of course, private facilities and many of our listed hotels have guest arrangements with local clubs or schools for use of their facilities. Here are some of the city-operated and private clubs offering services to keep you happy, healthy and shapely while you are on the road.

HEALTH CLUBS

AEROBICS CENTER, 12202 Preston (1 mile south of LBJ), 233-4832

Mon.–Sat. 5 A.M.–9 P.M. Closed Sunday. For a $5 guest fee you can have the most complete running facilities in town and a host of topnotch other athletic facilities as well. There are three running courses: ¼, ½ and a mile course, as well as an indoor track. There are four racquetball courts, outdoor tennis courts, a six-lane pool, stationary bikes and treadmills and an indoor basketball court. You can also have breakfast or lunch from 6:30 A.M. to 3:30 P.M. Despite a recent fire this is still the finest and most scenic athletic center in town.

ANATOLE HOTEL, 2201 Stemmons (Market Center), 748-1200

Open seven days: Mon.–Sat. 6 A.M.–10 P.M., Sun. 8 A.M.–5 P.M. This hotel has agreements with surrounding hotels for guest use of their facilities which are very complete. Included in the list of offerings at the Anatole are coed workout areas with stationary bikes, rowing machines, steam and sauna for men, sauna for women, men's and women's massage, racquetball courts and outdoor tennis courts at hourly rates, an indoor pool and Jacuzzi. AE, MC, V.

MARKET FITNESS CENTER, Park Lane, east of N. Central (North Central), 696-1300

Mon.–Fri. 10 A.M.–10 P.M., Sat. & Sun. 9 A.M.–9 P.M. This facility has memberships and will also allow guests and one-time users. They have four racquetball courts (with equipment rental), a weight room, steam room, sauna, whirlpool and an outdoor swimming pool. All facilities are coed. Reservations for racquetball courts should be made at least a day ahead especially for the hours right after work. MC, V.

RACQUETBALL AT NORTHPARK, 8878 N. Central, 692-6000

Open seven days 6 A.M.–10 P.M. Located right in the middle of office complexes this is a complete health facility including 14 racquetball/handball courts, whirlpool, sauna and steam room. All facilities are coed. There is a small guest fee but this club has agreements with NCCA Affiliate Clubs for reciprocity. MC, V.

YMCA-DOWNTOWN, Ross & Akard (across from the Fairmont), 741-4836

This YMCA is the gem of the national system and is the largest and most complete of its kind in the nation. Fees are lower for members of other Y's and arrangements can be made for billing through your hotel. It is open Mon.–Sat. 6 A.M.–9:30 P.M. and Sunday 9 A.M.–5 P.M. Some of the fantastic facilities include: a 25-meter 8-lane indoor pool; 13 handball/racquetball courts; 2 squash courts (hard to find in Dallas); a 16-lap indoor and 12-lap outdoor track; 3 full-size gyms; complete Olympic-style weight room with Nautilus and universals; complete men's and women's health facilities including sauna, whirlpool, steam room, and a health food bar. There is a pro shop, lounges and locker areas and a 140-car parking area. You can spend an hour or the entire day here and feel good afterwards!

TENNIS

The city of Dallas has some of the most impressive public tennis facilities in the nation and the fees even for out-of-town players are minimal. For complete information call 670-8897. The pro shops at major centers listed below can arrange to find you a partner and can rent or sell you equipment. All courts are outdoors (indoor courts in Dallas other than hotels are all part of private clubs and do not accept one-time reservations) and most courts are lighted. Reservations can be made a day ahead of time by calling 428-1501. The following courts are closest to our hotel zones:

FAIR OAKS, 348-1810
16 courts convenient to LBJ & N. Central

KIEST CENTER, 330-7234
16 courts convenient to Downtown

L. B. Houston, 247-5782
12 courts west of Stemmons (Market Center)

We think these public courts are the best bet, but you may want to try the courts at some of the health clubs we listed (which cost considerably more per hour) or at the Bear Creek Golf & Racquet center at D/FW Airport (see listing under Golf).

RUNNING

There are only two city-operated and maintained jogging paths in Dallas—White Rock Lake (9-mile trail) at the eastern edge of Dallas near Northwest Highway, and Bachman Lake (3-mile trail) near Love Field. The Cross Country Club of Dallas at 826-8260 can provide you with information about races and about running activities in Dallas. You can also get information about races and running events from Phidippides Sports Center at 361-6493.

The YMCA downtown has an indoor and an outdoor track and the Aerobics Center has indoor and outdoor tracks that would be convenient if you are staying in the LBJ-North zone. (See Health Club listings.)

Since the terrain in Dallas is flat you will see jogging almost anywhere around town. There are no specific routes around particular hotels. The best advice we feel is to ask at the front desk for directions to the safest streets nearby.

GOLF

As is true of most cities the main golf clubs are private and do not allow out of town people to use their facilities. There are two golf facilities operated by the city which are convenient to the hotels and also one hotel which has a complete golfing facility.

BEAR CREEK GOLF & RACQUET CENTER, D/FW Airport (Amfac Hotel Complex), 453-8400
This full country club facility located right at the airport is open to the public and honors all major credit cards. Their hours change according to the seasons so be sure to call to check. There are 36 holes of golf comprising two 18-hole courses. Carts for rental and daily green fees. You can get a half-price green fee after 4 P.M. There is equipment rental, shower and locker facilities and a snack bar and full bar. This center also has tennis facilities and 10 indoor air-conditioned racquetball/handball courts.

CITY OF DALLAS GOLF COURSES
There are two 18-hole public courses convenient to hotels and a 36-hole course. Green fees here are really low and cart rental is fairly reasonable. It is best to call ahead for reservations and for specific directions from your hotel since all are just a bit out of our coverage area. None are more than a 20- to 30-minute ride from Downtown.

L. B. HOUSTON PARK, 18 holes, 247-5778 (nearest Market Center)

STEVENS PARK, 18 holes, 946-5781 (nearest Downtown)

TENNISON PARK, 36 holes, 823-5350 (far to the east but worth it)

BICYCLING AND BOATING

WHITE ROCK LAKE (321-2125) is a city-maintained park area on the far east side of Dallas at Northwest Highway

(Loop 12). A nine-mile trail along the banks of White Rock Lake is a scenic route for bikers. Hundley's (823-6933), on the southwest side of the lake is open seven days from 10 A.M. to sundown all year. Hundley's rents three-speed bikes and two-seaters, paddleboats (with a three-person limit) and canoes. All rentals are charged by the hour. They also sell fishing supplies. No credit cards.

ICE SKATING RINKS

If the heat in Dallas has you wishing for the cooler temperatures of the North you might give yourself a break and go ice skating. There are two major rinks open year round, located near hotels. Both charge admission and skate rental is extra.

PLAZA OF THE AMERICAS–ICE CAPADES CHALET, 748-4001
Open seven days, 11 A.M.–5 P.M. and 7:30–10 P.M., MC, V.

PRESTONWOOD–ICE CAPADES CHALET, Belt Line & Dallas Pkwy., 980-8988
Open Sun.–Thurs. 11 A.M.–5 P.M.; Fri. 11 A.M.–11 P.M., Sat. noon–11 P.M., MC, V.

BOWLING

Another of Texas's large, larger, largest facilities—the bowling centers listed each have over 50 lanes and all of those we have chosen are open 24 hours. Each suggests that weekday evenings are almost always solidly booked for league bowlers. There are usually free lanes available on weekends and earlier in the day. None accept credit cards.

DON CARTER'S ALL STAR LANES, 6343 E. Northwest Hwy. (2 blocks east of N. Central), 363-9418; Stemmons at Walnut Hill, 358-1382

EXPRESSWAY LANES, 5910 N. Central (SMU Exit), 826-6930

SHOOTING RANGES

Now that you are in the Wild West you might feel the urge to try your luck at trapshooting or skeet or on the pistol range. The city of Dallas provides this service at L.B. Houston Park and has facilities to rent pistols, rifles and trap and skeet guns. Best to call ahead for range and time schedules. Skeet & Trap Range, 241-2421; Rifle and Pistol Range, 241-3889.

SIGHTSEEING

IF you are looking for history, you might find Dallas disappointing. Dallas is a "new" American city; not only is it only a hundred years old, but its growth into a major modern metropolis has come so quickly that most buildings of historical interest were leveled before there was a chance to preserve them. The Fair Park area east of Downtown houses most of Dallas's museums, and they too are a disappointment, with the exception of the art museum which will be moving soon to a major new building–one that will form the core of an important new center for the arts in Downtown Dallas. Fort Worth has several good museums, well worth a visit if you have time for the 40-mile drive. They are listed in the Fort Worth section of the book.

Another big disappointment to visitors seeking a glimpse of the old West is the fact that there is not an oil well, major ranch or any other typically Texan sight within an easy drive of Dallas. One of the most exciting sights of Dallas is the space itself, and you might want to go to the top of the Dome (the tall ball at the top of the Hyatt Regency Hotel, made famous by the opening scenes of *Dallas* on TV). From there, or the Cirrus Lounge at the top of the Doubletree Inn on North Central Expressway, there is nothing to obscure your view, and you will feel as though you can see tomorrow.

TOURS

AMERICAN ART & MUSEUM TOURS, 13500 Midway, 691-5242

Guided tours of local art collections and museums for both groups and individuals. Also city tours on request.

GRAY LINE TOURS, 824-2424

Tours for individuals and groups (eight or more). Tours leave from Downtown and North Dallas hotels and include such excursions as "Southfork Ranch and J.R.'s Dallas," "Dallas After Dark," and "Texas Barbecue and the Rodeo."

If you are in charge of arranging a group tour, try one of the following new services:

DESTINATION DALLAS, 528-7916

KALEIDOSCOPE, 522-5930

MUSEUMS AND SIGHTS

We have combined our listings by area, since distances in Dallas are always deceptively far. We have limited our listings to those within easy reach—including some east of Downtown. You may read about other places and while they are interesting, many of them are in transitional neighborhoods, areas difficult to reach because of construction or traffic congestion, or quite far from any of our zones.

DOWNTOWN

BRYAN'S CABIN, Elm, Main and Market
Reconstruction of the cabin built in 1841 by Tennessee pioneer and Dallas founder, John Neely Bryan. Not furnished.

DALLAS CITY HALL, Akard at Marilla
A striking I. M. Pei building with cantilevered front and a monumental Henry Moore sculpture in front. Free guided tours. Pei also designed the One Dallas Center office building.

DALLAS MUSEUM OF FINE ARTS, Parry and Second, 421-4188
Tues.–Sat. 10 A.M.–5 P.M., Sun 1–5 P.M. A wide-ranging collection of art works from pre-Columbian to modern. Also good visiting exhibits. At the moment still housed in its original Fair Park location, but soon to move into its magnificent new home in central Downtown. Free.

DALLAS ZOO, 621 E. Clarendon (off I-35, south of Downtown), 946-5155
Open seven days 9 A.M.–5 P.M. One of the top collections of mammals, birds, reptiles and amphibians, though the facility badly needs refurbishing. Also includes a petting zoo open in the summer. Admisson charge.

FAIR PARK, Parry and First, 565-9931
This huge city park located two miles east of Downtown is the scene of the annual Texas State Fair (a definite "must see" if you are in Dallas during October) as well as the Cotton Bowl football classic played every New Year's Day. The fair grounds encompass a number of different buildings each housing a major exhibit and though the buildings all need repair it is a great place to spend a free weekend afternoon. The area outside the Fair Park grounds is not safe for walking around but there is plenty of free parking inside the fairgrounds. If you take a taxi be sure to have them drop you off inside the fairgrounds and call for your return taxi from one of the exhibit halls.

DALLAS AQUARIUM, 428-3587
Mon.–Sat. 9 A.M.–5 P.M., Sun. noon–5 P.M. Small admission fee.

DALLAS CIVIC GARDEN CENTER, 428-7476
Mon.–Fri. 10 A.M.–5 P.M., Sat. & Sun. 2–5 P.M. Botanical gardens. Free.

DALLAS MUSEUM OF NATURAL HISTORY, 421-2169
Mon.–Sat. 9 A.M.–5 P.M., Sun. noon–5 P.M. Small charge.

TEXAS HALL OF STATE, 421-5136
Mon.–Sat. 9 A.M.–5 P.M., Sun. 1–5 P.M. A collection of Texas historical memorabilia including handwritten diaries of Dallas's original settlers. Free.

THE SCIENCE PLACE, 428-8351
Tues.–Sat. 9 A.M.–5 P.M., Sun. 1–5 P.M. Small charge.

FARMER'S MARKET, 1010 S. Pearl, 748-2082
Open seven days. Great place to buy fresh produce direct from the farmers who grow it. Spring and summer are the best seasons but there are festivals all year long.

JOHN FITZGERALD KENNEDY MEMORIAL, Commerce, Main & Record.

This memorial is actually four concrete walls which form a 50 sq. ft. space with a black marble marker engraved simply JOHN F. KENNEDY. It was designed by Philip Johnson, a personal friend of Kennedy's and is a short distance from the actual spot where the President was shot.

JOHN F. KENNEDY MUSEUM, 501 Elm, 742-8582

Open seven days 9 A.M.–5 P.M. Located across the street from the Texas School Book Depository so familiar to all Americans who watched in horror the events of Nov. 22, 1963. This museum includes photos, paintings and other historical items related to that terrible day. "The Incredible Hours" is an excellent audiovisual reconstruction of these historic events and the life of the late President. Admission charge.

OLD CITY PARK, 1717 Gano, 421-7800

Tues.–Fri. 10 A.M.–4 P.M., Sat. & Sun. 1:30–4:30 P.M. Located just a 10-minute walk from the Convention Center or central Downtown. You can also take the Ervay Street bus from Neiman-Marcus. This park-museum traces Dallas's history from 1840 to 1910 through buildings, objects and live craft demonstrations. Admission charge.

SWISS AVENUE (just north of Downtown toward Highland Park)

Several blocks of renovated mansions, fine examples of nineteenth-century prairie architecture.

UNION STATION, Young and Houston (opposite Hyatt Regency)

This beautiful railroad station designed in 1914 has been restored and now houses several restaurants. It is owned and operated by Hyatt and is connected to the hotel by an underground walkway. Also the location of the Dallas Visitor and Information Center (747-2355).

THANKSGIVING SQUARE, Bryan, Pacific and Ervay

This center city square in the heart of the Downtown business district serves as a monument to America's religious heritage and includes fountains, gardens and a nondenominational chapel.

NORTH CENTRAL

BIBLICAL ARTS CENTER, Boedecker at Park Lane (across from NorthPark Center), 691-4661
Tues.–Sat. 10 A.M.–5 P.M. This center houses three museums of biblical artifacts, a gallery and a gigantic mural *Miracle at Pentacost.* There is also an atrium with a reconstruction of Christ's tomb. You'll know you're in the Bible Belt. Admission charge.

BETWEEN DALLAS AND FORT WORTH

The following sights and museums are located along Route I-30 between Dallas and Fort Worth and are about a 20- to 30-minute drive from Downtown Dallas.

SIX FLAGS OVER TEXAS, I-30, Arlington, (817) 461-3524
This theme park is an exciting place to take your family, young and old, for a day of amusements, rides and just plain fun. Hours and days of operation vary according to the seasons so be sure to call ahead. AE, MC, V.

SOUTHWESTERN HISTORICAL WAX MUSEUM, 601 E. Safari (I-30), 263-2391
Open seven days 9 A.M.–9 P.M. (Memorial Day–Labor Day), 10 A.M.–5 P.M. (6 P.M. weekends) rest of year. Over 180 wax figures, historical, political, sports and a huge collection of antique guns. Main attraction is *The Last Supper* in wax figures. Admission charge.

TEXAS SPORTS HALL OF FAME, 401 E. Safari (I-30), 263-4255
Open seven days 10 A.M.–5 P.M. (6 P.M. weekends), 10 A.M.–9 P.M. daily during the summer. Everything relating to Texas sports and Texas athletes from Babe Zaharias to Ben Hogan. Electronic games, four theaters and numerous exhibits of professional and collegiate athletics. Admission charge.

EMERGENCIES

MEDICAL problems while in a strange city can be very upsetting–where do you find help and whom do you call? Most hotels have doctors and dentists available on referral but in an emergency you may need a hospital. We have given you a list of emergency numbers as well as a selection of major hospitals with emergency rooms within reasonable distance of major hotels. Unlike many other major U.S. cities, Dallas/Fort Worth does not use the 911 number for police and fire emergencies. Many hotels now have a card or other listing in each room with these numbers.

EMERGENCY TELEPHONE NUMBERS (DALLAS)

Fire 744-4444

Police 744-4444

Emergency Ambulance 744-4444

Dallas County Dental Society 386-5741

Dallas County Medical Society 526-5090
(If no answer call) 528-6125

Poison Control Center 429-9142

Rape Crisis Center 521-1020

AMBULANCE SERVICE

Should you need to be transported by ambulance to a hospital in Dallas there are two things you should know–only the Dallas Fire Department (744-4444) is authorized to perform transfers in emergencies and they will take you to the nearest hospital. For nonemergency service the following companies, operated privately, offer local ground transportation to the hospital of your choice and also can arrange air ambulance service when necessary. They will also transport you to the airport. All firms listed operate 24 hours a day and credit card policy is indicated.

AM CARE, 749-0734
No credit cards.

AMERICAN AIR-LAND, 644-1444
No credit cards.

CARE-FLITE, 826-7200
MC.

HUGHES AMBULANCE SERVICE, 388-0444
AE, MC, V.

PROFESSIONAL AMBULANCE SERVICE, 821-4100
MC, V.

HOSPITALS

There are lots of hospitals in the Dallas area but we have chosen the following because they offer 24-hour emergency care and are within reasonable distance of hotels and office buildings within the same zone. All have coronary care units and ophthalmic services. Many will accept credit cards in payment of emergency room services.

AIRPORT

The Dallas/Fort Worth Airport has a staffed medical clinic open Mon.–Fri. 8 A.M.–6 P.M. and Sat. 8 A.M.–noon. They are equipped to handle minor medical emergencies. Emergency service available around the clock is provided by six paramedics on duty at all times. Emergency cases are transported after on-site care to Hurst, Euless, Bedford Medical Center five miles away by the D/FW ambulance. Both the ambulance and the on-site care are provided at no charge to travelers using the airport. If you need emergency assistance while at the airport, dial 9911 from any free airport phone—there are phones located along hallways in each terminal.

MARKET CENTER

PARKLAND MEMORIAL HOSPITAL, 5201 Harry Hines, 637-8281
Major trauma and burn center. Accepts MasterCard and Visa for emergency care. Will accept personal check with valid driver's license.

ST. PAUL'S HOSPITAL, 5909 Harry Hines, 689-2000
Accepts MasterCard, Visa and American Express as well as personal check with valid driver's license.

DOWNTOWN

BAYLOR UNIVERSITY MEDICAL CENTER, 3500 Gaston (just east of Downtown), 820-0111
A major teaching hospital. Accepts American Express, MasterCard and Visa for emergency treatment.

METHODIST HOSPITAL, 301 W. Colorado, 944-8181
Accepts American Express, MasterCard and Visa in payment.

NORTH CENTRAL

DALLAS OSTEOPATHIC HOSPITAL, 5003 Ross, 824-3071
Also close to Downtown. Will accept MasterCard and Visa.

DOCTORS HOSPITAL, 9440 Poppy Drive (northeast), 324-6100
Accepts American Express, MasterCard and Visa for emergency care payment.

PRESBYTERIAN HOSPITAL, 8200 Walnut Hill (two blocks east of N. Central), 369-4111
Accepts American Express, MasterCard and Visa and personal check with valid driver's license.

LBJ-NORTH

BROOKHAVEN GENERAL HOSPITAL, 12100 Webbs Chapel at LBJ, 247-1701
Accepts American Express, MasterCard and Visa for emergency treatment.

MEDICAL CITY OF DALLAS, 7777 Forest (just south of LBJ), 661-7000
Accepts American Express, MasterCard and Visa.

DENTAL REFERRAL

For emergency dental care, call 637-5700. This number provided by the Dallas County Dental Society, furnishes 24-hour referral service. For nonemergency referrals call the society at 386-5741.

CONTACT LENS REPAIR

BARRETT CONTACT LENS SERVICE, Southland Center (Downtown), 741-4661
Mon.–Fri. 9 A.M.–5:30 P.M. and 24-hour message service. Complete service for hard and soft contact lenses and other eyewear including one-day replacement. Doctor available during store hours. Lab on the premises allowing the fastest service in Dallas. MC, V.

OPTICAL CLINIC
1313 W. Airport Freeway, 258-1216
2877 LBJ, 241-9055
3098 Stemmons (Market Center); 638-1320
All stores open Mon.–Fri. 8:30 A.M.–5:30 P.M.; Sat. 8:30 A.M.–1 P.M. Doctor on staff during store hours and emergency service available for hard contact lenses. MC, V.

SAN FRANCISCO OPTICAL CO., 5521 Greenville (N. Central), 361-6130
Mon.–Fri. 10 A.M.–6 P.M., Sat. 10 A.M.–4 P.M. MC, V.

TEXAS STATE OPTICAL, NorthPark Center (N. Central), 363-7864
Mon.–Sat. 10 A.M.–5:30 P.M. Doctor available during store hours. Emergency repair of eyewear and replacement of soft contact lenses if they have them in stock. All work is sent out but they do keep a good supply of soft lenses.

MEDICAL EQUIPMENT RENTAL

The following companies offer a full line of medical equipment and supplies. If you are a wheelchair traveler or have the misfortune of needing crutches or other medical equipment, the following places will help you.

ABBEY MEDICAL, 3614 Greenville (two blocks east of N. Central), 827-6991
Mon.–Fri. 8:30 A.M.–5 P.M.; Sat. 9 A.M.–4 P.M. 24-hour phone line. Wheelchair repair service and free delivery. MC, V.

HOME CARE MEDICAL EQUIPMENT, 8220 Walnut Hill, 696-2525
Mon.–Fri. 9 A.M.–5 P.M.; Sat. 9 A.M.–1 P.M. 24-hour phone line. Full line of equipment and also oxygen. Free delivery. MC, V.

LINDE HOMECARE, 2780 Irving, 630-3834
Seven days, 24 hours. Free delivery. No credit cards.

PARK PLAZA MEDICAL, INC., 3534 E. Main, 351-0908
Mon.–Fri. 8 A.M.–5 P.M. Oxygen, wheelchairs and a full line of medical equipment. Free delivery. No credit cards.

MISCELLANY

THIS chapter should serve as a handy quick reference of information, telephone numbers and organizations whose advice or services you might need.

TELEPHONE NUMBERS

American Automobile Association	526-7911
Better Business Bureau	747-8891
Chamber of Commerce	651-1020
City Offices (24 hours)	670-3011
Consumer Action Center	670-4014
County Information	749-8011
Emergencies (Fire, Police, Ambulance)	744-4444
Health Department	670-6141
Parking Ticket Information	670-5328
Passports	749-8691
Postal Service (General Information)	767-6727
Salvation Army (Traveler's Aid Services)	742-9131
Secret Service	767-8021
Small Business Administration	767-7614
State Highway Department	321-6421
Transit System (Schedule Information)	826-2222
Visitor Information	747-2355
Weather (Local and Forecast)	993-2626
Weather (Recreation and Travel)	357-4643
Western Union	742-4231
ZIP Code Information	647-2996

BUSINESS AND TRADE ORGANIZATIONS

AFL-CIO Council	742-9246
American Fashion Association	631-0821

American Federation of TV &Radio Artists 522-2080
American Institute of Architects (AIA) 748-4264
American Management Association 661-9611
Dallas Advertising League 559-2960
Dallas Bar Association 745-1227
Dallas Black Chamber of Commerce 941-6613
Dallas Chamber of Commerce 651-1020
Dallas Restaurant Association 521-1495
Hong Kong Trade Commission 748-8162
Japan External Trade Association 651-0839
National Alliance of Business 528-6130
Sales & Marketing Executives of Dallas 747-9675
Texas Society of Certified Public Accountants 750-6406

LEGAL SERVICES

If you need a lawyer in Dallas or just some guidance regarding legal issues, here are some referral services.

Dallas Legal Aid Society 742-7650
Dallas Legal Services Foundation, Inc. 742-1631
Lawyer Referral Service 745-1227
Legal Clinic 692-3562
Legal Services-D.A.'s Office 749-8511

LIBRARIES

Underwood Library at Southern Methodist University (SMU), 692-3216, is open to outsiders but you must sign in and indicate why you are using the library. It is well-equipped and well-staffed.

Central Branch, Dallas Public Library, 1954 Commerce (one block from Dallas Hilton), 748-9071. Mon.–Fri. 9 A.M.–9 P.M.; Sat. 9 A.M.–6 P.M.

MAJOR MEDIA

Dallas Morning News, Young & Houston, 745-8222
Dallas Times Herald, Pacific at Griffin, 744-6111
Wall Street Journal (Southwest Edition), 631-7250

COLLEGES AND UNIVERSITIES

Southern Methodist University (two blocks west of N. Central, north of Mockingbird), 692-2000

North Texas State University (in Denton northwest of Dallas), 267-7481

University of Dallas, 3113 University Drive, Irving, 445-0110

University of Texas
- Arlington Campus, 273-2011
- Dallas Campus, 690-2111

Dallas County Community Colleges, 746-2200
- Brookhaven (LBJ-North), 746-5100
- Cedar Valley (Lancaster), 746-4858
- Eastfield (Mesquite), 746-3100
- El Centro (Downtown), 746-2152
- Mountain View (Southwest Dallas), 746-4100
- Northlake (Irving), 659-5230
- Richland (Northeast Dallas), 746-4494

Dallas Baptist College, 3000 Forina (Southwest Dallas), 331-8311.

Bishop College, 3837 Simpson-Stuart (Southeast Dallas), 372-8000.

U. S. GOVERNMENT LISTINGS

Alcohol Tobacco and Firearms 767-2282

Central Intelligence Agency 741-7340

Commerce Department, Industry and Trade
- Domestic 767-0544
- International and Export 767-0546

Environmental Protection Agency—24-hour emergency 767-2666

Express Mail Information 767-6691

FBI 741-1851

Federal Communications Commission 767-0764

Federal Information Center 767-8585

Food and Drug Administration—Consumer Complaints 767-0312

Passports 749-8691

Small Business Administration 767-0600

U.S. Customs Service
- Aircraft Arrivals 574-2131
- Cargo Clearance 574-2136
- Customs Entry 574-2125
- District Director D/FW Airport 574-2170

FORT WORTH

FORT WORTH, known as the city where the West began, is a business-oriented city that is growing "great guns." It is located west of Dallas in Tarrant County and has a population of 400,000. While it is often spoken of as if it were a twin city to Dallas, Fort Worth is 40 miles west of Dallas (connected to it by Route 30, the Dallas–Ft. Worth Turnpike) and is very different and much smaller.

As the last major rest stop along the Chisholm Trail, the stockyards were the hub of activity for cattlemen from all over the West in the early 1800's. When the railroads came, so did the packing companies, and in 1853 the business of cattle processing began. By 1902, two companies–Swift and Armour–were perched in statuesque buildings overlooking the stockyards. In 1917 over 1.6 million cattle were processed.

Today a spaghetti restaurant occupies the old Swift headquarters and weeds grow over the tiled streets in front of the Armour Company. As the packing plants followed the cattle out to the range, the thriving Cowtown began a steady decline.

The stockyards are the main tourist attraction now in Fort Worth. Cowtown Rodeo, the world's first indoor rodeo, started in 1917 and, attracts crowds now in spring and fall. The rows of storefronts, scenes of Western history and the empty cattle pens are relics of a thriving past.

But Fort Worth is moving forward, and downtown Main Street and vicinity is getting a face lift that will make it much more attractive to business travelers. Sixteen turn-of-the-century buildings are being restored and a sleek skyscraper will tower above them. The Convention Center, Tandy Center and others are now the central buildings downtown and scene of many meetings and conventions. The city is smaller and unlike Dallas, downtown you can easily walk to and from business appointments, your hotel and many fine restaurants.

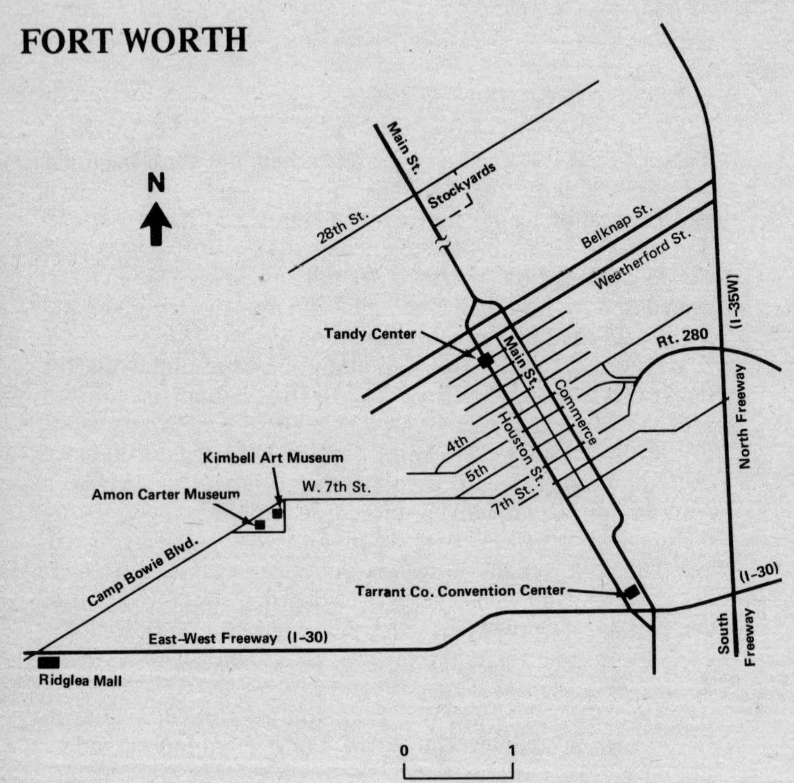
FORT WORTH
N
Main St.
Stockyards
28th St.
Belknap St.
Weatherford St.
(I-35W)
Tandy Center
Rt. 280
Main St.
Commerce
North Freeway
Houston St.
4th
5th
7th St.
Kimbell Art Museum
W. 7th St.
Amon Carter Museum
Camp Bowie Blvd.
Tarrant Co. Convention Center
(I-30)
East-West Freeway (I-30)
South Freeway
Ridglea Mall
0
1
Miles

Many of the restaurants we have reviewed are close to downtown hotels. Others are on Camp Bowie Boulevard, right off Route 30, a few minutes drive west of downtown, and the hub of nightlife in Fort Worth. All the services we list for Fort Worth are in the downtown area, which includes the new Tandy Center complex. Most other services and shops you might need are located in the Ridgelea Mall, only 5–10 minutes west of downtown.

Our entertainment section here is small, and for major sports events you will have to drive to Dallas. The same is true of shopping, outside the two areas we have mentioned above. Unlike Dallas, Fort Worth has wonderful art museums and you will see them listed in this section. You will also find a small section for emergency and miscellaneous information.

The *Fort Worth Star-Telegram* is the major daily newspaper and visitor information is available through the Fort Worth Convention and Visitors Bureau, 336-2491. The area code for Fort Worth is (817) but all phone numbers listed are local numbers. It is a long distance call from Dallas to Fort Worth.

HOTELS

You will want to review all our information about ratings and prices in the Dallas hotel introduction before making your choice of hotel.

★★★★ **AMERICANA HOTEL/TANDY CENTER**
$$$$ **200 Main Street**
(817) 870-1000; (800) 228-3278;
Telex 910 8935 089
All major credit cards

This new hotel is a study in understated elegance. From the sleek white exterior to the black gloss on the grand piano in the charming Van Cliburn suite, the designs are modern, sophisticated. The lobby is vast, accentuated by tall white pillars. A large bank of elevators is tucked under the staircase out of view of the front desk, but is adequately lit. The front desk is impeccable, no keys or mail anywhere; four crystal vases of fresh lilies provide the only distraction. Water cascades down from the next level along with soft piano music. The staff dresses in black tuxedo-like attire. Thick white marble walls create a formal feeling and can be a little intimidating, yet the service and attention by the friendly staff will take care of this. Check-in is efficient and your baggage will be carried from the front door to your room by one of the bellmen stationed at the carriage entrance.

The hotel is located in the heart of the city's historic district and there is a renovation project in progress. The project, known as Sundance Square, will occupy the 300 block of Main Street and include unique shops and galleries. Tandy Center, across the street connected by a skywalk, contains many retail stores as well as business services. The Americana has excellent meeting facilities including a grand ballroom with a private driveway and lobby.

Accommodations

Hallways are long and wide and elevators are well-lighted and have bells designed to aid the blind. The hotel has 510 rooms. All rooms are large and have the same decor—a lovely, low-key contemporary use of color and furniture, with beige carpet, white walls, museum posters on the walls, red or blue chairs and beige print bedspreads and window drapes. Each room has a butcher block table, dresser/vanity and an open closet and dressing area with full-length mirror. All rooms have either two double beds or one king, color TV with remote control, AM/FM radio and extra bathroom amenities such as shampoo, bath oil and extra towels.

All suites have either a terrace or balcony, some have a study. Every suite has a living room with wet bar, large bath with double sinks and mirrors, scale, bidet, bathrobe and TV. The hotel has two duplex suites, the most elaborate the Van Cliburn Suite (he stayed here during the famous competition and there is still a grand piano in here).

Personal Services

Full 24-hour room service and cashier are available. Same-day laundry and dry cleaning during the week. Baby-sitters and a doctor are on call. The Spa with outdoor tennis, weight room, Jacuzzi and a sundeck is available at no charge. The lobby newsstand is open seven days from 7 A.M. until 10 P.M., and there are a barber and a beauty shop in Tandy Center. There is a fulltime concierge to help with airlines reservations, theater and dinner arrangements and tours. The hotel maintains several cars on the premises for guests' rental.

Business Services

The meeting facilities are excellent at the Americana. The American Ballroom can accommodate up to 1,850 people for a reception. The walls are covered in soft gray suede in swirled patterns. There is another ballroom below which can accommodate about 900. Small conference rooms are nearby for breakout meetings. There is also a boardroom with dark paneling, high leather chairs and a long wooden conference table. A private valet service can be arranged for functions. There is also a patio for outdoor affairs. The catering department includes a kosher kitchen. Audiovisual and business machines are available for rental and a Telex machine is available Mon.–Fri. 7 A.M.–5 P.M.

Eating and Drinking

The hotel has three bars and two restaurants. The Brasserie La Salle stays open 24 hours. Reflections serves excellent French cuisine in an elegant setting for lunch and dinner Mon.–Sat. The nightclub, Ricochet, features live entertainment from 5 P.M. until 2 A.M. A lobby bar opens around 11 A.M. and stays open until 2 A.M. seven days. The Bridge Lounge features a seafood buffet on Fridays, and Sunday brunch from noon until 3.

★★★ FORT WORTH HILTON INN
$$ 1701 Commerce Street
(817) 335-7000
All major credit cards

Located conveniently right off Route 30, this fine hotel has recently gone through major renovation and the addition of an eight-story tower. The hotel is surrounded by warehouses but is across the street from Monnig's department store and is only a few short blocks from the Tarrant County Convention Center. The lobby has several seating areas with attractive plants and novel lighting fixtures. There is a lovely circular staircase leading from the lobby to the second floor meeting areas. An escalator and several elevators make ascending to the upper levels easy. The front desk is large and well-staffed and there are numerous bellmen available at the drive-up entrance. Safe-deposit boxes are available and a cashier is on duty from 8:30 A.M. to 5:00 P.M. daily. There are no chains on the doors but each has a peephole and a heavy-duty double lock against the passkey. There is 24-hour security.

Accommodations

Including the new tower the hotel has 450 rooms with 26 suites (at least one located on each floor). In the original tower the hallways are very bright with white and green predominating. The new tower is done in mauve and plum and has an elegant feeling. Rooms in the new tower seem slightly larger but all rooms are attractively wallpapered, have a desk, separate table with two side chairs, and AM/FM radio, color TV and an alarm clock. The baths and closet areas are the only shortcomings here—even suites have only single sinks and open hanging racks for clothes instead of closets. All bathrooms have tubs with showers and electrical outlets. Skirt hangers are supplied. There is one barrier-free room for handicapped guests. Suites have refrigerators and comfortable sofas. The 12th floor executive area, accessible only by key-operated elevator, offers separate concierge service and extra amenities such as better quality linens, bathrobes, newspapers and special soaps.

Personal Services

One nice touch is complimentary coffee and newspaper provided in the lobby Mon.–Sat. 7 A.M.–9 A.M. Room service is available seven days 7 A.M.–11 P.M. with $1 minimum charge. The hotel personnel are very gracious, including Daisy who has prided herself for years on keeping the rooms in perfect shape for "her guests." There is same-day laundry and dry cleaning available Mon.–Fri. if in by 8:30 A.M. Cribs and babysitters are available. Small pets are permitted and doctors and dentists are on call.

There is a National Car Rental referral phone in the lobby and a barber shop is open Mon.–Sat. 9 A.M.–5 P.M. The Non-Apothecary Shoppe sells liquor, drug products, newspapers including *The New York Times* and sundries seven days 7 A.M.–11 P.M. There is an indoor pool.

Business Services

With a large and a small ballroom, 10 large and 8 small meetings rooms this is a fine hotel to hold a meeting. There is a catering department and all types of audiovisual equipment is available. A notary public is on the premises and a photocopy machine is available for guest use during business hours. Secretarial services can be arranged.

Eating and Drinking

There are several bar areas in the hotel including the Way Station lobby bar overlooking the indoor pool and open seven days 1–8 P.M. The Waterworks Night Club with live entertainment is open Mon.–Sat. 11 A.M.–2 A.M.

The Greenery Cafe is open seven days 7 A.M.–11 P.M. and offers full menu service in an atrium-type atmosphere. For more gracious evening dining Mon.–Sat. try the Fountain Square which also serves Sunday brunch from 11:30 A.M.–2:30 P.M.

★★★★ HYATT REGENCY

$$$ 815 Main Street
(817) 870-1234; (800) 228-9000; Telex 794-826
All major credit cards

The Hyatt Regency is located in what used to be the old Hotel Texas. With its huge brick walls and white frame windows, it belongs more on the campus of some Ivy League school than in downtown Fort Worth. The entrance is grand with valets and bellmen everywhere. In the lobby, a registration desk is amply staffed. Keys and mail are hidden from view. Escalators lead to the mezzanine and atrium dominated by the bright shades of maroon, green and yellow in the modern Indian rug. High on a pedestal, a pianist fills the lobby with music.

The hotel is located across the parking lot from the Convention Center at the foot of Main Street. When the downtown restoration is completed, it will be a very fashionable address.

Accommodations

There are 530 rooms and 40 suites in the hotel. Rooms all have color TV with home box office, AM/FM radio and alarm clock. Furnishings are attractive in the standard rooms: light brown carpet, navy blue and red upholstery and one double or two single beds. There is a large desk and comfortable chair suitable for work. Deluxe rooms also have a couch. Bathrooms are large as in most Hyatt hotels, with an assortment of free toiletries. Closet areas are outside the bathroom and they do not have skirt hangers or full-length mirrors. All rooms have chains and double lock against passkey.

A typical suite has two bedrooms and a parlor with two bathrooms. Each bedroom has either two double beds or a king bed, an armchair and a coffee table. The parlor has a couch, desk with chair and lamp, and conference table for 6 to 10 people. Some suites have a wet bar. The couch in the parlor converts to a bed for extra sleeping space.

The Regency Club (floors 14 and 15) offers some extra amenities as well as a choice of room decor ranging from modern to antique. The center of activity for the club is its parlor on the 14th floor, an elegant area of dark green velvet couches, brass rails and antique tables and chairs. Complimentary breakfast around a sterling silver service and the honor bar in the evening, as well as separate check-in and check-out and the services of a very attentive concierge, are just a few of the amenities provided, and we think the additional cost is reasonable.

Personal Services

Room service is from 6:30 A.M. to 11:30 P.M. seven days. Same-day laundry and dry cleaning is available during the week. There is a doctor on call and babysitters, cribs and rollaways can be arranged. Safe-deposit boxes are available and the cashier stays open 24 hours. Foreign currency cannot be exchanged in the hotel. There is a car-rental agency and an airline office in the lobby, open weekdays from 9 A.M.–5 P.M. The hotel has no barber or beauty salon. Surtran buses to the airport leave every half hour seven days from 7 A.M.–10 P.M. A newsstand, which sells drugstore items, is open from 7 A.M. to 11 P.M. seven days.

Business Services

Eighteen meeting rooms accommodate from 12 to 1,300 people. The Grand Crystal Ballroom, the city's largest, is beautiful with large pink and blue diamonds on a rust carpet. The white ceiling is covered with dangling crystal slivers. Walls have a brass ballet bar and panels of rust suede in various tones lined with mirrors. There is a spacious pre-function area and four doorways. The catering department can handle any function. There is an audiovisual company on premises. Fifteen smaller meeting rooms on the third floor are equipped with conference tables, telephone, podium and blackboard. The Pavillion Exhibit Hall at the garage level can hold up to 250 display booths. The hotel can arrange secretarial services, and has a photocopy machine available 24 hours for a charge.

Eating and Drinking

The Cafe Centennial, the lobby coffee shop, serves from 6:30 A.M. to 11:30 P.M. The Crystal Cactus offers continental cuisine from 11 A.M. until 11 P.M. The hotel has three bars: the Skylight Court, above the lobby, serves drinks from 4–11 P.M., the Grotto Bar stays open from 11 A.M.–11 P.M. and the Crystal Cactus bar is open until 2 A.M. There is a spectacular Sunday brunch in the lobby from 11 A.M. until 3 P.M.

★ METRO CENTER HOTEL (Best Western)

$ 600 Commerce Street
(817) 332-6900; (800) 528-1234
All major credit cards

Located in the center of downtown Fort Worth, this hotel is convenient but lacks the class of a true center-city hotel. Its chief attraction is its closeness to the Tandy Center and the Convention Center as well as to the central business and shopping district. There is 24-hour security, and fire and safety information, including location of nearest exits, is provided in each room. There are several desk attendants but the lobby is merely a tiled entry foyer with small seating area.

Accommodations

There are 300 rooms and 12 suites in the Metro Center. Standard rooms have leatherette walls in beige and are adequate but not spacious. Bureau space in rooms is very sparse. Each room has a color TV, and metal hanging racks for clothes instead of closets. Bathrooms have single sinks and tub/showers and an electrical outlet next to the sink. There is no separate dressing area. Suites are actually two separate rooms without a common door, so you must go out into the hallway to get from living room to bedroom. The sitting room is comfortable with two sofas, coffee table, a desk with chair and a separate powder room. Hallways throughout are well lighted.

Personal Services

Room service is available seven days 6:30 A.M.–10:30 P.M. and same-day laundry and dry cleaning (in by 9 A.M. out by 3 P.M.) is available Mon.–Fri. A van is available to take you to Hertz and Budget car-rental agencies. The hotel offers free indoor parking. YeTeHay gift shop in the lobby is open seven days 8 A.M.–7 P.M. and sells liquor, sundries and snacks. Surtran service is available from the lobby. The most exciting part of this hotel is its Sundome, a 7000 sq. ft. covered area that includes a Jacuzzi, saunas, exercise room and electronic game room all surrounding a circular bar which is attractively decorated in yellow and green with gauze canopies.

Business Services

There are two large and three small meeting rooms available to handle 10 to 300 people and there is a catering department on the first floor right off the lobby. There is a meeting planner on staff but facilities are merely adequate. There are no business or audiovisual machines available.

Eating and Drinking

The Sundancer Restaurant is open from 6:30 A.M.–10:30 P.M. and has a fulltime pastry chef. The Sundancer Lounge has live entertainment and is open Mon.–Fri. 4 P.M.–2 A.M. and Sat. & Sun. 5 P.M.–1 A.M.

GETTING AROUND TOWN

As we said in our introduction to Fort Worth, you can walk anywhere downtown and this is really the easiest way to get around. To get to restaurants out on Camp Bowie Boulevard or any of the areas near Route 30 such as Ridgelea Mall, you will need a car or taxi.

As in Dallas, taxis do not really float, but you will find them waiting at most hotels and restaurants. If you are on Camp Bowie Boulevard, you may be lucky and be able to grab a taxi delivering new customers to the restaurant or club you are leaving. If not, you will have to call for a taxi to return to your hotel, but here, as in Dallas, there is no extra charge for this.

Walking around downtown Fort Worth at night is as safe as in any other major city, which for women means that you will probably be more comfortable in a taxi if you are alone. In the hotel area, there is quite a bit of traffic at all times, which makes it a pleasant area in which to walk. Stick with the crowds near Billy Bob's Texas at the end of Commerce Street; this is a big redevelopment area and there are many deserted buildings and lots.

Here is our list of car-rental agencies in Fort Worth:

AVIS, Hyatt Hotel Annex, 335-3211, (800) 331-1212

BUDGET, 2001 N. Forest Park, 334-0026, (800) 228-9650

HERTZ, 3017 W. 7th, 332-1864, (800) 654-3131

NATIONAL, 615 Commerce, 335-1030, (800) 328-4567

RESTAURANTS

You'll find the dining scene in Fort Worth enjoyable for several reasons. First, the variety of cuisine offered at the numerous restaurants ranges from Texas traditional (barbecued ribs) to four-star French. Next, most proprietors cater to the business traveler by providing friendly service, spacious seating and attractive surroundings. Finally, the convenience of dining in a hotel restaurant does not have to be a trade-off in the quality of food or service. The newer downtown hotels have excellent restaurants.

While you pay for what you get in every city, you seem to get a little more for a little less in Fort Worth. In general, entrees average between $1 and $2 cheaper than in Dallas.

★ **ANGELO'S**
$ **2533 White Settlement Road, 332-0357**
Closed Sunday
No credit cards

A trip to Fort Worth would not be complete or well-remembered without a visit to Angelo's for barbecue. The atmosphere is about as informal as you can get and three-piece suits are as prevalent as Harley-Davidson T-shirts in this famous smokehouse. The decor is bare but has its own charm. A stuffed bear greets you in the entrance.

Service is minimal. Grab a tray, get in line and select sliced brisket, ribs, hot links or a combination plate from the friendly chef's carving board. Choose a mild or extra hot sauce and a few side dishes, coleslaw, potato salad, beans (all marvelous) and maybe pick up a gigantic frosted mug of beer before moving to a table.

Part of the ambience at Angelo's is the people. Local politicians, cowboys, cheerleaders, celebrities, gather in the two dining rooms to enjoy the juicy, flavorful meat in large quantities. You may have to wait in line if you show up after noon for lunch but it is worth it.

★★ **THE BALCONY**
$$$ **6100 Camp Bowie Boulevard, 731-3719**
Closed Sunday
All major credit cards

Stale bread does not a good first impression make. But first impressions are often wrong as a recent trip to this revered restaurant proved. Mounting the stairs from the men's boutique below, we found the place in the midst of renovation with newly set tiles lining the entryway and sawdust, workbenches and blueprints everywhere. Inside, the food was exemplary and the soft sounds from the baby grand piano sounded fine.

Seating out on the balcony, away from the two main dining rooms, is more intimate. Service seems more attentive out here too, but service in the entire restaurant is generally slow. Don't expect to rush in and out—this is not that kind of a place. Overlook the basket of stale bread slices on the table, there are better things to come.

We began with soup, a hearty northern bean flavored with Canadian bacon and garlic and a hearts of palm salad. The house dressing is an unusual blend of oils covering pieces of cucumber, tomatoes and peppers from Texas plants. A hint of vinegar makes this dressing light and delicious. For entrees, we suggest the pepper steak or the tournedos of beef Lady Curzon, sautéed in sweet butter, and served with morels and wild rice and sauced with béarnaise dressing. Both dishes are accompanied by side dishes of broccoli au gratin and white asparagus (which comes from a can but tastes wonderful anyway). Fresh rolls are offered continually throughout the meal.

Bananas Foster was executed to perfection with a flourish we had not seen in a while. Four waiters assisted in the preparation of the dark sugar delight. We watched the addition of almond slivers, brandies, cinnamon with the interest of a child and the appetite of a gourmet. Both were satisfied.

★ CARRIAGE HOUSE

$$$ 5136 Camp Bowie Boulevard, 732-2873
Open seven days; brunch only on Sunday
All major credit cards

Three separate rooms comprise the dining areas at the Carriage House. We like the main dining room with all the intimate trimmings toned down for business yet perfect for the woman dining alone.

Liberty of London prints in green and brown on the walls, red plaid carpets, hunting scenes, muted glass on the low ceilings—the feeling is relaxed and comfortable. Service is friendly and attentive and the presence of regulars adds to the homey atmosphere. The next room is rustic with dark walls and red tablecloths, and is decorated with portraits of the owner's family. In the bar area, there's Monday night football and a casual decor.

You might want to start with a truly Western offering—calf fries, or mountain oysters, are bull's testicles. Cowboys eat them because they think they contribute to virility. They taste a little like liver. Or choose a baked brie, soft French cheese baked with almonds. For steaks and chops, the Carriage House is fine (an entree of lamb chops turned up pink in the middle, as requested, and char-broiled quickly on both sides of the thick cuts) but it fails when it comes to seafood and sauced dishes. Vegetable side dishes are limited to common, everyday choices. Crabmeat Lorenzo had everything the menu said, cream, lemon, wine, broccoli, but the small portion of crab was disappointing, and a veal dish was overcooked and overpowered by a bad sauce.

Cheesecake is not particularly fresh and none of the other desserts are homemade either. We opted for two espresso drinks with exotic Italian liqueurs and sharing a slice of cappuccino ice cream pie—a mellowing close to the evening. Passing through the bar on the way to the restrooms, we found a wall covered with eight tastefully painted portraits of nude women. An added dimension to this house.

★★ CRYSTAL CACTUS

$$$$ 815 Main Street (Hyatt Regency Hotel), 870-1234
Dinner seven days, lunch weekdays
All major credit cards

For a hotel restaurant, the Crystal Cactus offers a fine selection of steaks, veal and seafood in an elegant setting. Large etched-glass panels divide the dining room into smaller sections and tables are well-spaced for privacy. The walls are covered in dark green upholstery and touches of brass here and there create a relaxed, mellow feeling. Except when there is a convention in the hotel, at which time the noise level necessitates shouting, this restaurant offers polished, attentive service.

Appetizers range from lobster salad, expensive and

worth trying at least for the fine tarragon dressing, to onion broth with cheese and jalapenos. A charming interruption to the meal is the miniscoop of cactus-pear sherbet served in a cone between courses. In addition, piping-hot rounds of French bread are hollowed out and stuffed with roasted potato and served throughout the meal.

Two favorites from the limited entree menu are veal scallopini, served with spinach fettucini, and the sirloin steak. On our last visit, we tried the salmon which turned up dry and bland helped some by an herb butter dressing.

The desserts are not the most original and are limited to four choices all based on ice or whipped cream. The apple nut torte is fresh and comes with a bowl of Grand Marnier whipped cream. Pass on the others and opt for the huge cups of strong coffee or tea.

★ **EL RANCHO GRANDE**
$ **1400 North Main Street, 624-9206**
Closed Sunday
Most major credit cards

Next door, a one-story building with a non-descript brick facade and a neon sign is locked. This is the old El Rancho Grande. The two-story successor is inlaid with handpainted tiles and looks like a fashionable hacienda in Mexico. This is the new El Rancho Grande, a testament to the increasing popularity of the food.

The cantina has dark wood floors, stucco walls, high-beamed ceilings and a brick wall covered with ponchos. Long shutters, chairs covered in animal hide and an ornately carved bar form a pleasant backdrop for sipping margaritas before dining.

The dining room has terra-cotta tile floors and women flit about carrying steaming trays of tacos. The tables are close together and often pushed together to accommodate families with children. The emphasis is on good food, not privacy. Better to have a quiet discussion in the cantina beforehand.

The tacos al carbon are excellent. Another excellent entree is La Gran Fiesta, a sampling of enchiladas, flautas, rice and guacamole. We guarantee you will not be interested in dessert. Just as well since they are ordinary.

★ **HEDARY'S**
$ **3308 Fairfield (at Camp Bowie), 731-6961**
Dinner only; closed Monday
Most major credit cards

For something different, Hedary's offers some of the best Lebanese cooking we've ever had (even in the homes of our Arab friends). The small, family-run restaurant is located in the middle of a suburban shopping center next to a second-hand bookstore, and you'll see students absorbed in Hemingway while savoring grapeleaves, as well as eight-year-olds waiting tables. It's all part of the show and adds to the enjoyment of the wonderful cuisine.

Everyone in the family does something from baking pita bread at the ovens to crushing walnuts for baklava. Tables are well-spaced and the soft Eastern music does not obstruct conversation. In fact, the room is quiet. This is a very casual place as reflected in the functional, not fancy, decor.

We ordered the maza to start. Our tiny table was covered with dishes of tabbuli, hummus, cucumber in yogurt and much more. We dipped hot bread into the spicy salads to our hearts' content, alternating with the delicious dry yogurt. For dinner, we ordered the kafta, ground beef rolled into log shapes and baked, and raw kibbi, a garlicky steak tartare. Both were satisfying. One small gripe is the tendency to run out of baklava.

★★ **JOE T. GARCIA'S**
$ **2201 North Commerce Street, 626-4356**
Open seven days
No credit cards or personal checks

From the outside, there seems to be one small wall supporting a slanting frame house. But inside, up to 850 people can be accommodated. The fiesta garden is one of the loveliest spots in town with a thriving greenhouse, blue-tiled pool and strolling guitarist.

Lunch and dinner are fixed price. Courses include tostadas, meat tacos, side dishes of guacamole and beans, rice, delicious cheese enchiladas—all fresh from the kitchen (sometimes you have to walk through it to get to the dining room, a real treat). The decor is simple and interesting to observe. A large brick oven, used to smoke cabrito once a year, adds a charming touch. This is a locals' establishment but tourists invariably find their way here.

A visit is strongly recommended. Our only caveat: don't expect much privacy at peak hours.

★★★★ L'OUSTAU
$$$$ 300 Main Street, 332-8900
Closed Sunday
All major credit cards

This lovely French restaurant has been open only a few months. Located in a renovated section known as Sundance Square, there are two enclosed patios as well as an elegant dining room in a turn-of-the-century building.

The decor is decidedly feminine. Pale shades of pink and green are picked up everywhere—on the floral, high-backed chairs, in the tapestry carpeting, on the dust ruffle above the bar, even down to the Limoges china. Impressionist paintings in gold frames line the walls and a small deer's head hangs above the fireplace. Large French windows look out to a courtyard. Tables are spaced wide apart and soft classical music is piped into the room.

Service is flawless at L'Oustau; our waiter timed the delivery of courses perfectly, allowing time for conversation.

We started with coquilles St. Jacques and watercress soup. A tray of tiny puffed cheese pastries was offered with the appetizers. The champagne sorbet cleared our palate but nearly made us drunk. The veal medallion was tender, served with a light watercress sauce. Fillet of sole was tasty, covered with bits of delicious mussels and shrimp. Both entrees came with a puree of peas and a dollop of carrots—pretty but tasteless.

Don't leave without sampling something from the dessert cart. We liked the orange salad with raspberry and Grand Marnier sauce. When people can't make up their minds, the waiter will cut small pieces to try. Desserts are so popular, the restaurant serves pastries and tea for a few hours in the afternoon.

★★★ **THE OLD SWISS HOUSE**
$$$ **5412 Camp Bowie Boulevard, 738-8091**
Closed Sunday
Most major credit cards

Remembering names is one thing, but when the maitre d' remembers how much you enjoyed the veal on your last visit, (which was six weeks ago) that's something else. Things tend to be unchanging in this well-established, well-patronized restaurant. Only the flowers change daily.

In the main dining room (there are three) a team of waiters serve and engage in pointed conversation with the clientele. There is no music or entertainment for the simple reason that, for years, this has been known as a quiet place to enjoy excellent food and private conversation. The tradition continues, we discovered.

Tables are not close together. Courses are not far apart. There is a balance of rich sauces and grilled meats on the menu. The cold cucumber soup is perfect in the Texas summer heat, and the restaurant's version of fondue Suisse, slices of cheese crepes lightly breaded and fried is tasty. Our entrees of veal émincé, steamed in burgundy wine and served over spaetzel, and shrimp scampi were served with sliced new potatoes in their red skins and asparagus. A salad of Boston lettuce with an extraordinary vinaigrette dressing precedes this course.

The choice of desserts is very comprehensive ranging from flaming cherries to a single scoop of ice cream in a chocolate gravy. We chose champagne and strawberries. This request arrived at our table displayed on fine china and included small containers of powered sugar and orange liqueur. We dipped the plump strawberries into the condiments with pleasure since they were sweet and flavorful.

★★★★ **REFLECTIONS**
$$$$ **200 Main Street (Americana Hotel), 870-1000**
Dinner seven days, lunch weekdays
All major credit cards

Under the management of Jean Claude Prevot of Dallas, the restaurant enjoys the reputation of serving excellent cuisine. Service is always impeccable with two waiters for every table.

The decor is darkly elegant dominated by dark-navy-blue walls and three columns with artichoke-shaped caps letting off light. The tables are beautifully appointed in linen, china and crystal as well as silver. Although the room is not large, a unique arrangement of tables and booths puts a good distance between diners.

Be prepared to pay the price for this culinary pleasure. It's expensive and worth it. An appetizer of seafood came laced with cream sauce and containing tiny slivers of crab, scallops and shrimp. A champagne *sorbet* followed.

We liked the grenadins de veau, a visually delightful serving of tender veal slices in a delicate tarragon cream sauce. A puree of carrots was served as a side dish and we particularly liked the preparation—buttered, broiled, then sprinkled with caramel. A crisp breast of duckling with wild mushrooms and green peppercorn sauce was superb. Salads of watercress and several other types of lettuce were served next in a tangy oil and lemon dressing. A nice touch was the wedge of Camembert accompanying this course.

The dessert menu is imaginative offering a chance to satisfy any lingering appetites. We suggest the kiwi soufflé if you want something different. Its airy flavor is wonderful. If you are not worried about calories, indulge in the dark and white chocolate mousse topped with a thin raspberry sauce.

BUSINESS SERVICES

AUDIOVISUAL EQUIPMENT RENTAL

SIBONEY AUDIOVISUAL PRODUCTS,
3000 Montgomery, 731-8428
Mon.–Fri. 8 A.M.–5 P.M. Free delivery. Payment in advance. No credit cards. Company billing arranged.

TEXAS AUDIOVISUALS, 613 North Freeway, 332-5102
Mon.–Fri. 8:30 A.M.–5 P.M. Free delivery. Payment in advance. No credit cards.

CATERERS

CARRIAGE HOUSE CATERING, 5113 Pershing, 731-6181
Minimum 20 people. Chips and dip to gourmet meals. No credit cards. Company billing.

COLONIAL CATERING, 1700 Rogers, 335-9372
Private parties arranged. Company billing.

CONVENTION DISPLAYS (Trade Show Exhibits)

CHARLIE MANN DISPLAYS, INC., 2724 Tillar, 332-1561
Mon.–Fri. 8 A.M.–4:30 P.M. Company billing arranged.

HOLLAND DISPLAY CO., 2213 Delante, 831-0926
Mon.–Fri. 8:30 A.M.–5 P.M. Company billing arranged.

COPYING AND OFFSET PRINTING

JD'S KWIK PRINTING, 246 W. 15th St., 336-5181
Mon.–Fri. 8 A.M.–4:30 P.M. No credit cards. Company billing.

QUICK PRINT, 600 Houston, 336-2553
Mon.–Fri. 8 A.M.–5 P.M., Sat. 9 A.M.–1 P.M. No credit cards.

PRINTING CENTER, 701 E. 4th St., 335-9441
Mon.–Fri. 8 A.M.–4:30 P.M. No credit cards. Company billing. Delivery with minimum.

OFFICE SUPPLIES

ABC OFFICE SUPPLY, 3236 W. 7th St., 332-2155
Mon.–Fri. 8 A.M.–5 P.M., Sat. 9 A.M.–1 P.M. MC, V.

HOGAN'S OFFICE SUPPLY CO., 901 Houston, 332-1336
Mon.–Fri. 8 A.M.–5 P.M. No credit cards.

PANTHER CITY OFFICE SUPPLY Co., 3001 W. 7th St., 335-1221
Mon.–Fri. 8 A.M.–4:30 P.M. No credit cards.

TEMPORARY HELP

NORRELL TEMPORARY SERVICES INC., 2 Tandy Center, 870-1999
Mon.–Fri. 8 A.M.–5 P.M. 24-hour answering service. Secretarial, transcription, general office work, accounting, convention personnel. No credit cards. Company billing.

TEMPORARIES INC., 1 Tandy Center, 335-8588
Mon.–Fri. 8 A.M.–5 P.M., 24-hour answering service. General office, secretarial, data entry, convention personnel. No credit cards. Company billing.

TYPEWRITER AND OFFICE EQUIPMENT RENTAL

REMCO, 1917 West Freeway, 335-9588
Mon.–Fri. 8 A.M.–5 P.M. Typewriters, calculators, etc., by the month only. Free delivery. Payment in advance. No credit cards.

ROYAL OFFICE EQUIPMENT, 2517 8th Ave., 921-3631
Mon.–Fri. 8 A.M.–5 P.M., Sat. 9 A.M.–noon. Typewriters, calculators, etc. One-week minimum. Free delivery. Payment in advance. No credit cards.

XEROX REPRODUCTION CENTER, 416 Taylor, 338-0373
Mon.–Fri. 8:30 A.M.–5 P.M. Copiers, duplicating machines, telecopiers. Minimum 3-day rental. Free delivery. Payment in advance. No credit cards.

BANKING SERVICES

BANK OF COMMERCE, Throckmorton and 7th St., 332-3261
Mon.–Thurs. 9A.M.–2 P.M., Fri. 9 A.M.–2 P.M. & 4–6 P.M. Cash advance on MC, V.

CONTINENTAL NATIONAL BANK, 714 Houston (at 7th St.), 334-9000
Mon.–Thurs. 9 A.M.–4 P.M., Fri. 9 A.M.–6 P.M. Foreign currency exchanged. Cash advance on MC, V.

FIRST NATIONAL BANK OF FORT WORTH, Burnett Plaza, 390-6161
Mon.–Thurs. 9 A.M.–2 P.M., Fri. 9 A.M.–2 P.M. & 4–6 P.M. Cash advance on MC, V. Foreign currency exchanged.

FORT WORTH NATIONAL BANK, 500 Throckmorton, 338-8011
Mon.–Thurs. 9 A.M.–2 P.M., Fri. 9 A.M.–2 P.M. & 4–6 P.M. Foreign currency exchanged. Cash advance on MC, V.

AMERICAN EXPRESS CHECK MACHINE

AMERICAN EXPRESS, 1702 Green Oaks (Ridgemar Mall, west of downtown), 738-5441
Mon.– Sat. 10 A.M.–6 P.M.

DELIVERY AND POSTAL SERVICES

We are listing only local delivery services. For long-distance service refer to the listings in the Dallas delivery section.

LOCAL DELIVERY SERVICES

QUICK WAY COURIER, 1105 E. Vickery Blvd., 338-0631
Mon.–Fri. 8:30 A.M.–4:30 P.M. No credit cards.

RAPID DELIVERY, 3600 E. Orchard, 429-7243
Mon.–Fri. 8 A.M.–5 P.M. No credit cards.

WORTHINGTON DELIVERY, 220 W. Daggett, 336-3784
Mon.–Fri. 8 A.M.–5 P.M. No credit cards.

NATIONAL & INTERNATIONAL DELIVERY SERVICES

EMERY AIR FREIGHT, 574-6300
Open seven days, 6 A.M.–1 A.M. No credit cards.

FEDERAL EXPRESS, 332-6293
Mon.–Fri. 8:30 A.M.–7:30 P.M., Sat. 8:30 A.M.–1 P.M. All major credit cards.

POSTAL SERVICES

FORT WORTH MAIN POST OFFICE, 251 W. Lancaster, 334-2920
Open Mon.–Fri. 8:30 A.M.–5 P.M. Express mail information, 334-2035.

PERSONAL SERVICES

Our personal services section is limited, as are services in downtown Fort Worth (don't expect to find a newsstand with out-of-town papers here). We have chosen places close to hotels and know that with the rapid redevelopment of the downtown area, we will be adding many more to future editions.

CLEANERS

CLASSIC CLEANING CENTER, 1134 East Seminary (south of downtown), 927-5141
Open 7 days, 8 A.M.–8 P.M. A bit away from downtown, but absolutely the best hours of operation in the area. Specializes in suedes and leathers and also does alterations.

STACY LAUNDRY AND CLEANERS, 508 Commerce, 332-0186
Mon.–Fri. 7 A.M.–6 P.M., Sat. 9 A.M.–2 P.M. One-hour dry cleaning service. No credit cards.

DRUGSTORES AND PHARMACIES

HALL'S PHARMACY, 1008 Pennsylvania, 336-7281
Mon.–Fri. 8:30 A.M.–6 P.M., Sat. 8:30 A.M.–2 P.M. Citywide delivery. 24-hour emergency prescription service. MC, V.

REVCO, 504 W. Rosedale, 336-9779
Mon.–Sat. 9 A.M.–9 P.M., Sun. 10 A.M.–6 P.M. Open holidays. AE, MC, V.

WEAVER PHARMACY, 661 5th Ave., 332-9193
Mon.–Fri. 8 A.M.–8 P.M., Sat. 8 A.M.–6 P.M., Sun. 1–6 P.M. Delivery service. MC, V.

FLORISTS

ADERHOLT'S FLOWERS, 2805 8th Ave., 924-7987
Mon.–Fri. 8 A.M.–5 P.M., Sat. 8 A.M.–1 P.M. Most major credit cards.

FLOWERS FROM MARGARET, 912 Houston, 332-7507
Mon.–Sat. 8:30 A.M.–5 P.M. All major credit cards.

FLOWERS ON THE SQUARE, 311 Main, 870-2888
Mon.–Fri. 9 A.M.–6 P.M., Sat. 10 A.M.–3 P.M. AE, MC, V.

FORMAL WEAR RENTAL

AL'S FORMAL WEAR, 315 Throckmorton, 335-9493
Mon.–Sat. 8:30 A.M.–5:30 P.M. Men's formals only. No delivery or pickup. MC, V.

GROCERIES

MCCLOUD'S, 805 E. Belknap, 335-0045
Open seven days, 6 A.M.–midnight. Beer, snacks, sodas.

TURNER & DINGEE, 800 W. 7th, 332-9201
Mon.–Sat. 8 A.M.–6:30 P.M. Cold drinks, snacks.

HAIRDRESSERS

CHEZ CHARME BEAUTY SALON, Bank of Commerce Bldg. (Throckmorton at 7th St.), 336-7107
Mon.–Fri. 8 A.M.–5 P.M., Sat. 8 A.M.–noon. Women only. No credit cards.

HAIR ETC., 207 W. 8th St., 332-2643
Mon.–Sat. 9 A.M.–5 P.M. Men and women. MC, V.

HAZEL'S HAIR FASHION, 408 W. 4th St., 336-7692
Mon.–Fri. 8 A.M.–5 P.M., Sat. 8 A.M.–2 P.M. No credit cards.

LIQUOR STORES

BURKE'S PACKAGE STORE, 1908 East 4th St., 335-0157
Mon.–Sat. 10 A.M.–9 P.M. No credit cards.

CHICOTSKY'S PACKAGE STORE, 3437 West 7th St., 332-3566
Mon.–Thurs. 10 A.M.–7 P.M., Fri. & Sat. until 9 P.M. MC, V.

MAJESTIC LIQUORS, 3215 N. Main. 624-7172
Mon.–Sat. 10 A.M.–9 P.M. Most major credit cards.

OPTICIANS

GALLERIA OPTICIANS, 1 Tandy Center, 332-8262
Mon.–Fri. 9 A.M.–5 P.M., Sat. 10 A.M.–5 P.M. Emergency contact lens repair. AE, MC, V.

OPTICAL CLINIC, 304 Houston, 336-4549
Mon.–Sat. 9 A.M.–5 P.M. Emergency contact lens repair. MC, V.

SHOE AND LUGGAGE REPAIR

TANDY CENTER SHOE REPAIR, 1 Tandy Center, 332-7627
Mon.–Fri. 8 A.M.–5 P.M. Shoe, luggage and handbag repair service. Minor repairs while-u-wait. MC, V.

VAN'S SHOE SERVICE, 306 W. Main, 274-1409
Mon.–Fri. 8:30 A.M.–5:30 P.M., Sat. 8:30 A.M.–2 P.M. Minor luggage repair and full shoe repair service. No credit cards.

SPORTS AND ENTERTAINMENT

For most entertainment, including major sports, you will have to make the trip to Dallas. The Tarrant County Convention Center, right downtown and an easy walk from any of our hotels, periodically has top-name talent appearances, but last-minute tickets are hard to get. One thing Fort Worth has a lot of is nightclubs, and if lively saloons with everything from Country & Western to jazz are your thing, you're in for a treat here. Here are some of our recommendations for a night on the town in Fort Worth.

BILLY BOB'S TEXAS, 2520 N. Commerce, 625-6491
A legend in its own time, Billy Bob's brings in the best Country & Western stars nightly. A rodeo, a hat store and cowgirls to shine your boots—all in one sprawling, converted livestock building.

BLOSSOM'S, 5201 Camp Bowie, 732-3441
A lively nightspot in an old house featuring a changing menu of rock, blues and country music.

DADDIO'S, 111 E. 4th St., 332-0752
The jazz is the best in town provided by Nick Kitha's house combo and occasional visitors from out of town. Limited sandwich and Greek menu.

NEW WEST, 3105 Winthrop, 730-0872
The house band, Tommy Allsept and the New West Wranglers, provide humor as well as good music. No mirrored disco ball here, just a life-sized mirrored saddle over the bar.

WINFIELD'S '08, 301 Main, 870-1908
The Western saloon of the eighties with potent drinks and avid conversationalists.

WHITE ELEPHANT SALOON, 106 E. Exchange, 624-1887
Rustic right down to the picnic tables, this stockyard saloon offers country music and inexpensive drinks.

SIGHTSEEING

Despite its size and the fact that Fort Worth is not yet a major city in the sense of New York, Washington or Philadelphia, it does have some very significant sights to see. The following spots are worth your time and are quite close to the major downtown hotels—a brief cab ride for most. All are open free to the public.

AMON CARTER MUSEUM OF WESTERN ART, 3501 Camp Bowie, 738-1933
Tues.–Sat. 10 A.M.–5 P.M., Sun. 1–5:30 P.M. The largest collection of Western art with emphasis on collections of Frederic Remington and Charles Russell.

BOTANIC GARDENS, University, off I-30, 870-7686
Mon.–Fri. 8 A.M.–5 P.M., Sat. 9 A.M.–5 P.M., Sun. 9 A.M.–1 P.M. Famous for the Japanese gardens within.

FORT WORTH ART MUSEUM, 1309 Montgomery, 738-9215
Tues. 10 A.M.–9 P.M., Wed.–Sat. 10 A.M.–5 P.M., Sun. 1–5 P.M. Major works from ancient to modern times.

KIMBELL ART MUSEUM, Will Rogers Rd., West, 332-8451
Tues.–Sat. 10 A.M.–5 P.M., Sun. 1–5 P.M. The Louis Kahn designed building houses a wide range of exhibits.

STOCKYARDS, Main & Exchange
This hub of activity in Fort Worth includes shops, the Cowtown Coliseum and buildings restored to the cattle-driving days of yesteryear.

WATER GARDENS, I-20 at Main (across from the Fort Worth Hilton)
Open 24 hours, fountains operate seven days 8 A.M.–11 P.M.

ZOO, 2727 Zoological Park Drive (Forest Park), 870-7050
Open seven days. Can be reached by riding the 5-mile miniature steam trains along the Trinity River.

EMERGENCIES

Since Fort Worth is quite a drive from Dallas—as well as in a separate telephone area code—we are including a separate list of emergency information.

EMERGENCY TELEPHONE NUMBERS

Ambulance 335-1213

Fire 332-2131

Police 335-4222

Fort Worth Dental Association 336-3693

Poison Control Center 336-6611

Tarrant County Medical Society 732-2825

HOSPITALS

JOHN PETER SMITH HOSPITAL, 1500 S. Main, 429-5156 Fort Worth's major hospital with all services and 24-hour emergency room.

DALLAS INDEX

DALLAS RESTAURANTS

DALLAS RESTAURANTS (By cuisine)

FORT WORTH INDEX

FORT WORTH RESTAURANTS